Frontispiece **Christine Buchegger as Hedda Gabler, Rezidenztheater, Munich, 1979.**

A Routledge Literary Sourcebook on

Henrik Ibsen's *Hedda Gabler*

Variously denounced as the epitome of moral corruption and heralded as a great tragic heroine or figurehead of the Women's Movement, the character of Hedda Gabler has haunted generations of readers, critics, playgoers, and producers. This Routledge Literary Sourcebook explores Henrik Ibsen's revolutionary play, first performed in 1890.

Christopher Innes provides everything required for a well-rounded understanding of *Hedda Gabler*, exploring the play in carefully linked sections on Contexts, Interpretations, Key Passages, and Further Reading. In each section, reprinted source documents are balanced with introductory commentaries, and cross-references from section to section enable readers to follow up the issues that interest them most. The Contexts section will prove especially useful for its wealth of information on Norwegian nationalism, the Women's Movement, and Naturalist theater, while the Interpretations section traces the interwoven histories of the performance and criticism of the play. In the Key Passages, clear and comprehensive commentaries introduce important scenes, reprinted with extensive new footnotes to form the essential guide to the play. Finally, Further Reading suggests directions for additional study.

Drawing on many years of teaching experience and crucial research work on Naturalist theater, Christopher Innes offers the best available introduction to *Hedda Gabler* and its cultural, literary, and critical contexts.

Christopher Innes is Canada Research Chair in Performance and Culture, based at York University, Ontario. Among his recent publications are *Modern British Drama: The Twentieth Century*, *Avant Garde Theatre: 1892–1992*, and *A Sourcebook on Naturalist Theatre*.

Routledge Literary Sourcebooks

Series Editor: Duncan Wu, St Catherine's College, Oxford University

Also available are Routledge Literary Sourcebooks on:
William Shakespeare's *The Merchant of Venice* edited by S. P. Cerasano
E. M. Forster's *A Passage to India* edited by Peter Childs
Mary Wollstonecraft's *A Vindication of the Rights of Woman* edited by Adriana Craciun
Herman Melville's *Moby-Dick* edited by Michael J. Davey
Charles Dickens's *David Copperfield* edited by Richard J. Dunn
William Shakespeare's *Othello* edited by Andrew Hadfield
William Shakespeare's *King Lear* edited by Grace Ioppolo
Mary Shelley's *Frankenstein* edited by Timothy Morton
The Poems of W. B. Yeats edited by Michael O'Neill
Harriet Beecher Stowe's *Uncle Tom's Cabin* edited by Debra J. Rosenthal
The Poems of John Keats edited by John Strachan

A Routledge Literary Sourcebook on

Henrik Ibsen's *Hedda Gabler*

Edited by Christopher Innes

LONDON AND NEW YORK

First published 2003
by Routledge
11 New Fetter Lane, London EC4P 4EE

Simultaneously published in the USA and Canada
by Routledge
29 West 35th Street, New York, NY 10001

Routledge is an imprint of the Taylor & Francis Group

Typeset in Sabon and Gill Sans by RefineCatch Limited, Bungay, Suffolk
Printed and bound in Great Britain by
TJ International Ltd, Padstow, Cornwall

British Library Cataloguing in Publication Data
A catalogue record for this book is available from the British Library

Library of Congress Cataloging in Publication Data
A Routledge literary sourcebook on Henrik Ibsen's *Hedda Gabler* /
edited by Christopher Innes.
p. cm.—(Routledge literary sourcebooks)
1. Ibsen, Henrik, 1828–1906. Dukkehjem. I. Innes, C. D. II. Series.

PT8861 .A67 2003
839.8'226—dc21 2002155697

ISBN 0–415–23818–8 (hbk)
ISBN 0–415–23819–6 (pbk)

Contents

Illustrations

Series Editor's Preface

The Routledge Literary Sourcebook series has been designed to provide students with the materials required to begin serious study of individual literary works, all in a single volume. This includes an overview of the critical history of the work, including extracts from important critical debates of recent decades, and a selection of key passages from the text itself. Volume editors provide introductory commentaries and annotation for the reader's guidance. These handy books provide almost everything most students will need for the contextual and critical overview of literature expected in schools and universities today.

This aim is reflected in the structure of each Sourcebook. Section 1, 'Contexts', provides biographical data in the form of an author chronology and contemporary documents relating to the author and his or her work. In Section 2, 'Interpretations', the editor assembles extracts from the most influential and important criticism throughout the history of the work. In some cases this includes materials relating to performances or adaptations. The third section, 'Key Passages', gathers together the essential episodes from the literary text connected by editorial commentary and annotation so as to relate them to ideas raised earlier in the volume. The final section offers suggestions for further reading, including recommended editions and critical volumes.

Annotation is a key feature of this series. Both the original notes from the reprinted texts and new annotations by the editor appear at the bottom of the relevant page. The reprinted notes are prefaced with the author's name in square brackets, e.g. [Robinson's note.].

Routledge Literary Sourcebooks offer the ideal introduction to single literary works, combining primary and secondary materials, chosen by experts, in accessible form.

Duncan Wu

Acknowledgments

This Sourcebook was completed together with the Performance and Culture Group of the Canada Research Chair at York University, and with generous help of the Social Sciences and Humanities Research Council of Canada. Two research assistants, Stewart MacDonald and Chandrima Chakraborty, deserve particular mention. The contribution of these organizations and individuals was invaluable, and I am deeply grateful for their assistance.

I would like to thank the following publishers, institutions, and individuals for permission to reprint materials:

CAMBRIDGE UNIVERSITY PRESS, LISE-LONE MARKER, and FREDERICK J. MARKER for Frederick J. Marker and Lise-Lone Marker, *Ingmar Bergman: A Life in the Theatre*, 1992, © Cambridge University Press.

MANDER AND MITCHENSON THEATRE COLLECTION for studio portrait of Elizabeth Robbins as Hedda Gabler, London, 1891 (photographed by A. Ellis).

MUSEUM OF THE CITY OF NEW YORK for Alla Nazimova as Hedda Gabler (Act 4), New York, 1918, © Museum of the City of New York, The Theater Collection, gift of Mme. Alla Nazimova; Eva le Gallienne as Hedda Gabler, New York, 1939, Legitimate Theater Corp. of America, © Museum of the City of New York, The Theater Collection.

NEW YORK PUBLIC LIBRARY for Glenda Jackson as Hedda Gabler in the 1976 film (credit: Billy Rose Theatre Collection, New York Public Library).

NEW YORK TIMES for Elenore Lester, "Hedda – Frigid Woman or Life Bearer?", *The New York Sunday Times*, March 7, 1971.

NORVIK PRESS and KATHLEEN McFARLANE for James McFarlane, *Ibsen and Meaning*, Norwich: Norvik Press, 1989.

PALGRAVE MACMILLAN for Janet Suzman, "The Play in Performance" in Errol Durbach (ed.) *Ibsen and the Theatre*, Macmillan, 1980.

RANDOM HOUSE GROUP LTD. for extract from *Ibsen the Norwegian* by Muriel Bradbrook, 1948, published by Chatto & Windus. Used by permission of The Random House Group Limited.

RANDOM HOUSE INC. for extract reprinted from H. L. Mencken, *Eleven Plays of Henrik Ibsen*, Random House Inc., 1939.

ROBERT A. SCHANKE for Richard J. Beckley, "Interview with Janet Suzman" in Robert A. Schanke (ed.), *Ibsen in America*, Scarecrow Press, 1988, © 1988 Robert A. Schanke.

THE SOCIETY OF AUTHORS, on behalf of the Bernard Shaw Estate for Bernard Shaw, *The Quintessence of Ibsenism*, 1891.

The publishers have made every effort to contact copyright holders. Any omissions brought to our attention will be rectified in future editions.

Introduction

Hedda Gabler was published in December 1890 and first performed at the Residenztheater, Munich, in January 1891. Since then it has become the most frequently performed of all plays (with the possible exception of one or two by Shakespeare). With over sixty productions, many of which have enjoyed long runs or toured extensively, *Hedda Gabler* has appeared almost continuously somewhere on the American and European stage over the whole of the last century. First translated into English by Edmund Gosse (1890) and revised for its first English-language performance in 1891 by William Archer, it has been republished and retranslated more than fifteen times since then. New editions and translations of the play proliferated in the 1950s and 1960s – including one by America's leading actress of the time, Eva le Gallienne, who performed the role several times – and the significance of *Hedda Gabler* continues to grow. There have been a number of recent adaptations by playwrights: Charles Marowitz (1982), John Osborne and Christopher Hampton (both 1989). And new translations, such as those by Nicholas Rudall (1992) and Jon Robin Baitz (2000), continue to appear.

Its popularity is partly due to the opportunity the title role offers to actresses. But more than that – as its critical history shows – of all the early modern plays, its subject has retained a sharply contemporary edge, while its text has an ambiguity that allows for many different emphases or interpretations. Depicting the frustrated attempts by the title figure to escape from the constrictions of marriage and a paternalistic society, *Hedda Gabler* has been a key text for feminists from Emma Goldman (1914) onwards. Simultaneously passionate and frigid, daring and enervated, possibly pregnant yet rejecting the ties of motherhood, asserting masculine prerogatives but unable to overstep the bounds of propriety, Hedda is both a victim and demonic. Not surprisingly such complexity attracts psychological interpretations. Her struggles for self-realization destroy the only man she might have loved, her husband's rival for a coveted university post. To cover up her responsibility for his ignominious death, she burns the manuscript which is his life's work, only to find herself open to sexual blackmail. With her husband seduced into reconstituting his dead rival's book (together with the woman who had helped to write the original version) and ignoring her plight, Hedda shoots herself: suicide being the only form of self-assertion or escape left to her. The image of Hedda with her pistol is as iconic as Hamlet holding a skull, and the play has become a test case for modern tragedy.

As the most compressed and naturalistic of Ibsen's plays, combining subtextual depth with extreme simplicity of dialogue, *Hedda Gabler* is also a particularly rewarding play for stylistic analysis. And being open to so many types of critical approach, the text repays study, as much as the play's social impact throughout its stage history. It is one of the master-works of modern drama; and it is hoped that this volume will enhance understanding of the way in which text, performance, society, and criticism are inextricably linked, as well as helping readers to develop their own views and arrive at new interpretations of this "modern classic" play.

1

Contexts

Contextual Overview

To appreciate the nature of the play and its achievement, *Hedda Gabler* has to be seen in the wider context not only of Henrik Ibsen's career, but also against the political, social, and literary background of the period. Ibsen's development as a playwright can only be understood in terms of the cultural battle for Norwegian independence, and his own response which, by the time his major plays were written, asserted the preeminence of individual freedom over political liberty. Equally significant is the relationship of his mature dramas to the Women's Movement in Norway: the struggle for legal equality, financial independence, and the right to vote forms the subtext to *Hedda Gabler*. This paralleled, and even anticipated, similar movements in other Western countries towards the end of the nineteenth century; and Ibsen's involvement with these issues was echoed by other naturalistic playwrights across Europe. Indeed the nexus of ideas that gave rise to Naturalism, a literary movement that originated in France – and of which Ibsen became the leading theatrical exponent – is just as crucial, and provides the stylistic context for the play. This overview will deal briefly with each of these aspects. The Chronology (**pp. 16–22**) also lists relevant events by date and related documentation is printed in Contemporary Documents (**pp. 23–37**).

Norwegian Nationalism

Until 1814 Norway had been ruled by Denmark. It was then transferred to Sweden, in a union that again subordinated Norwegians to a foreign king, though they gained a limited local autonomy. Despite the political changes, during the first half of the century Norwegian art and literature remained almost exclusively Danish, while the Norwegian language itself was largely restricted to the peasants. But in the year of Ibsen's birth, 1828, the historian Rudolf Kayser had initiated a "new Norwegian history" by giving a series of lectures maintaining that linguistic evidence showed that Norway had been populated by "Nordic" tribes from the north, while the Danes and Swedes were originally "Goths" having come from the south. This played a crucial part in the struggle not only for a "Norwegian" culture but for a Norwegian nation.

The vital link between race and language in nation-building is outlined by Anne-Lise Seip, a contemporary Norwegian historian:

> Henrik Wergeland[1] wanted to enrich his prose and poetry with everyday expressions and words taken from the spoken language, which in many ways differed from the printed language, which was pure Danish. To create a genuine Norwegian language, he maintained, one had to go to those dialects which were less changed in the course of time, and which could bridge the gap with the old Norse language. This historical, etymological approach came to influence development immensely. Very soon a young genius took up the task of creating a Norwegian language. Ivar Aasen, son of a peasant on the west coast, started to collect samples of dialects in the vernacular, and also to prepare a grammar to create a common language. His motives were both national and social. Language was "the most distinctive mark of a nation," and Norway needed a language of its own. But the elements of such a language he found in his own social class, the rural population. He wanted to give it a language of its own [but] gave up his own first plan to base a written Norwegian language on the existing dialects. He succumbed to the theories of P. A. Munch,[2] who became his friend and mentor, and modeled his language on etymological principles, making it archaic and much less suited to the task he had set himself of creating a language that was easy to understand for the uneducated masses. Nevertheless, his Norwegian grammar, first published in 1848, as well as his dictionary of 1850 confirmed his theory that the vernacular was founded on the old Norse language, and was not, as hitherto believed, a distortion of Danish.[3]

This recovery of language was accompanied by a rediscovery and recording of folktales, songs, and fairy tales. Although long the object of scientific interest in other countries, including Denmark and Sweden, the first collection of Norwegian folk legends was not published until 1833. This was followed with folk songs collected by Jorgen Moe, M. B. Landstad, and their informant Olea Crøger, daughter of a country priest. As Seip concludes:

> All this gave occasion for pride, and in the year 1849 the national enthusiasm exploded, so to speak, in the capital. In a series of so-called "tableaux," the daughters of Christiana[4] acted as peasant girls against a background of curtains painted by Norwegian artists whom the revolu-

1 Wergeland (1808–45) was the first author to use Norwegian as a written language and one of the earliest to contest the Danish influence over Norwegian theater.

2 Peter Andreas Munch (1810–63) collected and published *Norse Mythology: Legends of Gods and Heroes* (1840, trans. 1927).

3 Seip, Anne-Lise. "Nation-building Within the Union: Politics, Class and Culture in the Norwegian Nation-State in the Nineteenth Century." *Scandinavian Journal of History*, 20(1), 1995, pp. 35–50.

4 Now Oslo.

tions of 1848 had forced back to Norway, while folk-music was played on the Hardanger fiddle and a choir of 100 men performed songs composed by musicians educated in Leipzig, but inspired by the "Norwegian tone" of the folk-songs.

These evening performances in 1849 were later on seen as the culmination of an epoch imprinted with national feeling.

It was a time in the latter part of the 1840s when we, who were then young, so to speak realized that we – in the concrete, and not only in the abstract – had a country (Vaterland), when we discovered that our people possessed a beautiful, big, common treasure of history, tales, songs, music, language, poetry and art, which all at once made it a cultured people (Kulturvolk) with a distinctive national stamp.

This was the verdict of an acute observer, the art historian Lorentz Dietrichson.[5]

Ibsen was just twenty years old in 1848, the "Year of Revolutions" – in which the proclamation of the French Republic led to violent uprisings from Berlin and Vienna to Milan and Rome (forcing the Pope to flee), and demands for national autonomy throughout the Austro-Hungarian empire – and the year of the first Norwegian grammar. In 1850, moved by the political passions that had swept Europe, Ibsen helped to establish a short-lived highly political newspaper, *Andrimmer*, which called for the dethroning of the Swedish King and the founding of a socialist republic in Norway. At this time, the theater was increasingly the focus of those fighting for a national literature and in 1850 the Norske Teater was founded in Bergen. Before this time no plays had been written in Norwegian – indeed up to then the written forms of the Danish and Norwegian languages were identical – and there were no Norwegian actors. The first Norwegian dramatist, Ludvig Holberg (1684–1754), whose plays Ibsen quoted continually in his letters, wrote exclusively in Danish for theaters in Copenhagen. The first all-Norwegian-speaking company appeared only in 1852, on the stage of the Norske Teater. Ibsen had joined the Teater the same year as resident dramatist. He had had a narrow escape the previous year when his *Andrimmer* co-founders, who had been responsible for the most revolutionary of the pieces in the newspaper, were arrested and sentenced to long prison terms. According to his first biographer, Edmund Gosse, this led to Ibsen's lifelong rejection of practical political involvement. However, by joining the Norske Teater in 1852, Ibsen placed himself at the forefront of the cultural struggle.

It is only fairly recently that historians have analyzed the social and cultural aspect of national development. Significantly, the areas considered crucial by historians are also integral elements in Ibsen's early plays: the recording of folklore and the historical glorification of the Vikings (which became the subject of his early heroic tragedies), and the development of the Norwegian language. From the first, Ibsen was associated with cultural independence, particularly as a result of his appointments as resident dramatist and later director at the Norske Teater.

5 Seip, "Nation-building Within the Union," pp. 43–4.

In choosing to write his poems and plays in Norwegian, Ibsen was making a political statement. At the same time, once he began writing naturalistic drama, he ensured that his plays were available for the world repertoire by having them immediately translated into German.[6]

His early historical dramas may have had nationalistic themes, but his study of history also formed a basis for his naturalistic plays. Just after completing *A Doll's House*, Ibsen commented in a letter to John Paulsen, a young Norwegian writer and protégé of his, that "An extensive knowledge of history is indispensable to an author; without it he is not in a position to understand the conditions of his own age, or to judge men, their motives and actions, except in the most incomplete and superficial manner."[7]

Another influence was the war of 1866 in which Prussia annexed the Danish provinces of Schleswig-Holstein. The lack of support for Denmark from Sweden and Norway confirmed Ibsen in his opposition to the nation-state, and in his pan-Scandinavian patriotism. His letters, and later public speeches, also show that as he turned to Naturalistic work, with its inherent criticism of society, he was less concerned with nationalism than individual freedom. In a letter to fellow Norwegian dramatist, novelist, and poet Bjørnstjerne Bjørnson, he writes, "It is said that Norway is an independent state, but I do not value much this liberty and independence so long as I know that the individuals are neither free nor independent," and rails against "prejudice, narrow-mindedness, wrong-headed notions, dependence and the belief in groundless authority."[8] Indeed Ibsen's dissatisfaction with the narrow morality, conservatism, and provincialism of Norwegian society had already led to self-imposed exile in 1864 (twenty-five years before *A Doll's House*); and while accepting a pension and public honors, the radicalism of his views caused him to reject both the state and any form of political action. As he put it in letters to critic and friend Georg Brandes, "there is absolutely no reasonable necessity for the individual to be a citizen. On the contrary – the state is the curse of the individual," following this up with "From special reforms I expect nothing. The whole race is on the wrong track."[9]

The Women's Movement

Another crucial element in Ibsen's plays, which only became central once he turned to Naturalistic subjects, was the position of women. The Naturalistic movement – particularly at the time when it reached the theater – coincided with the fight for women's rights, and indeed, in many ways, fostered the demands for legal equality, financial independence, and voting rights:

6 The German translator of most of Ibsen's plays, Ludwig Passarge (1825–1912), was also the first to write an extended critical essay on his early work, in 1883.

7 Letter to John Paulsen, September 20, 1879. Mary Morison (ed.) *Henrik Ibsen: Correspondence*, London: Hodder & Stoughton, 1905.

8 Letter to Bjørnstjerne Bjørnson, July 12, 1879, in Morison (ed.) *Henrik Ibsen, Correspondence*.

9 February 17 (see **p. 24**) and September 24, 1871. See also "To My Friend the Revolutionary Orator," **p. 24**.

> From Zola's *Thérèse Raquin* on, the number of naturalistic plays with women as their title figures or central characters is striking. These include, most notably: Nora in *A Doll's House*, Mrs. Alving in *Ghosts*, Rebecca West in *Rosmersholm* and the title figures of *Hedda Gabler*, Chekhov's *The Three Sisters*, Shaw's *Mrs Warren's Profession* and *Candida* (a direct response to Ibsen showing, in Shaw's terms, that in the typical doll's house "it is the man who is the doll"), as well as Strindberg's *Miss Julie* (despite Strindberg's well-known misogyny) and Hauptmann's *Rose Bernd* – also Becque's *La Parisienne*, Brieux's *Blanchette*, *The Three Daughters of M. Dupont* and *Maternity*. Of course there are examples of major female characters throughout theatre history, from Medea to Lady Macbeth and Cleopatra, to Racine's *Andromaque*, *Bérénice* and *Phèdre*. However, these are almost all presented as evil and immoral, or as tragic victims – generally distanced by being archetypes taken from history – implicitly condemned, or punished for playing an active male role or for achieving a prominence at odds with the traditional (male) ideals of submissive and self-effacing women. In sharp contrast, Ibsen's women are portrayed without moral bias, as figures striving for authenticity against the unconscious hypocrisy of the males in their patriarchal society. Each is an individualized and fully realized personality – set in a specific and recognizable contemporary context (rather than being historical) – and Ibsen even extends the dramatic franchise to female children: Hedvig, the young girl who is the most obvious analogue to *The Wild Duck*.[10]

The Naturalistic emphasis on women is something decisively new in theater and Ibsen led the way with his strong female characters. The factor that makes this new is not the number, or even the centrality of female characters, but the way female experience is presented. Ibsen's plays presented the ideology of the Women's Movement, but in theatrical images that resonated because they were immediately accessible, and the empathy created by stage performance encouraged identification. The female characters' views are given equal weight to those of the men in the plays. Indeed, since these women assert themselves in opposition to the male-dominated society ranked against them, even though in general they fail and must either withdraw completely from society (as Nora and, in a still more final way, Hedda do) or be trapped (as Mrs. Alving is in *Ghosts*), it is their voice that predominates. And Ibsen was widely followed. It was only after studying Ibsen's plays (in the series of lectures published as *The Quintessence of Ibsenism* – see **pp. 56–7** – in 1890) that Bernard Shaw turned to writing plays, and links may also be made with the emergence of female playwrights in England. Before the 1890s there had been very few and isolated examples of women who wrote plays: Mary Sidney in the Elizabethan period, Aphra Behn a century later. Now a whole group appeared, clearly linked to Ibsen. The most notable was

10 Christopher Innes, *A Sourcebook on Naturalist Theatre*, London: Routledge, 2000, p. 18.

Elizabeth Robins, who performed *Hedda Gabler* in 1891. Robins wrote *Alan's Wife* (1893) together with Florence Bell, and *Votes for Women!* (1906). Janet Achurch, the actress who first performed *A Doll's House* in England, went on to write *Mrs Daintree's Daughter* (1895). Others included Constance Fletcher (*Mrs. Lessingham*, 1894) and Dorothy Leighton (*Thyrza Fleming*, 1894).

The situation of women in Scandinavia had already become a subject of debate by 1854 (the date when Norwegian daughters were first given equal inheritance rights to sons). In the same year, two Swedish economists wrote of peasant women and servants: "woman in the North is the household beast of burden and the slave of man. We are so used to it that it does not arouse our shame."[11] Contemporary sociologists confirm that this extended throughout the social scale:

> Women of the middle classes although spared from drudgery, were even more cut off from really functional activity. They were either more intimate servants or decorative hothouse plants. If their fathers and husbands were rich enough to keep them in indolence, they might be given excellent formalistic educations, but they were separated from the world and from life by a Chinese wall of proprieties which usually served to frustrate any desires for active self-expression. The wall was built of modesty, helplessness, delicacy, gratitude, and a chastity valued the more as it approached ignorance. The supreme virtue was obedience. As far as their means permitted, the men of the lower middle classes demanded of their women the same behavior. Never so much as then was home the woman's place; never did poets so ecstatically eulogize the "beautiful, weaker sex." [. . .] If the lot of the daughter and the wife was drab, that of the unmarried woman was incredibly dreary. She was not even ornamental. Where she could perform some useful work in the house of her relatives she was able to maintain her self-respect and was often welcome. Otherwise she must become a burden, or seek refuge in some sort of foundation, or take employment as a servant.[12]

Although in 1810 the city physician of Copenhagen had published a proposal to combat prostitution by allowing women to seek employment in crafts and trades, it was not until 1866 that a law was passed in Norway giving women the right to work in any trade or profession. The conservatism of Norwegian society is indicated by the fact that equivalent laws had been passed significantly earlier by the other Scandinavian countries: Denmark in 1857 and Sweden in 1864.

The way ideals of femininity frustrated self-expression and isolated women from public life forms the context for almost all Ibsen's female characters, with Hedda Gabler as the most notable example. Similarly, although male

11 Agardh and Ljungberg, *Försök till en statsekonomisk statisik öfver Sverige*, Karlstad and Stockholm, 1854, vol. IV, pp. 415–16.

12 B. J. Hovde, *The Scandinavian Countries 1720–1865: The Rise of the Middle Classes*, Vol. II, Port Washington, NY: Kennikat Press, 1943, pp. 682–3. This picture is confirmed by many documents from the period, such as the diary entry of Camilla Collett reprinted on pp. 25–6.

guardianship of unmarried women was abolished in Norway in 1863, and after 1866 women had the right to earn an independent living, the situation facing unmarried women was still bleak, giving added weight to both the attitude of Mrs. Linde (who bemoans the life of a working woman) and Nora's famous decision to walk out on her marriage and make her own way in the world in *A Doll's House*. In addition Norwegian nationalism itself contained a symbolic representation of gender, which denied equality. For instance, at the May 17 celebration of statehood in 1827 the procession carried paintings of Nora – a female symbol of the Norwegian nation, hence the name of Ibsen's heroine in his most shocking early Naturalistic play – while the national anthem first performed on May 17, 1864 codified different roles for men and women. As one commentator wrote in 1996, "The song reflected the roles assigned to each gender in the construction of the national home: the strong father protecting his house, actively supported by his wife." She continued, "Against this background, it seems natural that men, as fathers and defenders of the nation, had the right to take part in political decisions." Women, as mothers, "had their special function in the national home, but to take part in active combat did not comply with their femininity."[13]

The Norwegian Women's Rights League was founded in 1884, just five years after the first performance of *A Doll's House*, and from 1886 on published a biweekly woman's suffrage magazine, *Nylaende*. Ibsen had associated himself with the Women's Movement in Norway shortly after *A Doll's House*. Writing in 1879 to Camilla Collett, one of the earliest and most influential advocates of women's rights in Norway, Ibsen recorded his "warm, complete sympathy with you and your life-task," and when the League invited Ibsen to address their Festival in Christiana in May 1888, it was in recognition of the role his drama had played in fostering public awareness of the position of women in Norwegian society (and generally in Europe). That Festival marked the campaign for the first constitutional proposal to give women the vote, which reached parliament in 1890. But it was typical that even though he had signed a petition for changing the law to allow married women the right to their own property and earnings, which was presented to the Storting (Parliament) in 1884, Ibsen's speech rejected any specific gender bias – just as he earlier denied the relevance of national liberation to individual self-fulfillment. Instead, he argued, "My task has been the description of humanity."[14]

Naturalism

It was only in mid-career, at the age of forty-nine, that Ibsen achieved more than a local Scandinavian prominence by a radical switch in his dramatic material and style. When he turned from his early verse tragedies, and the heroic historical

13 Ida Blom, "Nation–Class–Gender: Scandinavia at the Turn of the Century," *Scandinavian Journal of History*, 21(1), 1996, pp. 3–4.
14 See **p. 26** for an extract from this speech.

costume dramas (*The Vikings*, 1858, or *The Pretenders*, 1863) which counted as his contribution to the recuperation of national myth and folk legends, to the portrayal of ordinary people in contemporary Norwegian society (starting with his attack on financial corruption in *The Pillars of Society*, 1877), Ibsen joined the major literary trend of the nineteenth century: Naturalism. Already established by novelists like Émile Zola and the Goncourt brothers in France, this movement had not yet invaded the theater. Although Zola had written one superficially Naturalistic play, *Thérèse Raquin* (1873), this remained in many ways melodramatic; and it was Ibsen who created the first dramas that were recognizable examples of Naturalism. The eight plays he wrote over the fourteen years from *The Pillars of Society* and *A Doll's House* (1879) culminating with *Hedda Gabler* in 1891 broke new ground, making him the leading Naturalist playwright. This artistic context is no less important for understanding *Hedda Gabler*, in many ways Ibsen's most quintessentially Naturalistic play, than the political and social background.

On one level Naturalism was an aesthetic revolt against traditional styles of performance that had become outdated, and were no longer capable of representing social conditions in a rapidly changing world on the verge of the modern age. However, Naturalism was also the expression of a moral or social revolution. The primary influences on the Naturalistic movement were Charles Darwin's evolutionary theories of biology (*The Origin of the Species*, 1859), Claude Bernard's scientific observation of human physiology (*Introduction à l'étude de la médecine experimentale*, 1865), and Karl Marx's economic analysis of society (*Das Kapital*, 1867) – plus, somewhat later, Sigmund Freud's work on psychology (*On the Psychical Mechanism of Hysterical Phenomena*, with Charcot, 1893; *The Interpretation of Dreams*, 1900). It also reflected the emergence of materialistic capitalism and the rise of middle-class democracy.

There is general agreement that the crucial factors inspiring Naturalism were the perceptions that all life, human as well as animal, is in a process of continual evolution, and that human behavior can be explained through scientific analysis. These new ideas led to the assumption that people's character and personality are formed by a combination of heredity and their social environment, plus the value placed on the individual. This meant that ordinary citizens, including workers and the poor (who had traditionally played at best supporting or comic roles in literature, particularly drama) became the protagonists, and attention focused on the family. Perhaps even more significant, as we have already seen, is that Naturalistic drama, established in the 1880s and 1890s, coincided with the early Women's Movement and the new sense of national identity in Scandinavia. It also coincided with the liberation of the serfs in Russia. All this was directly reflected in Naturalistic plays.

Although this democratization of literary subjects in itself was not new, Naturalism represented a significant change in treatment, being overtly scientific, presenting characters as case studies in human behavior or social problems. In the hugely influential *Naturalism in the Theatre* (1881), Émile Zola called for "the study of reality" and "men of genius who can fix the naturalistic formula." In particular, he called for dramatists "to establish our new theatre" (see **pp. 27–8**). Ibsen was indeed the kind of dramatist Zola called for, but although Zola was writing two years after *A Doll's House* had first appeared, none of Ibsen's Naturalistic plays had yet reached France. And while it is doubtful if Ibsen was aware of Zola's dramatic criticism, it is hardly coincidental that just over a year later he renounced all verse and poetic speech in favor of "the straightforward, plain language spoken in real life" (letter to the actress Lucie Wolf, May 25, 1883).

Zola provided the theoretical manifesto for Naturalist theater; but on a practical level the stage had been moving towards greater realism throughout the nineteenth century. There was the development of the "well-made play" by Eugène Scribe, whose structural principles for introducing and developing interlinked dramatic situations, with a denouement that leads into the next situation, until all strands of the plot are neatly resolved in the conclusion, created an impression of logical coherence. Theatrically effective, this structuring rapidly became codified. It allowed Scribe to produce over 350 plays between 1813 and his death in 1861; and Scribe's "well-made" techniques were widely imitated during the mid-nineteenth century. His plays were staged – and copied – throughout Europe, from England to Norway, where Ibsen staged several Scribean pieces.

These developments in play-writing were accompanied by changes in stage lighting, culminating with the introduction of electric lighting in 1881 (the year of Zola's *Naturalism in the Theatre*), and in scenery, which for the first time began to present a three-dimensional and increasingly realistic physical context for dramatic characters. The next step was taken by the court theater of the small German state of Saxe-Meiningen, under the artistic direction of its duke, whose enthusiasm for Charles Kean's historically accurate stagings of Shakespeare in the 1850s led him to develop an ensemble dedicated to archeologically authentic productions. Each production was prepared in meticulous detail, with particular attention being paid to crowd scenes, and extensively rehearsed in costume and with full sets in order to make the performers so familiar with their dramatic environment that they would appear to "live" in it. The Meiningen Company gained an instant reputation with its first German tour in 1874. They also toured widely through Europe up to 1890, creating new standards of authenticity for the stage – even if this was largely limited to pictorial effect. Their productions were seen by Ibsen in Berlin, when they performed his early heroic play *The Crown Pretenders* in 1876.

Having been stage director at the Bergen theater, and from 1857 to 1862 manager of the Norwegian Theater in Christiana, Ibsen had practical experience of both the changes in dramatic construction, and the new scenic and lighting techniques. In addition Ibsen's involvement with the Meiningen Company had exposed him to the possibilities for using authentic detail in the setting. All these inform the sequence of plays initiated by *A Doll's House*. It is hardly coincidental that Ibsen's turn to Naturalism coincided with a significant change in stage practices – a difference that can be measured by the contrast in preparation for two early productions of his Naturalistic plays. Following the standard practice for Romantic or Scribean drama, the Royal Theatre in Stockholm allowed just two rehearsals for blocking, eight general rehearsals, and one dress rehearsal for *A Doll's House* in 1879. Four years later, in 1883 at the same theatre, *An Enemy of the People* was given a total of thirty-two rehearsals, twelve of which (reflecting Meiningen practice) were devoted solely to the crowd scene in Act 4.

For most of the nineteenth century – particularly in continental Europe – the standard style of acting was histrionic, using codified gestures to display heightened emotion, but the way in which the new dramatists perceived people was the opposite of the type of figure expressed in traditional acting. As August Strindberg, Ibsen's Swedish rival, explains in his Preface to *Miss Julie* (see **pp. 28–9**), modern characters acted on a series of sometimes ambiguous motives, not out of a simple, fixed nature. Moral judgments were precluded by the complex treatments given to central figures. Indeed, character was given primacy over plot – plot proceeded from the highly individual character first imagined by the playwright. And for the Naturalists, as the documents later in this section reveal, the visual aspects of a production and the acting had to be as "lifelike" as the new type of characterization. Zola's *Naturalism in the Theatre* set out an intimate link between personality and environment as one of the most crucial aspects of Naturalism. His highly influential essay attracted the attention of a young French actor/ director, André Antoine (1858–1943), whose Théâtre Libre became a model for the whole Independent Theatre movement (so-called because a subscription-audience freed these theaters from censorship and allowed them to produce "unpopular" or "scandalous" plays) that was the platform for the new Naturalistic drama. The Théâtre Libre's first production, in 1887, was an adaptation of a short story by Zola. The (at the time) striking elements of Antoine's production were a deliberate simplicity in scenery, using borrowed furniture that was solid and worn with use to create real-life surroundings on stage. His Théâtre Libre was followed by Otto Brahm's Freie Bühne in Germany (1889), John Grein's Independent Theatre in Britain (1891), the Irish Literary Theatre (1897) and the Irish National Dramatic Company (1902) in Dublin. So it was only around the time *Hedda Gabler* appeared that methods of staging caught up with Ibsen's dramaturgy. The output of the Théâtre Libre and its successor, the Théâtre Antoine, from 1897 to 1906 was typical of the Little Theatre movement as a whole. It included productions of Ibsen's *Ghosts* (1890) and *The Wild Duck* (1891), Strindberg's *Miss Julie* and Gerhart Hauptmann's *The Weavers* (both 1893) as well as Tolstoy's *Power of Darkness* (produced in 1878), plays by Eugène Brieux (such as *Maternité*, banned in 1901), and adaptations of Zola, such as *La Terre* (1902). During Ibsen's lifetime it was largely through these small independent theaters that his work was spread outside Norway. However, as letters reprinted in the Contemporary Documents section indicate, Ibsen sought to control or advise on key aspects of the staging of his plays both in Norway and abroad (see **pp. 30–2**).

It is worth noting that although each of Ibsen's plays marks a new development, he also saw an essential continuity, in the most general thematic terms, between his earlier heroic drama and his Naturalistic work, as he commented, looking back on his first play, *Catiline* (completed in 1849):

> Much that my later work concerns itself with – the conflict between one's aims and one's abilities, between what man purposes and what is actually possible, constituting at once both the tragedy and comedy of

mankind and of the individual – is already vaguely intimated in this work.[15]

Ibsen had already adopted the stylistic principles associated with Naturalism while still engaged with heroic historical plays; in an 1874 letter to his English translator, Edmund Gosse, he wrote of *Emperor and Galilean* that "the illusion I wished to produce was that of reality" (see **p. 30**). The general principles outlined are those that Ibsen followed in his subsequent plays dealing with contemporary society: the stress on modernity, the individualization of even minor characters, and the use of everyday language. Writing to August Lindberg, the director of *Ghosts*, a decade later, the same principles are restated: "The effect of the play depends a great deal on making the spectator feel as if he were actually sitting, listening, and looking at events happening in real life."[16]

15 Ibsen, Preface to *Catiline*, February 1, 1875, first translated by Anders Orbeck, in Henrik Ibsen, *Early Plays*, New York: The American–Scandinavian Foundation, 1921, p. 6.
16 Ibsen, letter to August Lindberg, August 2, 1883.

Chronology

- • indicates events in author's life and career
- * indicates contextual events

1828
• Henrik Ibsen born in Skien, Norway

1830
* First box set introduced on a stage in London.

1833
* First collection of Norwegian folktales published

1841
* Asbjörnsen and Moe, *Norwegian Folk Tales* published

1843
• Ibsen leaves home to work as an apothecary's apprentice in Grimstad

1846
• Else Sophie Birkedalen gives birth to Ibsen's illegitimate son

1848
• Ibsen writes his first play, *Catiline* (in verse and on Roman history), which the Christiana Theater rejects
* First Norwegian grammar published; the Thrane movement for reform in Norway (1848–51); the "Year of Revolutions" in Europe; Marx and Engels publish *The Communist Manifesto*

1850
• *Catiline* published privately under the pseudonym of Brynjolf Bjarme; Ibsen co-founds a political newspaper, *Andrimmer*, in Christiana; *The Burial*

Mound (a nationalistic historical romance) written under the pseudonym of Brynjolf Bjarme, and produced by the Christiana Theater

* First Norwegian theater founded in Bergen

1851

- Ibsen publishes poems and critical articles in periodicals; moves to Bergen to work at the newly founded Norwegian Theater as a "dramatic author"

1853

- *St. John's Night*, a three-act comedy, which Ibsen later disowned, is performed by the Norwegian Theater in Bergen

1854

- Revised version of *The Burial Mound* produced by the Norwegian Theater in Bergen, but is not well received

* Law passed to give women equal inheritance rights in Norway

1855

- *Lady Inger of Ostrat* (Ibsen's first prose play) produced by the Norwegian Theater in Bergen

* Dumas fils, *Le Demi-Monde*; Collet, *The Sheriff's Daughter*; David E. Hughes invents the telegraph

1856

- *The Feast at Solhaug* produced by Norwegian Theater in Bergen, under Ibsen's own direction; Ibsen meets his future wife, Suzannah Thoresen

1857

- *Olaf Liljekrans* produced at the Norwegian Theater in Bergen; Ibsen moves from Bergen to become artistic director of the Norwegian Theater in Christiana

1858

- *The Vikings at Helgeland* (a nationalistic saga-play) rejected by the Royal Theatre in Copenhagen, but is published and produced at Christiana Norwegian Theater; Ibsen marries Suzannah Thoresen

1859

- *In the Picture Gallery* is published; Ibsen's son, Sigurd, is born

* Darwin, *On the Origin of Species by Natural Selection* and Mill, *Essay on Liberty* published

1860

- The newspapers and the board of the Christiana Norwegian Theater mount a campaign against Ibsen

1862

- Ibsen records folktales and songs in western Norway; the Christiana Norwegian Theater bankrupt, Ibsen without regular income for two years; *Love's Comedy* (Ibsen's first play set in contemporary Norway) published as a New Year's supplement

1863

- Ibsen receives government grant to spend a year in Rome; *The Pretenders* (epic historical drama) published

* Law created in Norway to give unmarried women independence from male guardians

1864

- *The Pretenders* produced in Christiana; Ibsen leaves for Rome (where he remains for the next four years)

1865

- Ibsen completes *Brand* (epic religious tragedy)

* Abraham Lincoln assassinated

1866

- *Brand* published in Copenhagen; Ibsen awarded a lifetime grant from the government that allows him to concentrate on his writing

* Law created in Norway to allow women the right to work in any trade or profession; Prussia annexes Schleswig-Holstein from Denmark

1867

- *Peer Gynt* (a picaresque and highly symbolic comedy) published in Copenhagen

* Marx, *Das Kapital*

1868

- Ibsen leaves Italy and settles in Dresden

* Elizabeth Cady and Susan B. Anthony found the women's rights periodical, *The Revolution*

1869

- Ibsen honoured with the Vasa Order by the King of Sweden and Norway; invited to be Norway's representative in Egypt for the opening of the Suez Canal; *The League of Youth* (a political satire in colloquial language) is published

* Mill, *On the Subjection of Women*

1870

* Married Women's Property Act in Britain allows married women to keep £200 of their own earnings; Franco-Prussian War (1870–1)

1871

- Ibsen receives Denmark's Order of Dannebrog; poems published
- * Georg Brandes, "Inaugural Lecture"

1873

- Ibsen serves on jury of International Art Exhibition in Vienna; awarded the Norwegian Knight's Order of St Olaf; *Emperor and Galilean* (a trilogy of epic historical dramas on the conflict between Christianity and paganism) published
- * Zola, *Thérèse Raquin* (play) peformed

1874

- * First Impressionist salon in Paris: the Saxe-Meiningen Players' first tour of Germany

1875

- Ibsen moves from Dresden to Munich; travels to Berlin to see the Saxe-Meiningen production of *The Pretenders*
- * London Medical School for Women is founded

1876

- *Emperor and Galilean* translated into English; *Peer Gynt*, including incidental music by Grieg, opens at the Christiana Theater
- * Alexander Graham Bell invents the telephone; Wagner's theater, Bayreuth Festspielhaus, opens with *The Ring*

1877

- *The Pillars of Society* (Ibsen's first Naturalistic play) published
- * Thomas Edison invents the phonograph; Collet's novel, *From the Camp of the Dumb*, published

1879

- *A Doll's House* (the play that won Ibsen immediate international fame as a social realist) published, and first produced in Copenhagen
- * Nietzsche writes *Birth of Tragedy*; Thomas Edison invents electric light

1880

- *Quicksands*, an adaptation of *The Pillars of Society*, opens at the Gaiety Theatre in London (the first Ibsen play to appear in England)
- * Zola publishes *Naturalism in the Theatre*

1881

- *Ghosts* published – Ibsen's most controversial play, attacked as immoral due to its subjects: syphilis and incest

1882

- *The Child Wife*, an adaptation of *A Doll's House*, produced at the Grand Opera House in Milwaukee (the first Ibsen play to be performed in North America); *An Enemy of the People* (dramatizing the conflict between an idealistic doctor and corrupt society) published

* Nietzsche declares "the death of God" in *The Gay Science*

1883

- *An Enemy of the People* produced at Royal Theater in Stockholm

1884

- *The Wild Duck* (an attack on idealism balancing comedy with tragedy) published

* Married Women's Property Act in Britain deems that women are no longer "chattel" but are autonomous people

1885

- Ibsen returns for a trip to Norway, then settles in Munich for next six years

* Zola's naturalistic novel *Germinal* published

1886

- *Rosmersholm* (addressing freethinking and free love) published; Ibsen attends Saxe-Meiningen production of *Ghosts* in Germany – but play banned in Berlin

* Tolstoy writes *Power of Darkness* (banned in Russia until 1895)

1887

* Strindberg's Naturalistic play, *The Father*, is produced; André Antoine founds the Théâtre Libre in Paris

1888

- *The Lady from the Sea* (a drama of memory combining Naturalistic style with symbolism) published

* Strindberg's Naturalistic tragedy of sex and class, *Miss Julie*, performed

1889

- First British production of *A Doll's House*; Die Freie Bühne is founded by Otto Brahm in Berlin, opening with *Ghosts*

* Strindberg's Scandinavian Experimental Theater is founded

1890

- *Hedda Gabler* published and staged throughout Europe; *Ghosts* staged by Théâtre Libre in Paris

* Shaw lectures on Ibsen for the Fabian Society

1891

- • Ibsen moves to Christiana; J. T. Grein opens the Independent Theatre Club in London with *Ghosts*; *The Wild Duck* is staged by Théâtre Libre
- * The Symbolist Théâtre d'Art produces Maeterlinck's *Intruder* and *The Blind*; Norwegian movement for independence from Sweden grows

1892

- • *The Master Builder* (marking Ibsen's turn to psychological and more symbolic drama) published; Ibsen's son, Sigurd, weds Bjørnstjerne Bjørnson's daughter, Bergliot
- * Shaw's first play, *Widowers' Houses*, staged by the Independent Theatre Club

1893

- * Hauptmann's *The Weavers* and Strindberg's *Miss Julie* staged by Théâtre Libre; Freud (with Charcot) publishes *On the Psychical Mechanism of Hysterical Phenomena*

1894

- • *Little Eyolf* (exploring sexuality and guilt) published
- * Thomas Edison opens his Kinetoscope Parlor in New York

1896

- • *John Gabriel Borkman* published

1897

- * Théâtre Antoine, the successor to Théâtre Libre, founded; the Irish Literary Theatre founded; Moscow Art Theater founded by Constantine Stanislavsky

1898

- * Zola publishes "J'accuse"; Moscow Art Theater produces Chekhov's *The Seagull* (first performed unsuccessfully in St Petersburg in 1986); manhood suffrage first introduced in Norway at age twenty-five

1899

- • *When We Dead Awaken* ("a dramatic epilogue") published
- * Freud publishes *The Interpretation of Dreams*

1900

- • Ibsen suffers his first stroke and is no longer able to write

1901

- * Brieux's play *Maternité* (promoting women's issues) banned; women first allowed to vote in Norway (but only in local elections); Nobel Prize established

1902
- * Gorky's Naturalistic play, *The Lower Depths* performed; Zola, *La Terre* staged by Théâtre Antoine; Strindberg's *A Dream Play* performed (promoting a new form of drama: expressionism); Lenin publishes his revolutionary text, *What Is to Be Done?*

1903
- * Bjørnstjerne Bjørnson wins the Nobel Prize for Literature; Orville and Wilbur Wright successfully fly an engine-powered airplane; Women's Social and Political Union started in Britain to campaign for women's suffrage ("suffragettes")

1905
- * Albert Einstein formulates his Special Theory of Relativity; union between Norway and Sweden is dissolved; the crew of the battleship *Potemkin* mutiny

1906
- • Ibsen dies

1907
- * Norway becomes first European state to establish universal female suffrage

Contemporary Documents

Introduction

It is crucial to remember that a play only reaches full expression in performance on the stage, and the degree to which Ibsen was able to influence or dictate the first production of his plays is important. For this reason, many of the documents in this section explore the staging of his work. However, important documents relating to the cultural contexts of *Hedda Gabler* are also included below, following the structure of the Contextual Overview, to look first at Ibsen's views on nationalism or the state and the individual, then the Women's Movement, then Naturalism and the plays. Finally, documents on the evolution of *Hedda Gabler* are included.

Statehood and Individual Freedom

The poem below was addressed to Adolf Hedin (1834–1905), a journalist and member of the Swedish Parliament. Georg Brandes (1842–1927) was a leading literary critic and professor at the University of Copenhagen, and a long-time friend of Ibsen. His 1871 "Inaugural Lecture," published in his *Main Currents of Nineteenth-Century Literature*, was a significant factor in Ibsen's turn to Naturalistic drama, and Ibsen was in the habit of sending completed scripts to Brandes for commentary. The poem and letters reflect Ibsen's disillusionment with the state and any form of political action. As outlined in the Contextual Overview, he fought rather for individual liberty and did not consider state social reform as a feasible path to this goal. Though extreme, given the history of twentieth-century ideologies his comments might be seen as prescient – consider his comment on the Jews and statehood – but such views contributed to accusations of "nihilism" (the rejection of all religious beliefs or moral principles) in his plays.

From **Ibsen, "To My Friend the Revolutionary Orator"** (1869) in *Ibsen's Poems*, trans. John Northam (Oslo: Norwegian University Press, 1986), pp. 94–5.

You say I've become a 'conservative'.
I remain as I was, every day I live.
[. . .]
Just one revolution is worth repeating
that wasn't a matter of half-baked cheating.

It robs all the later attempts of their glory.
Of course I refer to the Deluge's story.
[. . .]
Let's try it again, but be more categorical;
We'll need real men though, not just rhetorical.

You fix up a flood to earth's farthest mark.
I'll gladly, myself, torpedo the Ark.

From **Ibsen, Letter to Georg Brandes**, December 20, 1870

[. . .] I must confess that the only thing I love about liberty is the struggle for it; I care nothing for the possession of it.

The great events of the day occupy my thoughts much at present. The old, illusory France has collapsed; and as soon as the new, real Prussia does the same, we shall be with one bound in a new age. How ideas will then come tumbling about our ears! And it is high time they did. Up till now we have been living on nothing but the crumbs from the revolutionary table of last century, a food out of which all nutriment has long been chewed. The old terms require to have a new meaning infused into them. Liberty, equality, and fraternity are no longer the things they were in the days of the late-lamented guillotine. This is what the politicians will not understand; and therefore I hate them. They want only their own special revolutions – revolutions in externals, in politics, etc. But all this is mere trifling. What is all-important is the revolution of the spirit of man [. . .]

From **Ibsen, Letter to Georg Brandes**, February 17, 1871

[. . .] I shall never agree to making liberty synonymous with political liberty. What you call liberty, I call liberties; and what I call struggle for liberty is nothing but the constant, living assimilation of the idea of freedom. He who possesses liberty other than as a thing to be striven for, possesses it dead and soulless for the idea of liberty has undoubtedly this character; that it develops steadily during its assimilation. So that a man who stops in the midst of the struggle and says: "Now I have it" – thereby shows that he has lost it. It is, however, this dead maintenance of a certain given standpoint of liberty that is characteristic of the communities which go by the name of states – and this it is that I have called worthless.

Yes, to be sure, it is a benefit to possess the franchise, the right of self-taxation, etc., but for whom is it a benefit? For the citizen, not for the individual. Now there is absolutely no reasonable necessity for the individual to be a citizen. On the contrary – the state is the curse of the individual. With what is the strength of Prussia as a state bought? With the merging of the individual in the political and geographical concept. The waiter makes the best soldier. Now, turn to the Jewish nation, the nobility of the human race. How has it preserved itself – isolated, poetical – despite all the barbarity from without? Because it had no state to burden it. Had the Jewish nation remained in Palestine, it would long since have been ruined in the process of construction, like all the other nations. The state must be abolished! In that revolution I will take part. Undermine the idea of the state; make willingness and spiritual kinship the only essentials in the case of a union – and you have the beginning of a liberty that is of some value. The changing of forms of government is mere toying with degrees – a little more or a little less – folly, the whole of it.

Yes, dear friend, the great thing is not to allow one's self to be frightened by the venerableness of the institution. The state has its root in Time: it will have its culmination in Time. Greater things than it will fall; all religion will fall. Neither the conceptions of morality nor those of art are eternal. To how much are we really obliged to pin our faith? Who will vouch for it that two and two do not make five up in Jupiter?

Ibsen and Women's Rights

From **Camilla Collett, Diary Entry**, cit. Karen Koht, *Norske Kvinder*, Oslo, 1914, Vol. I, p. 25

Camilla Collett (1813–95) was one of the earliest and most influential advocates of women's rights through her novels *The Sheriff's Daughter* (1855) and *From the Camp of the Dumb* (1877), friend and correspondent of Ibsen, and sister of the nationalistic historian and linguist Henrik Wergeland. She is reflected in the female protagonists of several of Ibsen's plays, most obviously in Hedda Gabler, and it is interesting to note that her novels attracted the same kind of criticism as Ibsen's work over twenty years later, being attacked both for their realism and for "feminine immodesty." Collett fell passionately in love with an intellectual rival of her brother and, when he rejected her because she offended his ideals of feminine propriety, married a dully respectable professor. The diary entry below indicates the boredom and enforced passivity of nineteenth-century women (see **p. 10**).

My life passes uselessly and without importance, suffocated by the eternal question whether this is really the kind of existence to which I am destined. It awakens me suddenly at night, I arise with it in the morning, and when I put on my night-cap in the evening and contemplate what I have done the whole day since I took it off I am saddened and ask myself why I dress at all, why I do not always wear it, for that would be most appropriate to such a night-cap life.

From **Ibsen, Speech at the Festival of the Norwegian Women's Rights League**, Christiana, May 26, 1888

Ibsen had clearly expressed his support for the women's rights movement in letters to Collett. And this short speech (from which only a few sentences of general compliment have been omitted) again reflects his desire for individual liberty and self-fulfillment for all – not just for women, but, as he says below, for "mankind in general." Since this speech was delivered barely a year before Ibsen started drafting *Hedda Gabler*, where the heroine not only burns a book that she clearly identifies as the intellectual equivalent of a baby, but also – though herself pregnant – rejects the constricting ties of motherhood in the most final way possible through her suicide, which also means the murder of her unborn child, his comments on the role of mothers has particular significance. (For further commentary on this speech, see **p. 11**.)

I am not a member of the Women's Rights League. Whatever I have written has been without any conscious thought of making propaganda. I have been more the poet and less the social philosopher than people generally seem inclined to believe. I thank you for the toast, but must disclaim the honor of having consciously worked for the women's rights movement. I am not even quite clear as to just what this women's rights movement really is. To me it has seemed a problem of mankind in general. And if you read my books carefully you will understand this. True enough, it is desirable to solve the woman problem, along with all the others; but that has not been the whole purpose. My task has been the description of humanity. To be sure, whenever such a description is felt to be reasonably true, the reader will read his own feelings and sentiments into the work of the poet. These are then attributed to the poet; but incorrectly so [. . .]

I do indeed recognize that women have an important task to perform in the particular directions this club is working along. I will express my thanks by proposing a toast to the League for Women's Rights, wishing it progress and success.

The task always before my mind has been to advance our country and to give our people a higher standard. To achieve this, two factors are important. It is for the mothers, by strenuous and sustained labor, to awaken a conscious feeling of culture and discipline. This feeling must be awakened before it will be possible to lift the people to a higher plane. It is the women who shall solve the human problem. As mothers they shall solve it. And only in that capacity can they solve it. Here lies a great task for woman. My thanks! And success to the League for Women's Rights!

The Principles of Naturalism

From **Émile Zola, *Naturalism in the Theatre***, 1881 (*Le Naturalisme au théâtre*) Paris: G. Charpentier, 1881, pp. 10–11, 14–15, 22–3, 123–4

Émile Zola (1840–1902) is best known for a monumental series of novels depicting French life during the Second Empire that made him the leading figure of the Naturalist movement. Zola here calls for a new drama based on realistic observation and scientific analysis, for which his best-known play *Thérèse Raquin* (1873) was intended as a model. His essays, collected in *Naturalism in the Theatre*, were some of the most influential documents of the period, providing a theoretical basis for Naturalistic drama. Ibsen never met Zola, but Zola's influence on the entire field of Naturalistic drama is clear.

It seems impossible that the movement of inquiry and analysis, which is precisely the movement of the nineteenth century, can have revolutionized all the sciences and arts and left dramatic art to one side, as if isolated. The natural sciences date from the end of the last century; chemistry and physics are less than a hundred years old; history and criticism have been renovated, virtually re-created since the Revolution; an entire world has arisen; it has sent us back to the study of documents, to experience, made us realize that to start afresh we must first take things back to the beginning, become familiar with man and nature, verify what is. Thenceforward, the great naturalistic school, which has spread secretly, irrevocably, often making its way in darkness but always advancing, can finally come out triumphantly into the light of day. To trace the history of this movement, with the misunderstandings that might have impeded it and the multiple causes that have thrust it forward or slowed it down, would be to trace the history of the century itself. An irresistible current carries our society towards the study of reality [. . .]

Naturalism alone corresponds to our social needs; it alone has deep roots in the spirit of our times; and it alone can provide a living, durable formula for our art, because this formula will express the nature of our contemporary intelligence. There may be fashions and passing fantasies that exist outside naturalism but they will not survive for long. I say again, naturalism is the expression of our century and it will not die until a new upheaval transforms our democratic world. Only one thing is needed now: men of genius who can fix the naturalistic formula. Balzac has done it for the novel and the novel is established. When will our Corneilles, Molières and Racines appear to establish our new theatre? [. . .]

The future is with naturalism. The formula will be found; it will be proved that there is more poetry in the little apartment of a bourgeois than in all the empty, worm-eaten palaces of history; in the end we will see that everything meets in the real: lovely fantasies that are free of capriciousness and whimsy, and idylls, and comedies, and dramas.

In addition to its scientific materialism, for Zola an essential element of the new theater will be stylistic consistency, where the visual aspects of a production and the acting had to correspond to the new type of characterization.

[. . .] everything is interdependent in the theatre. Lifelike costumes look wrong if the sets, the diction, the plays themselves are not lifelike. They must all march in step along the naturalistic road. When costume becomes more accurate, so do sets; actors free themselves from bombastic declaiming; plays study reality more closely and their characters are more true to life. I could make the same observations about sets I have just made about costume [. . .] Most of all we would need to intensify the illusion in reconstructing the environments, less for their picturesque quality than for dramatic utility. The environment must determine the character.

From **August Strindberg, Preface to *Miss Julie***, 1888, *Six Plays of Strindberg*, trans. Elizabeth Sprigge, Garden City, NJ: Doubleday & Company, Inc, 1955, pp. 63–5

August Strindberg (1849–1912) was a Swedish playwright, author of several Naturalistic plays including *Miss Julie*, and great rival of Ibsen. This Preface is often quoted in reference to the Naturalistic treatment of character. The ambiguity of motive asserted here is combined with a complex treatment of central figures. Although Naturalistic drama may contain explicit moral messages (for instance, plays campaigning for birth control, or dealing with the evils of prostitution) and strong social criticism, the way the characters are portrayed precludes moral judgments.

In real life an action – this, by the way, is a somewhat new discovery – is generally caused by a whole series of motives [. . .] I see Miss Julie's tragic fate to be the result of many circumstances [. . .]

I have made my people somewhat "characterless" for the following reason. In the course of time the word character has assumed manifold meanings. It must have originally signified the dominating trait of the soul complex, and this was confused with temperament. Later it became the middle-class term for the automaton, one whose nature had become fixed or who had adapted himself to a particular role in life . . . while one continuing to develop was called characterless, in a derogatory sense, of course, because he was so hard to catch, classify and keep track of [. . .]

Because they are modern characters, living in a period of transition more feverishly hysterical than its predecessor at least, I have drawn my figures vacillating, disintegrated, a blend of old and new.

Strindberg is typical in rejecting all moral judgment, describing his theme, elsewhere in the Preface, as:

[. . .] neither exclusively physiological nor psychological. I have not put the blame wholly on the inheritance from her mother, nor on her physical condition at the time, nor on immorality. I have not even preached a moral sermon [. . .]

Ibsen, On Objectivity, from *Morgenbladet*, January 14, 1882

In the stress on avoiding "messages," Strindberg was following Ibsen, who published this open letter in response to the uproar in the Scandinavian press that followed the first performance of *Ghosts*.

[. . .] They endeavour to make me responsible for the opinions expressed by some of the characters in the play. And yet [. . .] the method in itself, the technique which determined the form of the work, entirely precluded the author's appearing in the speeches. My intention was to produce the impression in the mind of the reader that he was experiencing something real. Now nothing would more effectively prevent such an impression than the insertion of the author's private opinions in the dialogue [. . .] It preaches nothing at all [. . .]

Ibsen, On the Primacy of Character, n.d., cit. Rudolph Lothar, *Henrik Ibsen* (1902)

The primacy of character over plot is one of the defining aspects of Naturalism. From the initial concept to the focus of the audience, Ibsen's Naturalistic drama – most particularly *Hedda Gabler* – centers on highly individualized and completely realized people.

Before I write a single word, I have to have each character in mind through and through. I must penetrate into the last wrinkle of his soul. I always proceed from the individual; everything else – the stage setting, the dramatic ensemble – comes naturally and does not cause me any worry, as soon as I am certain of the individual in every aspect of his humanity. But I also have to have his exterior in mind down to the last button: how he stands and walks, how he behaves, what his voice sounds like. Then I do not let him go until his fate fulfilled.

From **Ibsen, Letter to Edmund Gosse**, January 15, 1874, in Mary Morison (ed.) *Henrik Ibsen: Correspondence* (London: Hodder & Stoughton, 1905)

Sir Edmund Gosse (1849–1928) was Ibsen's first English translator and biographer, a critic of his work, and a personal friend. He became a major literary figure in England during the 1890s. In this letter to Gosse, written about the early history play *Emperor and Galilean*, Ibsen reveals the principles which continued to inform his work in his later Naturalistic stage.

The play is, as you must have observed, conceived in the most realistic style; the illusion I wished to produce was that of reality. I wished to produce the impression on the reader that what he was reading was something that had really happened. If I had employed verse, I should have counteracted my own intention and prevented the accomplishment of the task I had set myself. The many ordinary, insignificant characters whom I have intentionally introduced into the play would have become indistinct and indistinguishable from one another, if I had allowed them all to speak in the same rhythmical measure. We are no longer living in the days of Shakespeare. Among sculptors there is already talk of painting statues in the natural colours [. . .] I have no desire to see the Venus of Milo painted, but I would rather see the head of a negro executed in black than in white marble. Speaking generally the style must conform to the degree of ideality which pervades the representation. My new drama is no tragedy in the ancient acceptation; what I desired to depict were human beings, and therefore I would not let them talk the "language of the Gods".

Ibsen and the Naturalist Theater

Extracts from Ibsen's letters show the way in which he exercised control over the casting of his plays in Scandinavia (and to a lesser extent in Germany). He also advised directors on characterization and the way characters should be played, the setting and particularly the lighting, even the blocking of key scenes. Although the letters relating to this are relatively few for each production, and there are almost none relating to *Hedda Gabler* – which may indicate the degree to which Ibsen's principles had become generally accepted by that time – a composite picture of his intentions can be gained from the kinds of instruction he gives for a range of plays. His letters reflect a concern with casting and style of acting, lighting for emotional effect, exact positioning at key points (relating to *The Wild Duck*), and detailed realistic settings (for *Ghosts*), and he issues instructions to both directors and actors (as with *Rosmersholm*).

From **Ibsen, Letter to August Lindberg**, November 22, 1884, in Mary Morison (ed.) *Henrik Ibsen: Correspondence* (London: Hodder & Stoughton, 1905)

August Lindberg (1846–1916) was a Swedish actor and producer, who directed the Scandinavian premieres of several Ibsen plays. Particularly associated with Naturalistic drama, he also staged the plays of Strindberg. This letter advises on a production of *The Wild Duck*.

I have supposed Hjalmar will be played by Reimers. This part must definitely not be rendered with any touch of parody nor with the faintest suggestion that the actor is aware that there is anything funny about his remarks [. . .] His sentimentality is genuine, his melancholy charming in its way – not a bit of affectation [. . .]

The lighting too, has its significance; it differs from act to act and is calculated to correspond to the basic mood that characterizes each of the five acts [. . .] When Hedvig has shot herself, she should be placed on the couch in such a way that her feet are downstage, so that her right hand holding the pistol can hang down. When she is carried out through the kitchen door, I imagined Hjalmar holding her under the arms and Gina her feet.

From **Ibsen, Letter to Duke Georg II of Saxe-Meiningen**, November 13, 1886, in Mary Morison (ed.) *Henrik Ibsen: Correspondence* (London: Hodder & Stoughton, 1905)

Duke Georg (1826–1914) was founder of the Meiningen Company, which, with its unrivalled standard of realistic staging, performed *Ghosts* in 1886, to which Ibsen refers here.

The living rooms of the oldest family house of this type are sometimes covered with coloured, dark wallpaper. Below the paper the walls are lined with simple wainscoting [. . .] The stoves are big and massive, generally of cast iron. The furniture is kept to the style of the First Empire; however, the colours are consistently darker.

From **Ibsen, Letter to Sofie Reimers**, March 25, 1887, in Mary Morison (ed.) *Henrik Ibsen: Correspondence* (London: Hodder & Stoughton, 1905)

Sofie Reimers (1853–1932) was the first Norwegian actress to play Rebecca West in *Rosmersholm*. Her selection for the part shows Ibsen's control over casting. Hans Schroder, artistic director of the Christiana Theater, initially selected Laura Gundersen for the part – Ibsen objected that the role required a younger actress, and insisted she be replaced by Constance Bruun, who fell ill and had to be replaced in turn by Sofie Reimers.

[. . .] carefully observe what the other persons say about Rebecca. In earlier times our actors often committed the great mistake of studying their parts in isolation and without paying sufficient attention to the character's position in and connection with the work as a whole [. . .]

No declamation! No theatrical emphases! No pomposity at all! Give each mood credible, true to life expression. Do not ever think of this or that actress you may have seen.

From **Ibsen, Letter to Kristina Stern**, January 14, 1891, in Mary Morison (ed.) *Henrik Ibsen: Correspondence* (London: Hodder & Stoughton, 1905)

Ibsen's emphasis on the group of characters as a whole, which is particularly important in a play so apparently dominated by a central figure like Hedda, is restated in response to the refusal by Lucie Wolf, one of the lead actresses at the Kristiania Teater, to accept the minor role of the maid in *Hedda Gabler*.

Jørgen Tesman, his old aunts, and the elderly serving maid Berte together form a whole and a unity. They have a common way of thinking; common memories, and a common attitude to life. For Hedda they appear as an inimical and alien power directed against her fundamental nature. For this reason there must be harmony between them in performance.

Out of regard for Mrs. Wolf's good judgment I cannot seriously believe that she considers it beneath her dignity as an artist to portray a maid. After all, I have not considered it beneath my dignity to *create* this good-natured, simple, oldish person.

Hedda Gabler

From **Ibsen, Letter to Count Moritz Prozor**, December 4, 1890, in Mary Morison (ed.) *Henrik Ibsen: Correspondence* (London: Hodder & Stoughton, 1905)

Prozor [1849–?] was Ibsen's French translator. Ibsen's letters to Prozor contain illuminating comments on the themes, including the comment below.

The title of the play is *Hedda Gabler*. My intention in giving it this name was to indicate that Hedda as a personality is to be regarded rather as her father's daughter than as her husband's wife.

It was not my desire to deal in this play with so-called problems. What I principally wanted to do was to depict human beings, human emotions, and human destinies, upon a groundwork of certain of the social conditions and principles of the present day.

Ibsen, Preliminary Outline for *Hedda Gabler*, c.1889, in *The Works of Henrik Ibsen*, trans. William Archer (New York: 1912)

Taken as a whole, Ibsen's preliminary notes for *Hedda Gabler* are more detailed than for any of his other plays, and give a good picture of his working methods, as well as providing insights into his intentions. The initial concept (probably dating from late summer 1889) revolves around Camilla Collett (see **pp. 10** and **25–6**). The issue of a woman's lack of real outlets for personal fulfillment in a male dominated society was carried over into subsequent versions, together with the female protagonist's jealousy of a man with a mission in life, and contrasting male figures. In addition certain of the plot details from these first jottings survive into the final play – such as a misplaced manuscript, and a double suicide, botched by one of the participants. However, the protagonist was to change completely.

A married woman more and more imagines that she is an important personality, and as a consequence feels compelled to create for herself a sensational past –

If an interesting female character appears in a new story or in a play, she believes it is she who is being portrayed.

The masculine environment helps to confirm her in this belief.

The two lady friends agree to die together. One of them carries out her end of the bargain, but the other one who realizes what lies in store for her loses her courage. This is the reversal.

"He has such a disgusting way of walking when one sees him from behind."

She hates him because he has a goal, a mission in life. The lady friend has one too, but does not dare to devote herself to it. Her personal life treated in fictional form.

In the second act the manuscript that is left behind –

The "lost soul" apologizes for the man of culture. The wild horse and the race horse.

[. . .]

Revolution against the laws of nature – but nothing stupid, not until the position is secure.

Ibsen, Working Note for *Hedda Gabler*, c.1889–90, in *Playwrights on Playwriting*, ed. Toby Cole, trans. Evert Sprinchorn (New York: Hill and Wang, 1960)

This first note from a slightly later and much fuller outline encapsulates the central elements of the character who emerges as Hedda.

The pale, seemingly cold beauty. Great demands upon life and upon the joy of life.

He, who has now at last conquered her, is insignificant in person, but an honorable and gifted, liberal-minded man of science.

Ibsen, Scenario for Acts 2 and 3, c.1890, in *Playwrights on Playwriting*, ed. Toby Cole, trans. Evert Sprinchorn (New York: Hill and Wang, 1960)

Ibsen's subsequent scenario (probably written in spring 1890) indicates the type of social criticism embedded in the characters, but shows that the details of Hedda's personality are still developing and at this point some of her eventual attributes are shared by Thea (Mrs. R.). The contents of Løvborg's manuscript clearly echo views expressed in Ibsen's own letters (see above, **p. 24**), signaling that some later interpretations of Løvborg as a charlatan (as in Ingmar Bergman's 1964 production of *Hedda Gabler*: see below, **pp. 88–92**) are a distortion.

The manuscript that H.L. leaves behind contends that man's mission is: Upward, towards the bearer of light. Life on the present foundations of society is not worth living. Therefore he escapes from it through his imagination. By drinking, etc. – Tesman stands for correct behaviour. Hedda for blasé over-sophistication. Mrs. R. is the nervous-hysterical modern individual. Brack represents the personal bourgeois point of view.

[. . .]

N.B.! Brack had always thought that Hedda's short engagement to Tesman would be broken off.

Hedda talks of how she felt herself set aside, step by step, when her father had fallen out of favour, retired [from the army] and died leaving no property – She then felt, and felt bitterly, as if it had been for his sake that she had been feted – And she was already between 25 and 26. On the point of going downhill unmarried.

She thinks that Tesman in reality feels only a vain exultation at having won her. His care for her is like that which one expends upon a fine riding-horse, or a valuable sporting dog – She does not, however, feel indignant at this. She regards it simply as a fact.

Hedda says to Brack that she does not think one can call Tesman ridiculous. But in reality she does find him so. And later she finds him pitiful.

TESMAN. Could you not call me by my Christian name?
HEDDA. No, indeed, I can't – unless you had a different name from the one they have given you.

Tesman takes possession of Løvborg's manuscript, in order that it may not be lost. It is Hedda who afterwards, as if by a passing remark, intended to test him, suggests to him the idea of keeping it.

Then he reads it. A new train of thought is set up within him. But the situation becomes more tense. Hedda awakens his jealousy.

*

In the third act there comes one piece of news after another as to Løvborg's exploits during the night. At last he himself arrives, in quiet despair. "Where is the manuscript?" "Did I not leave it behind me here?" He knows that he did not. And, in any case, what use would the manuscript be to him now! He to write of "the ethics of the future"! He, who has just got out of the police cells!

Hedda's despair lies in the idea that there are surely so many possibilities of happiness in the world, but that she cannot discover them. It is the lack of an object in life that tortures her.

When Hedda tempts T. to lead E.L. to ruin, it is to test T.'s character.

It is in Hedda's neighbourhood that the irresistible craving for dissipation always comes over E.L.

Tesman cannot understand that E.L. should be willing to build his future on wrong done to another.

From **William Archer, Preface to *Hedda Gabler***, in *The Collected Works of Henrik Ibsen*, trans. Edmund Gosse and William Archer, New York: Charles Scribner's, 1906–12, Vol. X (1912), pp. xii–xvi.

Archer (1856–1924) was the English theater critic most responsible for introducing Ibsen to the English stage. As well as writing over 200 reviews and essays on Ibsen from 1878 to 1923, Archer directed many of the first London productions of Ibsen's plays. He got to know Ibsen well, translated most of his plays (some together with Edmund Gosse – see **p. 30**), and edited *The Collected Works*, from which this Preface is drawn. Archer's analysis of the genesis of the play, based as it is on his own observation of Ibsen at work and his various contacts with Ibsen, carries more than usual weight. His point in these extracts about Ibsen's increasing focus on Hedda helps to explain the general critical reception of the play over the first half of the twentieth century, which focused on the character of the heroine to the exclusion of social factors – while his description of the search for a real-life source for Hedda (and the self-identification of one man with Løvborg) is an indication both of the level of realism Ibsen achieved in the play, and of the degree to which contemporaries identified with the major characters. Indeed still other analogues have been suggested: for example that Løvborg was based on Julius Hoffory, a Norwegian professor who went insane in 1890. However, it has to be kept in mind that Ibsen insisted that his sources were subjective.

From the more detailed drafts it would appear that, in the poet's original conception, Tesman was to be much more of an active intermediary between Hedda and Løvborg than he became in the end. It was Tesman who, at her instigation, was to lure Løvborg to Brack's orgy; and it was apparently Tesman who was actually to make away with or misappropriate Løvborg's manuscript. Both Tesman and Mrs. Elvsted were to have known much more of the former "comradeship" between Løvborg and Hedda than they do in the finished play. There is no hint of any "Mademoiselle Diana" in the draft; when Hedda asks Mrs. Elvsted who the woman is whom Løvborg cannot forget, she replies point-blank, "It is yourself, Hedda." Mrs. Elvsted's luxuriant hair, Hedda's jealousy of it, and threat to "burn it off her head," are afterthoughts; so is the famous conception of Løvborg "with the vine-leaves in his hair." A curious touch, which I am at a loss to explain, occurs in the stage-direction for Hedda's burning of Løvborg's manuscript. It runs thus: "She goes to the writing-table, takes out the manuscript, seats herself in the arm-chair beside the stove; opens the packet, sorts out the white leaves from the blue, puts the white back in the cover again, and keeps the blue in her lap." Then she opens the stove door and gradually burns the blue leaves, with words very much like those of the final text. What the white leaves can have been I do not know; they must have belonged to some phase in the working-out of the play which has otherwise disappeared.

[. . .]

We cannot point to any individual model or models who "sat to" Ibsen for the character of Hedda.[1] The late Grant Allen[2] declared that Hedda was "nothing more nor less than the girl we take down to dinner in London nineteen times out of twenty"; in which case Ibsen must have suffered from a superfluity of models, rather than from any difficulty in finding one. But the fact is that in this, as in all other instances, the word "model" must be taken in a very different sense from that in which it is commonly used in painting. Ibsen undoubtedly used models for this trait and that, but never for a whole figure. If his characters can be called portraits at all, they are composite portraits. Even when it seems pretty clear that the initial impulse towards the creation of a particular character came from some individual, the original figure is entirely transmuted in the process of harmonisation with the dramatic scheme. We need not, therefore, look for a definite prototype of Hedda; but Dr. Brandes shows that two of that lady's exploits were probably suggested by the anecdotic history of the day.

Ibsen had no doubt heard how the wife of a well-known Norwegian composer, in a fit of raging jealousy excited by her husband's prolonged absence from home, burnt the manuscript of a symphony which he had just finished. The circumstances under which Hedda burns Løvborg's manuscript are, of course, entirely different and infinitely more dramatic; but here we have merely another instance

1 [Archer's note.] However, Dr. Brahm (*Neue deutsche Rundschau*, December 1906, p. 1422) says that after the first performance of *Hedda Gabler* in Berlin Ibsen confided to him that the character had been suggested by a German lady whom he met in Munich, and who did not shoot, but poisoned herself. Nothing more seems to be known of this lady. See, too, an article by Julius Elias in the same magazine, p. 1460.

2 Grant Allen (1848–99) was one of the major scientists and essayists of the period and had a reputation as an arbiter of fashion. A prolific novelist and frequent contributor to *The Strand* magazine, Grant also published naturalistic studies on insects and plants, topographical studies of England, books on scientific theory, psychology and theology, translations of Catullus, the first study of Charles Darwin (1886), and historical guidebooks to the principal cities of Europe.

of the dramatisation or "poetisation" of the raw material of life. Again, a still more painful incident probably came to his knowledge about the same time. A beautiful and very intellectual woman was married to a well-known man who had been addicted to drink, but had entirely conquered the vice. One day a mad whim seized her to put his self-mastery and her power over him to the test. As it happened to be his birthday, she rolled into his study a small keg of brandy, and then withdrew. She returned some time afterwards to find that he had broached the keg, and lay insensible on the floor. In this anecdote we cannot but recognise the germ, not only of Hedda's temptation of Løvborg, but of a large part of her character.

"Thus," says Dr. Brandes, "out of small and scattered traits of reality Ibsen fashioned his close-knit and profoundly thought-out works of art."

For the character of Eilert Løvborg, again, Ibsen seems unquestionably to have borrowed several traits from a definite original. A young Danish man of letters, whom Dr. Brandes calls Holm, was an enthusiastic admirer of Ibsen, and came to be on very friendly terms with him. One day Ibsen was astonished to receive, in Munich, a parcel addressed from Berlin by this young man, containing, without word of explanation, a packet of his (Ibsen's) letters, and a photograph which he had presented to Holm. Ibsen brooded and brooded over the incident, and at last came to the conclusion that the young man had intended to return her letters and photograph to a young lady to whom he was known to be attached, and had in a fit of aberration mixed up the two objects of his worship. Some time after, Holm appeared at Ibsen's rooms. He talked quite rationally, but professed to have no knowledge whatever of the letter-incident, though he admitted the truth of Ibsen's conjecture that the "belle dame sans merci" had demanded the return of her letters and portrait. Ibsen was determined to get at the root of the mystery; and a little inquiry into his young friend's habits revealed the fact that he broke his fast on a bottle of port wine, consumed a bottle of Rhine wine at lunch, of Burgundy at dinner, and finished off the evening with one or two more bottles of port. Then he heard, too, how, in the course of a night's carouse, Holm had lost the manuscript of a book; and in these traits he saw the outline of the figure of Eilert Løvborg.

Some time elapsed, and again Ibsen received a postal packet from Holm. This one contained his will, in which Ibsen figured as his residuary legatee. But many other legatees were mentioned in the instrument – all of them ladies, such as Fräulein Alma Rothbart, of Bremen, and Fräulein Elise Kraushaar, of Berlin. The bequests to these meritorious spinsters were so generous that their sum considerably exceeded the amount of the testator's property. Ibsen gently but firmly declined the proffered inheritance; but Holm's will no doubt suggested to him the figure of that red-haired "Mademoiselle Diana," who is heard of but not seen in *Hedda Gabler*, and enabled him to add some further traits to the portraiture of Løvborg. When the play appeared, Holm recognised himself with glee in the character of the bibulous man of letters, and thereafter adopted "Eilert Løvborg" as his pseudonym. I do not, therefore, see why Dr. Brandes should suppress his real name; but I willingly imitate him in erring on the side of discretion. The poor fellow died several years ago.

2

Interpretations

Critical History

Hedda Gabler was the first of Ibsen's "international" plays. His previous plays were performed first in Scandinavia. By contrast, not only was the premiere of *Hedda Gabler* in Germany, but almost simultaneous productions appeared in Munich, Berlin, London, and Copenhagen (all between January and April 1891), with a Paris production following before the end of the year (December 1891). And while Ibsen was more performed in Germany than anywhere else during the early period, subsequently *Hedda Gabler* has appeared more frequently and received more critical attention in Britain and America than even in Norway.

As with any play, the most important form of interpretation is stage performance, and critical responses and the history of the work in performance are inseparable. Actors and directors read critics in preparing any production of a "classic" – and *Hedda Gabler* quickly became a "modern classic" – so that their work can to some extent be seen as a reflection, or even as a way of testing the most recent critical consensus. But equally, those who write on a play will have seen one or more stagings; and the readings put forward in academic books or journal articles are frequently heavily conditioned by those performances. One example is Henry James, whose widely influential essay of 1891 (**pp. 63–4**), written after seeing Elizabeth Robins in the role, effectively imposed this performance as the standard view of Hedda's character for the early part of the twentieth century. Another instance is the way a production starring Joan Greenwood in 1960 inspired the critic and dramatist Nigel Dennis to see the play in terms of Greek tragedy (**pp. 83–4**), which then became a standard critical view in Britain during the 1960s. So throughout this section critical views of *Hedda Gabler* are interwoven with the comments of selected actresses and descriptions of key productions, in a chronological sequence which clearly shows the developing understanding of the play. The following overview offers a guide to the various, interrelated interpretations of Ibsen's play, by audiences, critics, and performers. Key interpretations are also represented in the documents which follow this overview.

Ibsen and His Public

In considering the reception and criticism of *Hedda Gabler*, it is important to have some idea of the initial response to Ibsen's work as a whole. From the slamming of the door as Nora walked out of her marriage in *A Doll's House*, almost all of Ibsen's Naturalistic plays were initially greeted with public outrage. This was particularly true in Britain where, although *Ghosts* was the only play refused public performance, the official view was that the society Ibsen portrayed so unpleasantly was too incredible to have any influence on the British public (see **p. 53**).

Defending his work against the outrage over *Ghosts*, Ibsen wrote a public letter to the leading Oslo newspaper, arguing that he was not responsible for the opinions expressed by the characters in his play. Rather, "My intention was to produce the impression in the mind of the reader that he was experiencing something real. Now nothing would more effectively prevent such an impression than the insertion of the author's private opinions in the dialogue."[1] Such a claim to objectivity is indispensable to the principles of Naturalism (see **p. 12**). However, in this case it was attacked as a "cowardly" evasion by both August Strindberg, Ibsen's fellow Naturalist playwright, and Georg Brandes, who had been the only Scandinavian commentator to defend the play. And indeed in the case of *Ghosts* the attack on the narrow morality of Norwegian society is immediately clear in the title itself, in images of syphilis and a fire that destroys an orphanage, and in the characterization of a parson whose moralistic actions and advice have led to the final disintegration of the family who represent the cultural core of Norway. His next play, *The Enemy of the People*, is generally taken as a direct response to the scandal, Ibsen identifying with its maligned hero.

Perhaps also as a reaction to the furor, thereafter his social criticism becomes less overt. While *Hedda Gabler* was considered disturbing and unpleasant, the major symbols – like Hedda's pistols, inherited from her father, or her husband's all too domestic slippers – are essentially personal, relating primarily to the characters. However, the critics of the time had come to expect the more obvious social criticism of Ibsen's previous plays. As William Archer, a major critic, producer, and translator of Ibsen's work pointed out, a primary "source of misunderstanding" for Ibsen's plays in general was "the facile hero-worship of those who saw in *A Doll's House* a sort of Woman's-Rights manifesto, and hailed Ibsen as the preacher of a social, one might almost say a social-democratic, gospel."[2] By contrast the absence of any identifiable ideology in *Hedda Gabler* was confusing for Ibsen's nineteenth-century audiences.

As a result, in Scandinavia and Germany at least, audiences rejected *Hedda Gabler* as incomprehensible and unpleasant, but it passed without public scandal – even though Ibsen's radical attack on society in his letters of 1870 and 1871 and his poem "To My Friend the Revolutionary Orator" (see above, **pp. 24–5**) is clearly expressed through Hedda's actions. The Munich and Christiana reviewers

1 *Morgenbladet*, January 14, 1882, reprinted on **p. 29**.
2 "The Real Ibsen," *International Monthly*, February 1901.

focused exclusively on the performance of whichever actress was playing the title role. Yet by contrast *Hedda Gabler* was the most successful of Ibsen's plays on the London stage in the 1890s, and the English critics, as Archer's summary in "The Mausoleum of Ibsen" shows (**pp. 62–3**), were hardly less outraged than by *Ghosts*.

Although Ibsen's plays both shocked and confused, his work became very popular. Interestingly, the major impact of his work came through publication, rather than stage performance. Ibsen refers in his letters to "readers" of his work. His first Naturalistic play, *The Pillars of Society*, was published in Norway a month before its first production and quickly sold 6,000 copies, with a second printing of 4,000 copies being required within two months. In English-speaking countries the effect was even more marked. The first play by Ibsen to reach the London stage was *The Pillars of Society*, given a single matinee in 1880. By 1892 five other plays had been staged in England; *Ghosts* and *Rosmersholm* (two performances each), *The Lady from the Sea* (three performances), *Hedda Gabler* (ten matinees), plus *A Doll's House* (one week, but extended to twenty-four performances, in 1889) – though *A Doll's House* had also been presented in two short-lived and very distorted adaptations, *Breaking a Butterfly* (1884) and *Nora* (1885). Up to 1893 fewer than 10,000 people in England would have seen staged performances of any play by Ibsen. In contrast, by the same year over three times as many copies of Ibsen's plays had been bought by the British public. In the *Fortnightly Review* of July 1, 1893, William Archer suggested that, by adding together the sales of individual plays and of every play within an anthology, "we are well within the mark in estimating that one hundred thousand prose dramas by Ibsen have been bought by the English-speaking public in the course of the past four years."

Given such publication figures – and following Janet Achurch's success in an extended run of *A Doll's House* – it is perhaps not surprising that in London during 1893 there were successful productions of *The Master Builder*, Beerbohm Tree's staging of *An Enemy of the People*, and an Ibsen "season" at the Opera Comique (which included a re-staging of *Hedda Gabler*). From that point on, Ibsen's Naturalistic plays became a standard feature of the English-speaking repertoire, as they had a decade earlier in Germany. *Hedda Gabler* has been one of the most frequently performed plays, and a tabled "performance history" in this section charts the major productions (**pp. 49–52**).

Gosse and Archer: Setting the Critical Agenda

Ibsen repeatedly refers to the conceptual unity of his mature plays; and *Hedda Gabler* is usually considered as the seventh in a series of twelve later plays initiated by *The Pillars of Society*. Some contemporary commentators see all of Ibsen's later plays as a single sequence, united by common themes, expressed in progressively more forceful terms. However, most divide the plays into separate groups, taking their cue from Georg Brandes, Ibsen's friend and contemporary. Brandes labeled the first six of these plays "polemical," the second six "psychological." A contemporary critic, James McFarlane (see **pp. 102–5**), goes even further in *Ibsen and Meaning* (1989), subdividing the plays into four groups: "Drama and Society" (*The Pillars of Society*, *A Doll's House*, *Ghosts*); "Drama and the Person" (*An Enemy of the People*, *The Wild Duck*, *Rosmersholm*); "Drama and the Mind" (*The Lady from the Sea*, *Hedda Gabler*, *The Master Builder*); "Drama and Individual Integrity" (*Little Eyolf*, *John Gabriel Borkman*, *When We Dead Awaken*).

By contrast, when the plays first appeared, commentators like Sir Edmund Gosse (in the earliest essay on *Hedda Gabler* in English – see **p. 54**) and William Archer (in his Preface nearly twenty years later – see **pp. 36** and **65**) saw *The Lady from the Sea* as a "falling-off" – its failure to meet the standard of the first six plays signaling a new departure in theme and stylistic approach, picked up again in *The Master Builder* and subsequent plays – whereas *Hedda Gabler* was greeted as a return to the Naturalism of *A Doll's House* and *Ghosts*.

Hedda Gabler, then, can be seen as the culminating play of Ibsen's trend-setting Naturalistic period; and the connection that Gosse makes between Hedda and the proto-feminist Nora of *A Doll's House* had already become a commonplace by the time of a 1918 revival of *Hedda Gabler* in America, with one reviewer describing it as "the companion-piece, or rather the negative pendant, of *A Doll's House*,"[3] though other more recent critics (such as McFarlane, see **pp. 102–5**) find closer parallels with Rebecca in *Rosmersholm*.

Gosse was also the first to appreciate the extreme conciseness of the speeches in *Hedda Gabler* – an aspect also remarked by Janet Suzman, the only actress to play the role on the English stage who was able to read the original Norwegian text (see **pp. 98–100**) – although Gosse saw this as simply a mark of expert workmanship, rather than appreciating the way such minimalism opens up the play to allow the critique of wide social issues beneath the apparently normal surface. However, he does point to the extent of the "pre-history" that gradually emerges, revealing hidden depths of motivation; and this aspect of the play too was later picked up in performance, notably by Blanche Yurka, who played the role in New York in 1929 (see **pp. 70–1**). A further level of interpretation, mentioned in passing by Gosse, links Hedda with the romantic decadence of *fin-de-siècle* Europe, which was only much later brought to the fore in Eva le Gallienne's 1964 National Repertory Theatre production (see **pp. 71–4**), and has since been explored in detail by the critic Errol Durbach in *Ibsen the Romantic* (1982).

Overlooking the wider implications of his insight about Hedda as a representative of late nineteenth-century decadence, Gosse sees Ibsen's focus in *Hedda Gabler* as "strictly psychological." As Gosse's 1891 article and Archer's Preface show, being unable to identify a clear social message, both translators concluded that it presented a study of individual character. This was echoed by Henry James in his 1891 review (**pp. 63–4**), and continued to be the accepted reading of the play until recently, still being promoted by one leading Ibsen scholar of the 1940s and 1950s, Muriel Bradbrook (see **pp. 77–9**). The problem with interpreting *Hedda Gabler* as "a portrait play,"[4] as the extract from Bradbrook's *Ibsen the*

3 John Corbin, "From the New Plays," the *New York Sunday Times*, April 14, 1918, section 4, p. 5.
4 Eva le Gallienne's description, *Civic Repertory Magazine*, December 1930.

Norwegian shows, is that it relegates all the other figures who surround Hedda to insignificant ciphers. This view also makes it possible for a critic like G. Wilson Knight to give a heroic reading of Hedda (see **pp. 80–1**), even though this sort of symbolic inflation is specifically rejected by actresses who have played the part (see Nazimova's commentary, **pp. 66–9**).

It was not until Glenda Jackson's 1975 performance that this view was seriously challenged. Jackson, in the title role, clearly perceived Hedda to be as much a victim as a villain, surrounded and manipulated by a group of "incredibly self-centred people" (see **pp. 95–8**). In the same decade, contemporary feminist interpretations began to appear, pointing to the patriarchal nature of the society surrounding Hedda as the source of her apparently psychotic behavior – and reinstating Hedda as a "heroine" though in very different terms to Knight.

Interpreting *Hedda Gabler*

It has been said that the role of Hedda is to contemporary actresses what Hamlet has always been for male actors; and throughout the twentieth century this has been one of the most frequently performed of all plays. The exotic Russian actress Alla Nazimova, who performed *Hedda Gabler* in America in 1906, the year of Ibsen's death, was still playing the role in 1936. In 1928–9 there were two versions of the play, one starring Blanche Yurka (presenting a whole season of Ibsen) and the other Eva le Gallienne, on Broadway simultaneously. Between 1970 and 1971 *Hedda Gabler* was staged in London, New York (twice), and Stratford, Ontario; and in 1981 there were at least four different productions of the play in the same year in North America alone – as there were in Germany in 1997. *Hedda Gabler* was one of the first Ibsen plays to be filmed – by Nance O'Neill in 1917 – and it has become a favorite stage vehicle for film stars like Mai Zetterling (1960), Joan Greenwood (1960 and 1964), Claire Bloom (1971), Liv Ullman (1975), Glenda Jackson (1975), and Susannah York (1981), while Ingrid Bergman appeared in a 1963 television production. It has also been translated in modern versions by two leading British playwrights – John Osborne (1972) and Christopher Hampton (1989) – as well as being used by Charles Marowitz as a basis for his *Hedda* adaptation (1980).

The early reception of *Hedda Gabler* in England was widely recognized as a vindication of Ibsen's theater despite the attacks on what was seen as the immorality and pessimism of the play's vision. This was largely due to the psychological character study on which Elizabeth Robins based her performance (outlined forty years later in her autobiography, *Ibsen and the Actress*: see **pp. 57–61**). The feminist implications of her interpretation were indeed overlooked (as she indicates); even Lady Bell, whom she mentions as one of her strongest women supporters, focused solely on the "corrosiveness" and "tragic" nature of the characterization.[5] In America this interpretation of the play as a portrait of

5 *Landmarks*, London: E. Benn, 1929, pp. 110–11.

perverse psychology was emphasized even more strongly by Alla Nazimova's melodramatic portrayal of evil.

Ibsen himself had deliberately set *Hedda Gabler* in the past, setting the action (as Archer points out in his Preface) back a whole generation. By contrast, during the middle decades of the century, the continuing relevance of the play was emphasized by contemporary dress productions: in 1927–8 by Eva le Gallienne, who was recorded as clothing Hedda "in the current mode – even to a jaunty mourning frock" as well as consuming "several cartons of cigarettes,"[6] and by Nazimova in 1936. Although le Gallienne rejected this type of "modernization" for a second production in 1964, such updating led to American interpretations of Hedda in the 1950s as a type of the bored suburban housewife: "Hedda as a woman with a Ladies Home Journal 'Freudian' problem" as a later critic remarked.[7] Other forms of updating include transposing the action to Ireland (1991) or Scotland (in the 1976 film of the Glenda Jackson production).

As Ibsen's plays became firmly established on mainstream stages – regularly performed in the West End and on Broadway, as well as at the American National Repertory Theatre and the Royal Shakespeare Company – and with *Hedda Gabler* being staged possibly even more often than *Hamlet* over the twentieth century, two distinct lines of criticism emerged, replacing the earlier moral emphasis. The first, starting with H.L. Mencken in the 1930s, was to dismiss all moral issues and instead concentrate on Ibsen's techniques and dramatic method (see **pp. 74–6**). Particularly associated with America, this morally neutral, work-aday depiction of Ibsen went along with Blanche Yurka's interpretation of Hedda as a contemporary woman and Eva le Gallienne's modern dress production. The view, stressed by Mencken, of Ibsen as a craftsman is also acknowledged by one of the most highly regarded modern American dramatists, Arthur Miller (see **pp. 76–7**), who started his career with a modern version of Ibsen's *The Pillars of Society* – *All My Sons* (1947) – and later pointed to the connection between his own plays and Ibsen's by adapting *An Enemy of the People* (1977). And since *Hedda Gabler* is recognized as one of the most technically sophisticated, from this viewpoint it gained central significance among the Naturalistic plays – which may also explain why *Hedda Gabler* became one of the most frequently performed plays on the American stage throughout the middle decades of the century.

Secondly, critics began to analyze Ibsen's work along the traditional criteria for "classics." This led to a re-evaluation of his plays in terms of poetic drama and tragedy. Although there were some transatlantic voices, this line was mainly pursued by British commentators. Following Halvdan Koht's 1928 biography which opened with the assertion that "Henrik Ibsen was a poet. This would seem self-evident; yet . . . too many have attempted to make him a thinker or a philosopher, a social critic or a social reformer,"[8] they focused on Ibsen's "use of symbols or

6 J. Brooks Atkinson, "The Play: Eva le Gallienne," the *New York Times*, March 27, 1928, p. 30.

7 Elenore Lester, "Hedda – Frigid Woman or Life Bearer?," the *New York Sunday Times*, March 7, 1971, section 2, pp. 3, 29.

8 Halvdan Koht, *Life of Ibsen*, trans. Einar Haugen and A. E. Santaniello, New York: American Scandinavian Foundation, W. W. Norton, 1931, p. 1.

symbolic motifs to suggest a surging unconscious of the will."[9] This led to an almost exclusive emphasis on Ibsen's early verse plays and the last group of overtly symbolic and psychological dramas, at the expense of the Naturalistic plays. Even when a less "literary" concept of poetry became accepted – as in the assertion that in Ibsen's "characters, the events and actions, the setting" all create "a unified pattern of metaphor and symbol"[10] – the concision and apparent flatness of the dialogue in *Hedda Gabler* meant that it was largely passed over, although the insights are equally applicable.

Allied with this was the measurement of Ibsen by the criteria of tragic theory, first mooted in *The Modern Theatre* (1948) by the eminent American critic, Eric Bentley (see **p. 82**) – even if, in his view, the combination of Naturalism with tragedy was an "uneasy" accomplishment from which Ibsen "retreated." This made Ibsen a key figure in the search for a viable form of modern tragedy, for which his work became an exemplar in the late 1950s and 1960s. Although this type of analysis tended to generalize on the basis of his plays as a whole – as with George Steiner (*The Death of Tragedy*, 1961 – see **pp. 84–5**), and Geoffrey Brereton (*The Principles of Tragedy*, 1968 – see **pp. 85–6** – many of the comments also apply directly to *Hedda Gabler*.

This critical elevation, while bringing out one level of ambiguity – the tension between surface realism and psychological depth – completely obscured another central aspect of the play: the harsh comedy that underlies many of the scenes. When the original Copenhagen and Munich audiences had laughed at *Hedda Gabler* in 1891 it was out of defensive scorn, a way of ridiculing Ibsen's "unnatural" woman.[11] In 1929 Blanche Yurka intended her production to have a comic edge, but (as her memoirs attest) it went completely unrecognized, the critics' mind-set being blinkered by the received view of the play.

More recently the play's true comic elements have been brought out. One of the earliest to stress the "black comedy" was a feminist critic, Elenore Lester, writing in 1971 (see **pp. 92–5**); and this formed the focus of a production just four years later, with Glenda Jackson – who played the title role in Los Angeles in 1975 – referring to Hedda as "not banal enough to be truly evil. She doesn't have enough passion for evil. She could say she hates something, for instance, but not know what hate is. Nothing works for her the way it should. I think the play is really a black comedy. It's really about someone marvelous who got away."[12] (For Jackson's further comments, see **p. 98**.) Significantly, since it shows how in the developing interpretation of a play at any given time there will be a consensus, reflecting the views of that particular era and conditioning the meaning of the text, in exactly the same year but completely independently, Janet Suzman's performance of the role also emphasized that there is "a lot of comedy" in *Hedda Gabler* (see **pp. 100–1**).

Ingmar Bergman's 1964 production, which could be counted as the first "postmodern" interpretation of the play, is illustrated by a study of its three

9 Peter Tennant, *Ibsen's Dramatic Technique*, Cambridge: Bowes & Bowes, 1948, p. 46.
10 Ronald Peacock, *The Art of Drama*, London: Routledge & Kegan Paul Ltd., 1957, p. 217.
11 Karl Frenzel, *Deutsche Rundschau*, April–May–June 1891.
12 Interview with Robert Shanke, May 13, 1982, reprinted in Robert Shanke, *Ibsen in America: A Century of Change*, Metuchen, NJ: The Scarecrow Press, 1988, pp. 266–71.

versions (**pp. 88–92**): in Stockholm, and again in London (1970) and in Munich (1979). The stripped-down text used by Bergman removed all temporal and social locators to focus exclusively on the play's emotional core, representing Hedda's internal state – as well as the moment of her suicide – physically on stage. It cut all realistic references, making the performative quality of theater overt by introducing an image of Hedda as actress, and presented a vision of spiritual paralysis and meaningless existence, in which even Løvborg's manuscript is reduced to irrelevance. And his interpretation remained in vogue: the symbolic blood-red setting, together with the visual references to Edvard Munch's paintings of interior emotions that had characterized Bergman's production, as well as the view of Hedda as "a force of nature confined in an airless existence"[13] being copied – albeit in a far more conventional staging by Yale Rep – a whole generation after its first appearance.

The most recent approach, which presents a balance between the various opposing views, is represented by Janet Suzman's commentary on the role, and by James McFarlane's 1989 analysis of *Hedda Gabler* (based on his 1966 Preface for the Oxford edition – see **pp. 102–5**).

The texts selected for inclusion in the performance and criticism sections below are listed in chronological order. Almost all these commentaries relate to the British and American reception of *Hedda Gabler*. Since the play itself is a modern text, the division between early and modern criticism and performance is somewhat arbitrary. But the transition here has been placed in 1906, the year of Ibsen's death, by which time the first biographies and complete editions of his plays were beginning to appear, encouraging more comprehensive critical approaches. It is also around this period that the view of Ibsen, and particularly of *Ghosts* and *Hedda Gabler*, shifted. In the 1890s and even through the first decade of the twentieth century, Ibsen was a revolutionary and his plays like *Hedda Gabler* were heaped with invective, fought over, and even censored. By contrast, from the 1920s on Ibsen had become accepted, and plays like *Hedda Gabler* became part of the standard theatrical repertoire.

13 Mel Gussow, "Theatre: 'Hedda Gabler' by Yale Rep," the *New York Times*, March 11, 1981, p. C22.

Hedda Gabler: Production History

Date	*Theater (city)*	*Director, translator (t) or adapter (a)*	*Actor playing Hedda*
January 1891	Residenztheater (Munich)	Ludwig Passarge	Marie Conrad-Ramlo
February 1891	Lessing Theater (Berlin)		Anna Haverland
February 1891	Danish Royal Theatre (Copenhagen)		Betty Hennings
April 1891	Vaudeville Theatre (London)	Elizabeth Robins William Archer (t)	Elizabeth Robins
December 1891	Théâtre du Vaudeville (Paris)		Marthe Brandès
May 1893	Opera Comique (London)		Janet Achurch
March 1898	5th Avenue Theatre (New York)	Edwin Knowles	Elizabeth Robins
February 1899	Moscow Art Theatre (Moscow)	Stanislavsky	Maria F. Andreeva
October 1903	Adelphi Theatre (London)	Eleonora Duse	Eleonora Duse
October 1903	Manhattan Theatre (New York)		Minnie Maddern Fiske
November 1906	Komissarzhevskaya Theatre (St. Petersburg)	Vsevolod Meyerhold	Vera Komissarzhevskaya
November 1906	Princess Theatre (New York) and then on tour	Alla Nazimova (t)	Alla Nazimova
March 1907	Royal Court (London) and on tour in England and America	Mrs. Patrick Campbell	Mrs. Patrick Campbell
May 1911	Kingsway Theatre (London)		Lydia Yavorska (Princess Bariatinsky)
November 1912	Court Theatre (London)	J. P. Grein Edmund Gosse (t)	Eve Balfour Hulston (replaced by Hilda Gilbert, then by Octavia Kenmore)
July 1917	(Silent film version)		Nance O'Neill
April 1918	Plymouth Theatre (New York)	Arthur Hopkins Alla Nazimova (t)	Alla Nazimova
September 1919	Neighborhood Theatre (New York)		Octavia Kenmore

Date	*Theater (city)*	*Director, translator (t) or adapter (a)*	*Actor playing Hedda*
August 1922	Brixton Theatre (London)	Mrs. Patrick Campbell William Archer (t)	Mrs. Patrick Campbell
May 1924	48th St. Theatre (New York)	Robert Edmond Jones	Clare Eames
April 1925	Comédie Française (Paris)		Mme. Piérat
January 1926	Comedy Theatre (New York)	Dudley Digges William Archer (t)	Emily Stevens
March 1928	Everyman Theatre (London)		Laura Cowie
March 1928–April 1931	Civic Repertory Theatre (New York)	Eva le Gallienne Eva le Gallienne and Paul Leyssac (t)	Eva le Gallienne
February 1929	49th St. Theatre (New York)	Blanche Yurka	Blanche Yurka
March 1931	Arts Theatre (London) then transferred to the Fortune Theatre (London)	Michael Orme William Archer (t)	Jean Forbes-Robertson
December 1934	Broadhurst Theatre (New York)	Eva le Gallienne	Eva le Gallienne
March 1936	Criterion Theatre (London)	Irene Hentschel	Jean Forbes-Robertson
October 1936	Colonial Theatre (New York)	Alla Nazimova	Alla Nazimova
January 1942	Longacre Theatre (New York)	Luther Greene Ethel Borden and Mary Cass Canfield (t and a)	Katina Paxinou
September 1942	Mercury Theatre (London)		Sonia Desdel
February 1948	Cort Theatre (New York)	Margaret Webster Eva le Gallienne (t)	Eva le Gallienne
July 1950	Masterpiece Playhouse TV		Jessica Tandy
January 1951	Arts Theatre (London)	Irene Hentschel	Jean Forbes-Robertson
June 1954	Lyric Theatre, Hammersmith (London) transferred to the Westminster Theatre (London)	Peter Ashmore Max Faber (a)	Peggy Ashcroft
March 1955	New Theatre (Oslo)	Peter Ashmore	Peggy Ashcroft

November 1960	Fourth Street Theatre (New York)	David Ross Michael Meyer (t)	Mai Zetterling (collapsed during previews, replaced by Anne Meacham)
October 1960	Oxford Playhouse	Minos Volankis	Joan Greenwood
July 1963	BBC TV	David Susskind	Ingrid Bergman
March 1964	National Repertory Theatre (New York)	Eva le Gallienne	Signe Hasso
April 1964	New Arts Theatre (London)	Minos Volankis	Joan Greenwood
October 1964	Kungliga Dramatiska Teater (Stockholm)	Ingmar Bergman	Gertrud Fridh
June 1968	Aldwych Theatre (London)	Ingmar Bergman	Gertrud Fridh
January 1970	The Actor's Playhouse (New York)	Ted van Griethuysen	Rebecca Thompson
June 1970	Stratford Festival (Stratford, Ontario)	Peter Gill Christopher Hampton (a)	Irene Worth
July 1970	National Theatre (London)	Ingmar Bergman Michael Meyer (t)	Maggie Smith
February 1971	Playhouse Theatre (New York)	Patrick Garland Christopher Hampton (a)	Claire Bloom
June 1972	Royal Court Theatre (London)	Anthony Page John Osborne (a)	Jill Bennett
April and July 1975	(??) Los Angeles, (Kennedy Center) Washington, and Aldwych Theatre (London) – filmed 1976	Trevor Nunn Trevor Nunn (a)	Glenda Jackson
May 1975	Classic Theatre Preview (NEH) TV		Janet Suzman
February 1977	Schiller Theater (Berlin)	Niels-Peter Rudolph	Gisela Stein
July 1977	Duke of York Theatre (London)	Keith Hack	Janet Suzman
1978	Bergen Festival (Bergen)	Charles Marowitz Charles Marowitz (a), *Hedda*	Unknown
April 1979	Residenztheater (Munich)	Ingmar Bergman	Christine Buchegger
August 1980	Round House Theatre (London)	Charles Marowitz Charles Marowitz (a), *Hedda*	Jenny Agutter

Date	*Theater (city)*	*Director, translator (t) or adapter (a)*	*Actor playing Hedda*
March 1981	Yale Repertory Theatre (New Haven, Conn.)	Lloyd Richards Rolf Fielde (t)	Dianne Wiest
May 1981	Roundabout Theatre (New York)	Michael Kahn Christopher Hampton (a)	Susannah York
October 1981	Hartman Theatre (New York)	Edwin Sherin Eva le Gallienne (t)	Jane Alexander
April 1984	Almeida Theatre (London)	Tim Albery	Deborah Findlay
February 1987	Haymarket (Leicester)	Michael Boyd Michael Meyer (t)	Sian Thomas
October 1988	Hampstead Theatre (London)	John Dove Trevor Nunn (a)	Lindsay Duncan
January 1989	Pearl Theatre (New York)	Richard Fancy Henry Beissel (t)	Joanne Camp
February 1989	Olivier Theatre (London)	Howard Davies	Juliet Stevenson
September 1991	Playhouse Theatre (London)	Deborah Warner	Fiona Shaw
July 1994	Roundabout Theatre (New York)	Sarah Pia Anderson Frank McGuinness (t)	Kelly McGillis
March 1999	Geffen Playhouse (Los Angeles)	Daniel Sullivan Jon Robin Baitz (a)	Annette Bening
October 2001	Royal Exchange Theatre (Manchester)	Graham Murray	Amanda Donohoe

Early Performance and Criticism

Ethical Approaches

From **E. F. S. Piggott, Testimony to the Select Committee on Censorship**, in Minutes of the Select Committee on Censorship, 1892

The Lord Chamberlain's office in England was responsible for upholding public morality on the stage, and all dramatic scripts had to be approved by the Examiner of Plays – at the time, E. F. S. Piggott. Due to the theme of incest, *Ghosts* had only been licenced for private performance. But (surprisingly) all of Ibsen's other plays, including *Hedda Gabler*, were allowed in the commercial theater – if only because the picture of society they presented was, in the official view, too eccentric to be recognizable.

I have studied Ibsen's plays pretty carefully, and all the characters seem to me to be morally deranged. All the heroines are dissatisfied spinsters who look on marriage as a monopoly, or dissatisfied married women, in a chronic state of rebellion [. . .] as for the men, they are all rascals or imbeciles [. . .] [Apart from *Ghosts*, Ibsen's plays] have not been censored as too absurd altogether to be injurious to public morals.

From **Edmund Gosse, "Ibsen's New Drama"** in *The Fortnightly*, vol. XLIX, January–June, 1891, 5–7, 9–10

Edmund Gosse (see **pp. 30, 44**) was the first to write in any language an extended critical analysis of *Hedda Gabler*. Completed before the play was produced, this served as an introduction to his translation of the text (though this was only published in 1900), and raised many of the points that have continued to preoccupy later critics. For instance, the reference to Ibsen only presenting his characters at the point where their fortunes are already determined is picked up by William Archer in his book *Play-making* where *Hedda Gabler* is described as the play "in which a sound proportion between the past and the present is most successfully preserved. The interest of the present action is thoroughly vivid; but it is rooted in facts and relations of the past."[1] It is also echoed by the director and critic Harold Clurman, who singled out Ibsen's "ability to make the exposition of conditions preceding the immediate action of his plays dramatic in themselves."[2]

The new drama is the longest which Ibsen has published, with the exception of *The Wild Duck* [. . .] In style it is a return to Ibsen's old realistic manner, without a trace of the romanticism which cropped up so strangely in *The Lady from the Sea*, and even in *Rosmersholm;* while the dialogue is more rapid and fluent, and less interrupted by long speeches than it has ever been before. In the whole of the new play there is not one speech which would require thirty seconds for its enunciation. I will dare to say that I think in this instance Ibsen has gone perilously far in his desire for rapid and concise expression. The *stichomythia*[3] of the Greek and French tragedians was lengthy in comparison with this unceasing display of hissing conversational fireworks, fragments of sentences without verbs, clauses that come to nothing, adverbial exclamations and cryptic interrogatories. It would add, I cannot but think, to the lucidity of the play if some one character were permitted occasionally to express himself at moderate length, as Nora does in *A Doll's House*, and as Mrs. Alving in *Ghosts*. None the less is the feat of combining a story with a play, and conducting both in meteoric bursts of extremely colloquial chat, one which Ibsen deserves the highest praise for having performed. And, on the stage, no doubt, this rapid broken utterance will give an extraordinary sense of reality.

As is known, Ibsen, like Euripides, does not present his characters to the public until their fortunes are determined. The heightened action of a third act in a "well-made" play is no luxury which he offers himself [. . .] He has to explain the situation out of the mouths of his characters, and this he has an unrivalled adroitness in doing. We are never conscious of being informed, but, as we read on, the situation gradually and inevitably becomes patent to us.

[. . .]

Action, in the ordinary sense, is not the strong point of the drama, the interest of which, indeed, is strictly psychological. It consists, mainly, of the revelation of the complex and morbid character of Hedda Gabler, attended by the satellites of Mrs. Elvsted, Brack, and Løvborg, the husband, Tesman, being in reality a semi-comic character, not much more subtle than Helmer in *A Doll's House*, but no whit the less closely studied.

1 William Archer, *Play-making: A Manual of Craftsmanship*, London: Chapman & Hall, 1912, p. 85.
2 Harold Clurman, *Ibsen*, New York: Macmillan Publishing Co., Inc., 1977, p. 155.
3 Dialogue used to indicate sharp disputation, in alternating lines, marked by antithesis and rhetorical repetition.

Hedda is one of the most singular beings whom Ibsen has created. She has a certain superficial likeness to Nora, of whom she is, indeed, a kind of moral parody or perverted imitation. Hedda Gabler is a spoilt child, whose indulgent father has allowed her to grow up without training of any kind. Superficially gracious and pleasing, with a very pretty face and tempting manners, she is in reality wholly devoid of moral sense. She reveals herself, as the play proceeds, as without respect for age or grief, without natural instincts, without interest in life, untruthful, treacherous, implacable in revenge. She is a very ill-conditioned little social panther or ocelot, totally without conscience of ill or preference for good, a product of the latest combination of pessimism, indifferentism and morbid selfishness, all claws and thirst for blood under the delicate velvet of her beauty.

[. . .]

Hedda Gabler is a more pronounced type of the *fin de siècle*[4] woman than Ibsen has hitherto created [. . .] In depicting Hedda Gabler, Ibsen seems to have expended his skill on the portrait of a typical member of that growing class [. . .] peculiarly frequent nowadays – the simple and masculine doctrines of obedience to duty, of perseverance, of love to mankind, are in danger of being replaced by "a complicated and sophisticated code which has the effect of making some of us mere cowards in the face of difficulty and sacrifice, and of disgusting all of us with the battle of life." In Hedda Gabler we see the religious idea violently suppressed under the pretext of a longing for liberty. She will not be a slave, yet is prepared for freedom by no education in self-command. Instead of religion, morality, and philosophy her head is feverishly stuffed with an amalgam of Buddhism and Schopenhauer.[5] Even the beautiful conventions of manners are broken down, and the suppression of all rules of conduct seems the sole road to happiness. In her breast, with its sickly indifferentism, love awakens no sympathy; age no respect, suffering no pity, and patience in adversity no admiration.

[. . .]

What the moral of *Hedda Gabler* is, what "gospel" it preaches, and what light it holds out to poor souls tossing in our sea of "hysterical mock-disease," I will not pretend to conjecture. Doubtless there will be scarcely less discussion over the ethics of Hedda's final resolve than there was over those of Nora, when she slammed the front-door so vigorously eleven years ago. These are matters which, I conceive, interest the great magian[6] at Munich less than they do his disciples. He

4 Literally "the end of a century," *fin de siècle* referred to the exhausted, over-sophisticated sensibility associated with the final phase of an era. It reflected the fading of Victorian certainties, and was used as a label for art that appeared decadent: perverse, erotic or anti-social, substituting decorative ornament for moral values or (like the Symbolists) subjective vision for external realities.

5 The Idealist and pessimistic philosophy of Arthur Schopenhauer (1788–1860) influenced both the Romantics and the Symbolists, as well as anticipating Freud's theories of sexuality and repression. For Schopenhauer any separate individual will was an illusion, being subsumed in the universal and noumenal Will, which led to his calling for a withdrawal from life and questioning the validity of reality: a position that can be linked with Buddhism.

6 "Magian" (metaphorically a seer or magician who points the way forward; a follower of the Magi, the three wise men who came bearing gifts to Christ) was Gosse's admiring nickname for Ibsen. At the time he was writing, Ibsen's ability to represent society realistically was seen by his admirers as something magical – and Elizabeth Robins also refers to him as a "wizard" (see **p. 58**).

takes a knotty situation, he conducts it to its extreme logical conclusion, he invites the world to fight over it, and then he retires for another two years of solitary meditation.

From **George Bernard Shaw, "The Lesson of Ibsen's Plays"**, 1891, in *The Quintessence of Ibsenism*, New York: Hill and Wang, 1913, pp. 59, 108–9, 113, 176, 180–1

Bernard Shaw's extended essay *The Quintessence of Ibsenism* – originally presented as a series of lectures for the Fabian Society and, like Gosse's article, written before *Hedda Gabler* had been performed – is perhaps the single most influential piece written about Ibsen's plays. Stressing the "moral" themes of the plays, and the attack on "idealism" – as well as asserting that the key to Ibsen's new technique was the substitution of "discussion" for the traditional action at the climax of the drama – it became a reference point for actresses as well as later critics, which is still cited today.

A typical Ibsen play is one in which the leading lady is an unwomanly woman, and the villain is an idealist. It follows that the leading lady is not a heroine of the Drury Lane type [i.e. immoral]; nor does the villain forge or assassinate, since he is a villain by virtue of his determination to do nothing wrong.

[. . .]

In the new plays, the drama arises through a conflict of unsettled ideals rather than through vulgar attachments, rapacities, generosities, resentments, ambitions, misunderstandings, oddities and so forth as to which no moral question is raised. The conflict is not between clear right and wrong: the villain is as conscientious as the hero, if not more so: in fact, the question which makes the play interesting (when it *is* interesting) is which is the villain and which the hero. Or, to put it another way, there are no villains and no heroes. This strikes the critics mainly as a departure from dramatic art; but it is really the inevitable return to nature which ends all the merely technical fashions. Now the natural is mainly the everyday; and its climaxes must be, if not everyday, at least everylife, if they are to have any importance for the spectator.

[. . .]

Hedda Gabler has no ethical ideals at all, only romantic ones. She is a typical nineteenth-century figure, falling into the abyss between the ideals which do not impose on her and the realities she has not yet discovered. The result is that though she has imagination, and an intense appetite for beauty, she has no conscience, no conviction: with plenty of cleverness, energy, and personal fascination she remains mean, envious, insolent, cruel in protest against others' happiness, fiendish in her dislike of inartistic people and things, a bully in reaction from her own cowardice. [. . .] She admits that the virtuous heroics with the pistol were pure cowardice; but she is still so void of any other standard of conduct than conformity to the conventional ideals, that she thinks her cowardice consisted in not daring to be wicked. That is, she thinks that what she actually did was the right thing; and since she despises herself for doing it, she gets a passionate feeling that what is wanted is the courage to do wrong. This unlooked-for reaction of idealism, this monstrous but very common setting-up of wrong-doing as an ideal, and of the wrongdoer as a hero or heroine *qua* wrongdoer, leads Hedda to conceive that [in the pre-history of the play] when Løvborg tried to seduce her he was a hero, and that in allowing Thea to reform him he has played the recreant. In acting on this misconception she is restrained by no consideration for any of the rest. Like all people whose lives are valueless, she has no [. . .] sense of the value of Løvborg's or Tesman's or Thea's lives.

[. . .]

If people's souls are tied up by law and public opinion it is much more tragic to leave them to wither in these bonds, than to end their misery and relieve the salutary compunction of the audience by outbreaks of violence. Judge Brack was, on the whole right when he said that people dont do such things. If I they did, the idealists would be brought to their senses very quickly indeed.

But in Ibsen's plays the catastrophe, even when it seems forced, and when the ending of the play would be more tragic without it, is never an accident; and the play never exists for its sake [. . .] As to the deaths in Ibsen's last acts, they are a sweeping up of the remains of dramatically finished people [. . .] Ibsen's dead bodies are those of the exhausted or destroyed.

The First English Production

From **Elizabeth Robins, "On Playing Hedda"** in *Ibsen and the Actress*, London: The Hogarth Press, 1928, pp. 18 ff.

Elizabeth Robins, who served her theatrical apprenticeship in America with the famous actor-managers Edwin Booth, Lawrence Barrett, and James O'Neill, became the primary interpreter of Ibsen on the stage after moving to England in 1888. After playing in *The Pillars of Society* (1889), during the 1890s she produced and starred in the premieres of *Hedda Gabler*, *The Master Builder*, *Brand*, *Little Eyolf*, and *John Gabriel Borkman*, as well as reviving *A Doll's House* and *Rosmersholm*. She also introduced *Hedda Gabler* to America in 1898 and her presentation of the role – as "unsympathetic," pitiable, and lonely, rather than evil – conditioned the way the play was interpreted by (the few) sympathetic critics of the time like Shaw (who commented "You were sympathetically unsympathetic, which was the exact solution of the central difficulty of playing Hedda"[1]) and William Archer. They were instrumental in setting the agenda for twentieth-century commentators on the play. Henry James was so impressed that he immediately started persuading Robins to take the role of the heroine in

1 Letter to Elizabeth Robins, April 20, 1891 in Dan H. Laurence (ed.) *George Bernard Shaw, Collected Letters 1874–1897*, Vol. 1, London: William Clowes & Sons Ltd., 1965, p. 292.

his own play, *The Americans*, which opened later the same year. Her reputation also brought George Meredith, who generally expressed scorn for London theater, and Thomas Hardy to see *Hedda Gabler*. As an indication of the continuing influence of her production, following the advice of Archer who was concerned about the 1891 audience reaction, she cut all references in the text to Hedda's pregnancy, creating an ambiguity – unsupported by the text – which was still current in 1975, as the actress Janet Suzman indicates by her comment that "I have actually heard it said that Hedda's pregnancy is in dispute" (see **p. 99**). The way Robins's interpretation anticipated later critics can also be seen in her explanation of the call for Løvborg to have "vine leaves in his hair," which is later proposed by the critic Wilson Knight (see **pp. 80–1**).

The press notices were a palpitating excitement, especially those we jeered at – with anxiety in our hearts. But we put on a bold front. Mr. Clement Scott[2] understand Hedda? – any man except that wizard Ibsen really understand her? Of course not. That was the tremendous part of it. How should men understand Hedda on the stage when they didn't understand her in the persons of their wives, their daughters, their women friends? One lady of our acquaintance, married and not noticeably unhappy, said laughing, "Hedda is all of us."

Hedda was not all of us, but she was a good many of us – so Mr Grant Allen[3] told the public. Anyway, she was a bundle of the unused possibilities, educated to fear life; too much opportunity to develop her weakness; no opportunity at all to use her best powers [. . .]

Hedda is first represented to us as an enviable person. We hear of what General Gabler's daughter had "been accustomed to"; how fond she was of dancing, and shooting at a mark and riding with her handsome father "in her long black habit and with feathers in her hat." "So beset with admirers," Aunt Julia says – who would have dreamt she would marry a mere professor? Well, she wasn't on the scene sixty seconds before it was clear she knew there was joy in life that she hadn't been able to grasp, and that marriage only emphasised what she was missing.

It was never any wish of mine to whitewash General Gabler's somewhat lurid daughter. Even in the heat and glamour of that first personal contact with a great Ibsen part, I was under no temptation to try to make her what is conventionally known as "sympathetic." One surviving recollection bears witness to that. Among those who never much cared about Ibsen, but always came to see him

2 The drama reviewer of the *Daily Telegraph* and *Illustrated London News* – a highly conservative critic, he attacked Ibsen and became a particular target of Bernard Shaw, whose work Scott also opposed. His is one of the negative reviews of *Hedda Gabler* (in the *Illustrated London News*) cited by William Archer (see **pp. 62–3** below).

3 Grant Allen, also referred to by Archer, dominated English intellectual life in the 1890s. See note on **p. 36** above.

Figure 1 **Hedda as the girl next door: studio portrait of Elizabeth Robins as Hedda Gabler, London, 1891. (Mander and Mitchenson Theatre Collection. Photographed by A. Ellis.)**

acted, was Lady Bell.[4] At the first performance of *Hedda* she was thought by her companion to be in danger of lending herself too much to the glamour of the play; so this friend of Lady Bell's youth warned her: "It's all very exciting, but I wouldn't trust her round the corner – that woman playing Hedda."

I had the best of reasons for not trying to mitigate Hedda's corrosive qualities. It was precisely the corrosive action of those qualities on a woman in Hedda's circumstances that made her the great acting opportunity she was – in her revolt against those commonplace surroundings that the book-worm she had married thought so "elegant"; her unashamed selfishness; her scorn of so-called womanly qualities; above all, her strong need to put some meaning into her life, even at the cost of borrowing it, or stealing the meaning out of someone else's.

Hedda's first and dearest dream had been to find contacts with life through the attractive young man of letters, Eilert Løvborg. That hope ended in driving him from her at the point of a pistol – not, as one eminent critic has said, "in the ostentation of outraged purity which is the instinctive defence of women to whom chastity is not natural." Hedda drove Løvborg from her in disgust; disgust at the new aspects of vulgar sensuality which her curiosity about life had led him to reveal. She never denied it was her doing that he revealed these things; it was not her doing that he had them to reveal. They made her gorge rise. The man who had wallowed in that filth must not touch Hedda Gabler – certainly not fresh from the latest orgy: The effect of that experience, plus the conditions of her own life and upbringing, was to throw her into marriage with the least ineligible man she can find who is decent, and no one can deny that poor Tesman was entirely decent.

The result was not peculiar to Ibsen characters. In one form or another, as we all know, it is a commonplace in the history of people whose nervous system generates more force than the engine of their opportunity can use up. Hedda speculates, like many another woman, on the opportunity politics would give to her husband, and, through him, give to her; but she is too intelligent to have much hope of Tesman in that direction. She is no sooner home from her boring honeymoon than she finds that a girl she had looked down on and terrorised at school – shrinking, gentle Mrs Elvsted – has reclaimed the dissipated Løvborg. More than that, largely by her faith in him, she has helped him to write what they are calling a work of genius. The timid Thea Elvsted has actually left her husband and her home to watch over Løvborg, so that he may not fall into evil courses again. How on earth had it all come about? Hedda, by turns, worms and coerces the facts out of Thea; "He gave up his old habits not because I *asked* him to, for I never dared do that; but he saw how repulsive they were to me – so he dropped them."

As simple as that! None of those shady stories told to Thea – but the pretty little fool has his dreams in her keeping; she has helped to turn them into reality. And Hedda has lost him. For Hedda there would be "others." The insinuating Judge Brack, with his aristocratic profile and his eyeglass, is already at the door – but

4 Lady Florence Bell (1851–1930) was a well-known essayist, who wrote a number of "chamber comedies," *A Chance Interview*, *A Joint Household*, *The "Swiss Times"* (published in Chamber Comedies: A Collection of Plays and Monologues for the Drawing Room, London: Longmans, Green, and Co., 1910), and a sociological study of an English manufacturing town (*At the Works*, London, Edward Arnold, 1907).

never the man whose faith in his own genius, faith in life, had given Hedda the one respite she had known from mean standards, mean fears.

Those had been times for Løvborg, too, of respite from his meaner self. Hedda's passion for external material beauty was not the only kind of beauty that swayed her. Løvborg in his moods of poetic exaltation had given her, too, a glorious sense of freedom, of daring. She had her phrase for those high moods of his. It was the phrase that, with a truly Ibsenite irony, became famous in England in a totally different sense. When Hedda asks eagerly, "Did he have vine leaves in his hair?" she was not inquiring whether Løvborg was drunk with the fiery Scandinavian punch, but whether he had been tasting a diviner draught. She was using her symbol for his hour of inspired vision, which had had for her, too, its intoxication. Now she has lost all that – unless – unless she can break the hold of this irritating little goose. Thea had said she'd been so frightened of Hedda at school. Well, she should be frightened again!

It is a commentary on actress psychology that though in those days I accepted, and even myself used, the description of Hedda as a "bloodless egoist," I was under no temptation to play her like that. Here I was in debt to Ibsen's supreme faculty for giving his actors the clue – the master-key – if they are not too lofty or too helplessly sophisticated to take it. Ibsen's unwritten clue brought me close enough to the "cold-blooded egoist" to feel her warm to my touch; to see Hedda Gabler as pitiable in her hungry loneliness – to see her as tragic. Insolent and evil she was, but some great celebrators of Ibsen have thought more meanly of Hedda than the text warrants [. . .]

It is perhaps curious Ibsen should have known that a good many women have found it possible to get through life by help of the knowledge that they have power to end it rather than accept certain slaveries. Naturally enough, no critic, so far as I know, has ever noticed this governing factor in Hedda's outlook, her consciousness of one sort of power, anyway – the power of escape. The reason men have not noticed the bearing this had on Hedda's character and fate seems plain enough. Certainly the particular humiliations and enslavements that threaten women do not threaten men. Such enslavements may seem so unreal to decent men as to appear as melodrama.

Ibsen not only knew better; he saw further than the special instance. He saw what we at the time did not; I mean the general bearing of Hedda's story.

From **William Archer, "The Mausoleum of Ibsen"** in *The Fortnightly Review*, July 1, 1893, 80–2

The reaction, described by William Archer, to the 1891 London production of *Hedda Gabler* was echoed by the American critics when Elizabeth Robins took her production to New York in 1898. In contrast to German and Scandinavian reviews of the first performances of *Hedda Gabler*, which almost completely ignored the underlying social criticism in the play, in English-speaking countries it initially aroused the same furor as *A Doll's House* or *Ghosts*; and the perceived threat to the social order is well indicated by Archer's selection of the reviews.

Ghosts was produced at the first performance of the Independent Theatre.[1] The frenzy of execration with which it was greeted must be within the memory of all my readers [. . .]

Nothing daunted by the tempest, Miss Elizabeth Robins and Miss Marion Lea produced *Hedda Gabler* only five weeks later [April 20th, 1891]. This time the "suburban Ibsen," the "egotist and bungler," was found by the *Daily Telegraph* to have produced a "ghastly picture beautifully painted." "It was like a visit to the Morgue. . . . There they all lay on their copper couches, fronting us, and waiting to be owned. . . . There they all were, false men, wicked women, deceitful friends, sensualists, egotists, piled up in a heap behind the screen of glass, which we were thankful for. . . . There were the dead bodies, and no one could resist looking at them. Art was used for the most baleful purpose. It is true that the very spectacle of moral corruption was positively fascinating. . . . Would indeed that, after this Morgue inspection, after this ghastly spectacle of dead bodies and suicides, after this revolting picture of human frailty and depravity, there could be a break in the cloud. . . . But alas! there is no gleam to be seen in the dark raincloud of Ibsenite pessimism! . . . What a horrible story! What a hideous play!" Most of my readers are probably aware that there is only one dead body in *Hedda Gabler*, seen for something like a quarter of a minute just as the curtain falls. But what must the readers of the *Daily Telegraph* have gathered from the outburst I have just quoted? "I should like so much to see the piece you're in," a lady said to Mr. Scott Buist, the excellent Tesman of the cast, "but I don't think I could stand anything so horrible." "Horrible! How do you mean?" he inquired. "Why, you have the Morgue on the stage, haven't you?" was the reply. And I have no doubt many thousands of people were under the same impression, on that 21st (not 1st) of April. The other critics, if less imaginative, were no less denunciatory.

"Ibsen's plays [may be] regarded as masterpieces of genius by a small but noisy set of people, but . . . the tastes of English playgoers are sound and healthy, and the hollowness and shams of the Ibsen cult need only be known to be rejected." – *Standard*.

"Dr. Ibsen's social dramas have yet to prove their power to interest cultivated audiences; for the limited number of worshippers who proclaim these productions as masterpieces of art and stagecraft . . . cannot be accepted as a fair sample even of the educated public." – *Daily News*.

"Robust common-sense of ordinary English audiences will confirm the adverse judgment pronounced upon the morbid Norwegian dramatist by all save a clique of faddists anxious to advertise themselves by the aid of any eccentricity that comes first to hand. . . . Already; we fancy, the craze has had its day." – *Sporting and Dramatic News*.

"One left the theatre filled with depression at the sorry spectacle that had been set before them *(sic)*." – *Reynolds' Newspaper*.

"A few steps out of the hospital-ward and we arrive at the dissecting-room. Down a little lower and we come to the deadhouse. There, for the present, Ibsen

1 Modeled on Antoine's Théâtre Libre, the Independent Theatre Society was founded in 1891 as a private club specifically to perform plays that had been banned by the censor.

has left us. . . . Miss Elizabeth Robins has done what no doubt she fully intended to do (!). She has made vice attractive by her art. She has almost ennobled crime. She has glorified an unwomanly woman," &c., &c. – Mr. C. SCOTT in the *Illustrated London News*.

"Hideous nightmare of pessimism. . . . The play is simply a bad escape of moral sewage-gas. . . . Hedda's soul is a-crawl with the foulest passions of humanity." – *Pictorial World*.

"The piece is stuff and nonsense; poor stuff and 'pernicious non-sense.' It is as if the author had studied the weakest of the Robertsonian[2] comedies, and had thought he could do something like it in a tragic vein." – *Punch*.

"It is not, possibly, so utterly repulsive as others that have been seen, but, nevertheless, it is offensive." – *Lloyd's News*.

"The more I see of Ibsen, the more disgusted I am with his alleged dramas." – *London*.

"Utterly pessimistic in its tedious turmoil of knaves and fools. . . . Other plays from the same tainted source." – *The People*.

"Full of loathsomeness." – *The Table*.

"Things rank and gross in nature alone have place in the mean and sordid philosophy of Ibsen. . . . Can any human being feel happier or better from a contemplation of the two harlots at heart who do duty in *Hedda Gabler*? . . . Insidious nastiness of photographic studies of vice and morbidity. . . . The blusterous little band of Ibsen idolaters. . . ." – *Saturday Review*.

"Strange provincial prigs and suburban chameleons. . . . The funereal clown who is amusing us . . . is given to jokes in very questionable taste. We are reminded again and again of Goethe's famous stage direction, '*Mephistopheles macht eine unabständige Geberde*,'[3] and it is a coarseness of this sort which, I fear, constitutes Ibsen's charm for some of his disciples. . . . For sheer unadulterated stupidity, for inherent meanness and vulgarity, for pretentious triviality . . . no Bostonian novel[4] or London penny novelette has surpassed *Hedda Gabler*." – Mr. ROBERT BUCHANAN in the *Illustrated London News*.

From **Henry James, "On the Occasion of *Hedda Gabler*"** in *The New Review*, June 1891, 519–30

Because of his literary stature, Henry James's views on *Hedda Gabler* had a lasting impact on the study of the play. He defined Ibsen's "great quality" as "dealing essentially with the individual caught in the fact" and Ibsen's characteristic atmosphere as parochialism in "the ugly interior on which his curtain inexorably rises . . . the pervasive air of small interests and standards, the sign of

2 Referring to T. W. Robertson (1829–71), whose plays gained a reputation for realism because of their close attention to detail.
3 "Mephistopheles makes an obscene gesture."
4 A reference to Henry James's novels.

limited local life." Both his view of Hedda (even though modified by his admiration for Elizabeth Robins in the role) and the absence of humor, which James identified with such bourgeois characters, is certainly something that shaped the critical views of *Hedda Gabler* up until relatively recently.

Hedda Gabler is probably an ironical pleasantry, the artistic exercise of a mind saturated with the vision of human infirmities; saturated above all, with a sense of the infinitude, for all its moral savour, of *character*, finding that an endless romance and a perpetual challenge [. . .] We are free to imagine that in this case Dr. Ibsen chose one of the last subjects that an expert might have been expected to choose, for the harmless pleasure of feeling and of showing that he was in possession of a method that could make up for its deficiencies.

The demonstration is complete and triumphant, but it does not conceal from us – on the contrary – that his drama is essentially that supposedly undramatic thing, the picture, not of an action but of a condition. It is the portrait of a nature, the story of what Paul Bourget[1] would call an *état à âme*, and of a state of nerves as well as soul, a state of temper, of disappointment, of desperation. *Hedda Gabler* is in short the study of an exasperated woman [. . .] We receive Hedda ripe for her catastrophe, and if we ask for antecedents and explanations we must simply find them in her character. Her motives are just her passions. What the four acts show us is these motives and that character – complicated, strange, irreconcilable, infernal – playing themselves out [. . .] And then one isn't so sure she is wicked, and by no means sure (particularly when she is represented by an actress who makes the point ambiguous) that she is disagreeable. She is various and sinuous and graceful, complicated and natural; she suffers, she struggles, she is human, and by that fact exposed to a dozen interpretations, to the importunity of our suspense.

[. . .]

[Ibsen's] people are of inexpressive race; they give us inescapably a *bourgeois* impression; even when they are furiously nervous, and, like Hedda, more than sufficiently fastidious, we recognize that they live, together with their remarkable creator, in a world where selection has no great range [. . .] They are all too busy learning how to live – humour will come later, when they know how.

1 Paul Bourget (1852–1935) was a French literary critic and travel writer, also known for his domestic dramas, who published *Essais de psychologie contemporaine* in 1883, which James is referring to here.

Hedda as "Modern Woman"

From **William Archer, Preface to *Hedda Gabler*** in *The Collected Works of Henrik Ibsen*, trans. Edmund Gosse and William Archer, Vol. X, New York: Charles Scribner's, 1906–12, pp. xii, xvi, xviii–xix

As well as working on the translation of *Hedda Gabler* for Elizabeth Robins's performance, Archer was the first to issue a "collected" volume of Ibsen's plays (in his own translation) with prefaces. These prefaces therefore carried a particular weight in "fixing" the interpretation of the texts. His point about the deliberately "old-fashioned" society (even for 1891) is crucial: possibly Ibsen was concerned to show that, despite the recent political advances won by women in Norway, little had changed, or perhaps Ibsen wished his audiences to look beyond current issues (which had distorted the reaction to *A Doll's House*) to the underlying, more universal problems. Either way the action is intended to be "distanced."

It has been suggested, I think without sufficient ground, that Ibsen deliberately conceived *Hedda Gabler* as an "international" play, and that the scene is really the "west end" of any great European city. To me it seems quite clear that Ibsen had Christiania in mind, and the Christiania of a somewhat earlier period than the 'nineties. The electric cars, telephones, and other conspicuous factors in the life of a modern capital are notably absent from the play. [. . .] This "suburbanism" which so distressed the London critics of 1891 was characteristic of the Christiania Ibsen himself had known in the 'sixties – the Christiania of *Love's Comedy* – rather than of the greatly extended and modernised city of the end of the century. Moreover, Løvborg's allusions to the fjord and the suggested picture of Sheriff Elvsted, his family and his avocations, are all distinctly Norwegian. The truth seems to be very simple – the environment and the subsidiary personages are all thoroughly national, but Hedda herself is an "international" type, a product of civilisation by no means peculiar to Norway.

[. . .]

Some critics have been greatly troubled as to the precise meaning of Hedda's fantastic vision of Løvborg "with vine-leaves in his hair." Surely this is a very obvious image or symbol of the beautiful, the ideal, aspect of bacchic elation and revelry. Antique art, or I am much mistaken, shows us many figures of Dionysus himself and his followers with vine-leaves entwined in their hair. To Ibsen's mind, at any rate, the image had long been familiar. In *Peer Gynt* (Act IV. sc. 8), when Peer, having carried off Anitra, finds himself in a particularly festive mood, he cries: "Were there vine-leaves around, I would garland my brow." Again, in *Emperor and Galilean* (Pt. ii. Act I) where Julian, in the procession of Dionysus, impersonates the god himself, it is directed that he shall wear a wreath of vine-leaves. Professor Dietrichson relates that among the young artists whose society Ibsen frequented during his first years in Rome, it was customary, at their little festivals, for the revellers to deck themselves in this fashion. But the image is so obvious that there is no need to trace it to any personal experience. The attempt to place Hedda's vine-leaves among Ibsen's obscurities is an example of the firm resolution not to understand which animated the criticism of the 'nineties.

[. . .]

Of all Ibsen's works, *Hedda Gabler* is the most detached, the most objective – a character-study pure and simple. It is impossible – or so it seems to me – to extract any sort of general idea from it. One cannot even call it a satire, unless one is prepared to apply that term to the record of a "case" in a work on criminology. Reverting to Dumas's[1] dictum that a play should contain "a painting, a judgment, an ideal," we may say that Hedda Gabler fulfils only the first of these requirements. The poet does not even pass judgment on his heroine: he simply paints her full-length portrait with scientific impassivity. But what a portrait! How searching in insight, how brilliant in colouring, how rich in detail! Grant Allen's remark [see p. 36] was, of course, a whimsical exaggeration: the Hedda type is not so common as all that, else the world would quickly come to an end. But particular traits and tendencies of the Hedda type are very common in modern life, and not only among women. Hyperaesthesia[2] lies at the root of her tragedy. With a keenly critical, relentlessly solvent intelligence, she combines a morbid shrinking from all the gross and prosaic detail of the sensual life. She has nothing to take her out of herself – not a single intellectual interest or moral enthusiasm. She cherishes, in a languid way, a petty social ambition; and even that she finds obstructed and baffled. At the same time she learns that another woman has had the courage to love and venture all, where she, in her cowardice, only hankered and refrained. Her malign egoism rises up uncontrolled, and calls to its aid her quick and subtle intellect. She ruins the other woman's happiness, but in doing so incurs a danger from which her sense of personal dignity revolts. Life has no such charm for her that she cares to purchase it at the cost of squalid humiliation and self-contempt. The good and the bad in her alike impel her to have done with it all; and a pistol-shot ends what is surely one of the most poignant character-tragedies in literature. Ibsen's brain never worked at higher pressure than in the conception and adjustment of those "crowded hours" in which Hedda, tangled in the web of Will and Circumstance, struggles on till she is too weary to struggle any more.

It may not be superfluous to note that the "a" in "Gabler" should be sounded long and full, like the "a" in "garden" – not like the "a" in "gable" or in "gabble."

From **Alla Nazimova, "Ibsen's Women"** in the *Independent*, October 17, 1907

Despite her emphasis on Hedda Gabler as an ordinary woman, Alla Nazimova, who continued to play the role for over thirty years after her 1906 American debut in the part, established the interpretation of Hedda as an image of evil. Standard critical responses praised her performances as "malignant," bringing

1 Archer is referring to Alexandre Dumas *fils* (1824–95), the author of *La Dame aux camellias* (originally published in novel form as *Camille*) and *Le Demi-monde*.

2 Excessive and morbid sensitivity of the nerves, a popular medical diagnosis of women in the period.

Figure 2 Alla Nazimova: Hedda as vamp (Act 4), New York, 1918. (© Museum of the City of New York. The Theater Collection, gift of Mme. Alla Nazimova.)

out "all the unhealthy, morbid, depraved phases of this utterly worthless and unfruitful being [. . .] with exquisite precision and directness" (*New York Times*, November 14, 1906); "as an incarnate she-devil" (*New York Times*, April 28, 1918); and as embodying "a creature beyond human life in the monstrous evil of her perceptions [. . .] a preternatural figure, a phantom of malevolence [. . .] Nazimova takes Hedda out of the play into the sphere of fiendish imagination [. . .] demoniac and cobra-like" (*New York Times*, November 17, 1936).

You do not have to go to the theater to meet Ibsen's women. They are to be found everywhere. You may have met Nora on the street or taken Hedda Gabler down to dinner. But you did not recognize them because Ibsen was not at hand to introduce them to you. That is why you have to go to the theater to see them. Just as the stage is merely a room with one wall gone, so Ibsen opens a window into the soul of his characters thru which you can look and see them as they are – and often see something of yourself, too.

It is a mistake to talk of "Ibsen's heroines." Ibsen has no heroines; he has women. Shakespeare has heroines. There is a simplicity and grandeur about them that make them seem very remote from us and very difficult for us to interpret and present on the stage [. . .] Shakespeare's women seem more like types, ideals, than real persons. They are clear and definite, either good or bad, coquettish or demure, vixenish or humble, and what they are at the beginning of the play that they stay till the curtain falls.

Perhaps women really were like that three hundred years ago and Shakespeare drew them as he saw them. But the position of women has changed so much since then and we ourselves have changed. Our Russian women three hundred years ago were good housewives and slaves and nothing else. Now, see, they are leaders of the revolution. The modern woman is more complex and she lives in a more complex world. She knows more; her nerves are exaggerated. Little things loom larger in our lives. Our characters are apt to be swamped in the mass of petty details.

Now Ibsen's women mean more to us of today than Shakespeare's, because they are complex instead of primitive. They are in a way difficult to understand, it is true, not because they are artfully mysterious, but because they are real and therefore like all real people not to be classified by a simple formula. They are full of the pettinesses, the peculiarities, the inconsistencies, the contradictions that we find in everybody we know intimately. That is what makes them so fascinating; that is why we want to learn more of them. Take Hedda, for example. She has a little of all women in her. She is weak and strong, capricious and determined, petty and powerful, yet always herself, always real. She is true to life. Ibsen did not exaggerate her. No, he had to make her smaller to get her on the stage.

I know that some critics, especially William Archer and John Corbin,[1] have found fault with my interpretation of Hedda Gabler on the ground that I exagger-

1 Corbin (1870–1959) was a New York theater reviewer who later became a respected social and political commentator.

ated her physiological condition[2], but I cannot change my conception of the part to suit them. Her condition does not change Hedda's character, it only serves to accentuate her natural peculiarities and make them more dramatic. Ibsen might just as well have left that point out, only it would have been more difficult then to make the character effectual.

2 Nazimova is referring to Hedda's pregnancy.

Modern Criticism and Performance

Updating Hedda for the 1920s

From **Blanche Yurka, "Acting Hedda Gabler"** in *Bohemian Girl: Blanche Yurka's Theatrical Life*, Athens, Ohio: Ohio University Press, 1970, pp. 141, 142–3

Blanche Yurka's complete 1928–9 season of Ibsen plays on Broadway marked the acceptance of *Hedda Gabler* as mainstream theater in America. Her interpretation (like Eva le Gallienne's the same year) was in conscious opposition to the rendering that Nazimova had established (see **pp. 66–9**). A modern woman out of place in her era was Yurka's contribution to the developing image of Hedda. Significantly, she used the "prehistory" of the action as a basis for focusing on the social context, and attempted (though unsuccessfully) to introduce comedy into the play.

I had some ideas about Hedda which were somewhat at variance with the interpretations I had seen. Almost always played as the embodiment of evil from the start, she usually became a ruthless witch, from whom Tesman would, in my opinion, have fled in terror. But I saw her rather differently: as a woman of potentially forceful character who, in another era, given an outlet for her energies, might have been a vital and entertaining member of society; moreover, one whose humor would certainly have been a distinct social asset among the sophisticates of today. But Hedda's restless energies were not viable in the society in which she lived; they festered and eventually destroyed her. She was an example of that evil which is primarily the negation of good, "*une vie manquée*," as Mme. Lillie[1] expressed in discussing my concept of the role with me.

In studying the part, I gave considerable thought to Hedda's background. Ibsen

1 Lillie Sang Collins was a teacher at the French Opera School and a well-known voice coach of the period, who effectively became Yurka's manager.

has a wonderful way of building up unseen characters in his plays. How clearly one can visualize the two maiden aunts who brought up Hjalmar Ekdal[2] (or Rosmer's dead wife in *Rosmersholm*) from Ibsen's few telling phrases. Yet not once does he mention Hedda's mother; always the reference is to "General Gabler's beautiful daughter." One may infer, therefore, that she was a motherless child, brought up extravagantly by an indulgent father, feted and spoiled on the assumption that she would, of course, make a good marriage. I can imagine them living up to the hilt of his income, a large one which ceased after his death. Hedda's casual requirement that Tesman provide a villa beyond his normal means, her bored indifference to it on the very first day of her incumbency, indicate a capricious extravagance accustomed to being indulged, with little consideration for ways and means.

[. . .]

There was one piece of business in the scene, with Løvborg, in Act III, where he tells her he has lost his precious manuscript, which seemed to me to mark the turning point in her character. I staged the situation a little differently from the productions I had seen.

Usually the manuscript is placed on the desk upstage. Ibsen directs it so. But I put it in a large box on the centre table across which we played Løvborg and Hedda's scene. Hedda listens with clinical detachment to his torrent of remorse and despair over his "lost child." Then, smiling indulgently at him as she lifts the lid of the box where she had concealed it, she is about to return his precious manuscript to him and end his agony, when he utters the words: "Thea's pure soul was in that book."

I used to pause for a second, my face stiffening with jealous fury, then, withdrawing my hand, I let the heavy lid fall with a soft, dull thud, a sound which John Anderson said in his review "was like the closing of a coffin lid." It marked the end of Løvborg's hope of regeneration and the end of Hedda's hope of salvation. From that moment her feet are set on the path of destruction. She sends him away with her pistol to kill himself, then burns the manuscript in that marvelous curtain to Act III. Using a fireplace instead of a stove, we got a wonderful effect by my thrusting the edges of the manuscript against an electric hot plate concealed by bits of colored glass which looked like glowing coals. In the slow flames which rose one could almost smell burning flesh as Hedda whispered: "I'm burning your child, Thea! Your child and Løvborg's! Burning your child!"

Usually this scene is regarded as the high peak of the play. Here again I differ. I see this scene rather as the springboard into the mounting tragedy of the last act, where Hedda is driven to her self-inflicted doom [. . .]

2 In *The Wild Duck*.

From **Eva le Gallienne, "Ibsen's *Hedda Gabler*"**, *Souvenir Program of the National Repertory Theatre*, 1964–5 Season, New York, 1964, n.p.

Eva le Gallienne, the founder of the Civic Repertory Theatre in the 1920s and one of the leading actors and directors of the National Repertory Theatre in the 1960s, performed the role of Hedda in six different New York productions of the play between 1928 and 1964, as well as playing in three national tours, and making the first American recording of it. Like Yurka, le Gallienne emphasized the contemporaneity of *Hedda Gabler*, and she points out the influence of the play on American dramatists of the 1920s and 1930s.

I suppose it was the first play of its kind; a complex, very complete and many-faceted psychological study of a woman; an unpleasant woman, a tortured, tormented creature, who brought destruction upon herself and everyone she came in contact with. When you compare this original study with some modern plays that have followed the pattern, such as "Craig's Wife" or "The Little Foxes,"[1] Ibsen's genius dazzles one with its brilliance. The other women seem two-dimensional, black-and-white cutouts, in comparison with Hedda. There seems to be no end to the subtleties and infinite variety of Ibsen's woman.

What an extraordinary experience it must have been to see "Hedda Gabler" when it was first performed! The penalty a work of art pays for becoming famous is incalculable. Such "classics" are very much taken for granted; this is true of great music, poetry and paintings, as well as plays and novels. They seem so familiar to us that we cease really to see them, or hear them, or give them the courtesy of thought.

But try to imagine the impact of "Hedda Gabler" on an audience that knew nothing about it; an audience that had not been told for seventy years by innumerable learned critics what to expect, what to think, what to feel; that simply came to the theatre to see a new play by the most daring playwright of his time. The suspense must have been almost unbearable.

The play is so modern in essence and always will be that. When I first played it in 1927–28, I thought it would bring the play closer to modern audiences if one dressed it in modern clothes. I felt that "costume" would distract from the core of the matter. I was mistaken in this. Modern audiences are so literal-minded that they were disturbed, for surely Tesman would have telephoned Løvborg; and Aunt Julia wouldn't have sent a note, she too would have picked up the telephone. A woman of our emancipated age would never have found herself in Hedda's position, or if she had, she would easily have been able to escape from it, etc. This last objection is sheer nonsense. In spite of the plodding millions of "emancipated" women, the Hedda type persists – the inevitable parasite. She could never have earned her own living unless she became a great *demi-mondaine*;[2] but her

1 The Pulitzer Prize-winning *Craig's Wife*, by George Kelly (1887–1974), depicted a heartless wife's obsessive search for perfection. Lillian Hellman (1906–84) was labeled a "second Ibsen," and her attack on the rapacity of the rising bourgeoisie in America in her 1939 play *The Little Foxes* centers on an evil, sexually manipulative woman.

2 *Demi-mondaine*: an apparently respectable woman who prostitutes herself as a high-priced courtesan and so exists on the moral outskirts of society. (From the Dumas novel: see **p. 66n1**.)

Figure 3 **Eva le Gallienne: Hedda Gabler as modern socialite, New York, 1939. (Legitimate Theatre Corp. of America, © Museum of the City of New York, The Theater Collection.)**

fastidious and conventional nature would never have allowed her to be that. She is, above everything else, a "great lady." There still exist many women of this sort; it is ignorance to deny it. [Yet] it seems wiser to play the play in the 1890's. There is an element in Hedda that is more easily understood when seen against the backdrop of the '90's: her incurable romanticism. She is a real "*romantique*". [. . .] I'm sure she must have loved "*Les Fleurs du Mal*"[3] and Beardsley's illustrations for *Salome*.[4] The theme of the double suicide – of the death in beauty – belongs to this part of her background.

The sense of "noblesse oblige," in spite of her lack of nobility in the simple things of life, is yet a strong factor in behavior. Her refusal to lie about the pistol, for instance. Her answer to Brack's "One could always declare that the pistol was stolen" comes as quick as a flash: "It would be better to die." And of course the fact that though a "terrible coward" she still has the courage to shoot herself – and beautifully and with a gallantry touched with bravado – belongs to this theme in her nature. Iris March in "The Green Hat"[5] killed herself by driving her Hispano Suiza at seventy miles an hour into a tree. I suppose perhaps a Hedda of 1964 would take off in a plane and lose herself by flying at four hundred miles per hour straight into the sun. Pistols are old-fashioned in this day of the Nuclear Missile. But this doesn't prevent the vital point, the reasons for her having to die, from being ageless and universal.

Ibsen as Craftsman

From **H. L. Mencken, Introduction to *Eleven Plays of Henrik Ibsen***, New York: The Modern Library, 1935, pp. vii–xi, xii–xiv

The reaction against the earlier view of Ibsen as a social iconoclast and moralist, which Yurka and le Gallienne had been implicitly promoting through the updated perspective of their productions, was put in its most explicit form by H. L. Mencken (1880–1956), the most famous American journalist and social commentator of the 1920s and 1930s.

3 "*Poisonous Flowers*," a cycle of Symbolist poems by Charles Baudelaire (1821–67), which gained a reputation for decadence and late-Romantic perversion. This connection with the *fin de siècle* was also used as a subtextual basis for interpreting the play by Janet Suzman: see **pp. 98–100** below.

4 Oscar Wilde's play *Salome*, written in 1892 and performed in 1896 by the Théâtre Libre, was immediately recognized as a core text of *fin-de-siècle* sensibility – while Aubrey Beardsley's exquisite and erotic Art Nouveau black-and-white drawings had already come to epitomize decadence in the leading art journals of the period.

5 The scandalous 1942 novel by Michael Arlen (1895–1956), also turned into a play, in which the heroine Iris March embarks on a series of promiscuous affairs after her syphilitic husband commits suicide on their wedding night rather than infect her. When she re-meets her girlhood love, Iris deliberately crashes her luxury car, choosing to die rather than wrecking his life.

Ibsen, like Wagner and Manet, has lived down his commentators, and is now ready to be examined and enjoyed for what he actually was, namely, *a first-rate journeyman dramatist*, perhaps the best that ever lived. Twenty years ago he was hymned and damned as anything and everything else: symbolist, seer, prophet, necromancer, maker of riddles, rabble-rouser, cheap shocker, pornographer, spinner of gossamer nothings. [. . .] No such Ibsen, of course, ever really existed [. . .] On the contrary, he was a man whose salient quality was precisely his distrust of, and disdain for, any and all such facile heresies; a highly respectable gentleman of the middle class, well-barbered, ease-loving and careful in mind; a very skilful practitioner of a very exacting and lucrative trade; a safe and sane exponent of order, efficiency, honesty and common sense. From end to end of his life there is no record that Ibsen ever wrote a single word or formulated a single idea that might not have been exposed in a newspaper editorial.

[. . .]

When this began to be understood, then he began to make his way, and all the serious dramatists of Europe began to imitate him. But they saw him, with their keener professional eyes, more clearly than the early and so absurd Ibsenites had seen him. They saw that he was not a brummagem[1] prophet, but a play-maker of astounding skill – one who had a new and better method to teach them. And so, when they set out to follow him, what they imitated was not the imaginary mystifications that foolish fuglemen had read into his dramas, but his direct and adept manner of clothing simple and even self-evident arguments in unusually lucid and brilliant dramatic forms – in brief, his enormously effective technique as a dramatist. He didn't teach them to think extraordinary thoughts; he taught them to put obvious thoughts into sound plays.

All this must be plain to anyone who goes through his so-called social dramas today; despite the confusing memory of all the gabble that went about in the high days of the Ibsen uproar. What ideas does one actually find in them? [. . .] They are without exception, ideas of the utmost simplicity. There is nothing mysterious in them; there is not even anything new in them. Above all there is no idiotic symbolism in them. They mean just what they say.

[. . .]

Ibsen's chief interest, from the beginning to the end of his career as a dramatist, was not with the propagation of ethical ideas, but with the solution of aesthetic problems. He was, in brief, not a preacher but an artist, and not the moony artist of popular legend, but the alert and competent artist of fact, intent upon the technical difficulties of his business. He gave infinitely more thought to questions of practical dramaturgy – to getting his characters on and off the stage, to building up climaxes, to calculating effects – than he ever gave to the ideational content of his dramas. Almost any idea was good enough, so long as it could be converted into a conflict, and the conflict could be worked out straightforwardly and effectively. Read his letters and you find him tremendously concerned, from the start,

1 Dialect slang for Birmingham, the industrial center of England, "brummagem" became the term for shoddy mass-produced goods.

with technical difficulties and expedients – and never mentioning morals, lesson, symbols, and that sort of thing at all.

[. . .]

[D]ramatists, once they could shake off Scribe tradition, began to imitate Ibsen – Jones and Pinero and later Shaw in England; Hauptmann and Sudermann in Germany; Gorky and many another in Russia; Hervieu, Brieux and their like in France; a swarm of lesser ones in Italy, Scandinavia and Austria.[2] Ibsen, in brief completely overthrew the well-made play of Scribe, and set up the play that was a direct imitation of reality. He showed that the illusion was not only not helped by the elaborate machinery of Scribe, but that it was actually hindered – that the way to sure and tremendous effects was by the route of simplicity, naturalness, ingenuousness. In *A Doll's House* he abandoned all of the old tricks save two or three; in *Ghosts* he made away with the rest of them, and even managed to do without a plot; by the time he got to *Little Eyolf* there was nothing left of the traditional dramaturgy save the act divisions.

[. . .]

He depicted the life of his time and he made use of the ideas of his time; he had no desire to change those ideas, not even, in the main, to criticize them. "A dramatist's business," he used to say, "is not to answer questions, but merely to ask them." He asked a question in *A Doll's House*. He asked another, ironically, in *Ghosts*. He asked others in *The Lady from the Sea, The Wild Duck* and *Little Eyolf*. In *The Master Builder*, rising, so to speak, to a question of personal privilege, he abandoned his habit and ventured upon a half-answer. But is there any answer in *Hedda Gabler*? Surely not.

From **Arthur Miller, Introduction to *Collected Plays***, Vol. 1, New York: Viking Press 1957, p. 21

The importance of Ibsen's dramaturgy as a technical model was confirmed by Arthur Miller (1915–), who achieved international fame with *Death of a Salesman* (1949) and still counts as America's greatest living playwright. In his Introduction to his own *Collected Plays* he singles out the structural effectiveness of Ibsen's plays, which is brought to its highest point in *Hedda Gabler*.

There is one element in Ibsen's method which I do not think ought to be overlooked, let alone dismissed as it so often is nowadays. If his plays, and his method, do nothing else they reveal the evolutionary quality of life. One is constantly aware, in watching his plays, of process, change, development. I think too many modern plays assume, so to speak, that their duty is merely to show the present countenance, rather than to account for what happens. It is therefore wrong to imagine that because his first and sometimes his second acts devote so much time to a studied revelation of antecedent material, his view is static compared to our

2 All the playwrights mentioned are (somewhat loosely) part of the Naturalist movement.

own. In truth, it is profoundly dynamic, for that enormous past was always heavily documented to the end that the present be comprehended with wholeness, as a moment in a flow of time, and not – as with so many modern plays – as a situation without roots. Indeed, even though I can myself reject other aspects of his work, it nevertheless presents barely and unadorned what I believe the biggest single dramatic problem, namely, how to dramatize what has gone before. I say this not merely out of technical interest, but because dramatic characters, and the drama itself, can never hope to attain a maximum degree of consciousness unless they contain a viable unveiling of the contrast between past and present, and an awareness of the process by which the present has become what it is. And I say this, finally, because I take it as a truth that the end of drama is creation of a higher consciousness and not merely a subjective attack upon the audience's nerves and feelings. What is precious in the Ibsen method is its insistence upon valid causation [. . .]

Hedda as "Heroine"

From **Muriel Bradbrook, "The Humanist"** in *Ibsen the Norwegian: A Revaluation*, London: Chatto & Windus, 1966, pp. 97, 116–18, 119–20

In the first half of the century, critics tended to focus on the central figure of Hedda to the exclusion of the society around her. This approach is represented by Muriel Bradbrook's comments in her highly influential study of Ibsen. It effectively removes any sense of social criticism – or indeed wider meaning – from the play, though at the same time Bradbrook does raise the issue of the comedy in the play, anticipating the interpretations by Glenda Jackson and Janet Suzman almost thirty years later (see **pp. 98, 101**). She classes *Hedda Gabler* (together with *The Wild Duck*, *The Lady from the Sea*, and *Rosmersholm*) as a "humanist" play, meaning that it focuses objectively on human nature, on the grounds that "Ibsen had ceased to be polemical."

Hedda's game with the pistols is a very different use of conventional material from Nora's dancing of the tarantella [in *A Doll's House*]. The pistols are consciously theatrical to herself and to the others, they are part of her "life-craving". The melodrama of the pistols is set against the background of Aunt Julle's domesticities and Tesman's solicitudes, and the implications are ironic. The four plays show indeed a progressive severity of control, until in *Hedda Gabler* the screw is turned so tightly that Ibsen has achieved the perfect specimen piece. [. . .]

There is no answer to Hedda. Even the Ibsenites could not find a problem in this play.

[. . .]

Hedda Gabler is strong in her intellectual dishonesty. She will not face her life, her limitations or her creditors. Hedda has neither self-awareness nor responsibility. Unlike Rebekke and Rosmer [in *The Lady from the Sea* and *Rosmersholm*[1]] she has in their sense no inner life at all: *love* is a word she does not understand and cannot use. There is neither progression nor conflict in her character. From the beginning she is shown as eaten up by envy and pride, in all the malignancy of impotence. Hedda loathes life. When she sees the cosy affection of Jørgen and Aunt Julle or the mutual trust of Løvborg and Thea she must strike, like a cobra. Her actions are instinctive: she herself admits to Brack that she does not know why she had to "mistake" Aunt Julle's bonnet for the servant's. So, too, she strikes at Løvborg who has forgotten her, and Thea who has supplanted her. "It's now I am burning thy bairn, Thea. Thou, with the curls! The bairn that is thine and his! I'm burning it – I'm burning the bairn now!"

The impulse to murder, which turns inevitably to self-murder, is in itself an inverted form of the life-craving (*livs-kravet*) which had linked Hedda to Løvborg. It is the most primitive form of self-assertion, and frustrated as she is, Hedda is ruled by her militant blood. The cobra strikes, and misses. For each time, her ignorance miscalculates and her attempts to impose her will on circumstances are deflected by some trivial accident in the external fabric of events.

The only person on whom she does get her revenge is Judge Brack. And perhaps on the unborn child, whose life too is ended by the final pistol shot.

Never is Hedda shown as suffering. She is hardly self-conscious enough to suffer. Although she is once or twice seen alone, there is nothing in the play that could be called a soliloquy from her: she is shown entirely in action. [. . .] There is no frame, no comment. No judgment is passed upon Hedda, or even invited. The audience is not asked to respond with a verdict, and this objectivity of presentation, this neutral response is the most discomfiting thing about the play. It was not at all characteristic of the age. Zola or Brieux painted life black enough, but, like the early Ibsen, they invited a judgment: they called aloud for horror or disgust or clinical excitement: they implied a scientific explanation and therefore a potential scientific remedy. [. . .]

In *Hedda Gabler* there is no such counterpoise. Jørgen the painful pedant, Løvborg, the debased Dionysius, and Brack, the suave bureaucrat, are equally unpleasant and unimportant, and the two minor women's parts are only "feeds". [. . .] The whole play pivots upon Hedda but she herself is neither "placed" nor judged. She is a study in a vacuum. Every speech in the play is directed towards the main purpose, the revelation of Hedda's character, although there is no longer the rigid interlocking through implication of speech with speech. As, however, the centre of the play is not a problem but a personality there is less emphasis on the story – on the links of cause and effect. The play proceeds rather by episodic development. Act I gives a full picture of the Tesman menage and sets out all the main problems. Act II introduces the rivals, Løvborg and Brack, and Hedda's first attempt to play with destiny and to thwart Thea. Act III is given up to the story of the manuscript and ends with Hedda's triumph. Act IV springs the trap, undoes

1 *Rosmersholm*, produced four years before, has been particularly compared to *Hedda Gabler*. The heroine, Rebecca West, falls in love with an apostate priest, lures his wife to her death, and enters into a suicide pact with him. Her actions prefigure Hedda's, though her intellectual honesty and capacity for passion are in sharp contrast.

the triumph, and forces Hedda to accept her own counsel and use the second pistol.

Archer noted long ago that the play "raised no special problems", but the fact that it also evokes no emotions, no judgment from the spectators means that there is no longer a tragic catharsis. Rather the attitude is akin to that of *Troilus and Cressida*, a sardonic depth of scepticism where the only satisfaction is to see the biter bit, and the engineer hoist with his own petard. We do not feel, with the final pistol shot, that Hedda has her deserts, nor yet that like Osvald [in *Ghosts*], she is necessity's victim. Whilst unsurpassed technical resources have been brought to bear, there is a kind of arrest or barrier upon the comment, the connexions, the threads which should reach out to ordinary life, its complexities and judgments. For the play is highly selective. Any strong character set up against Hedda would disrupt it: if Eilert Løvborg had been allowed to develop, he might have become positive enough to throw the play out of focus, and so he is used very sparingly and given two hysterical scenes to minimize his force as a character, and prevent any strong feeling for him which would endanger the neutrality of response. He becomes instead a recognizable type, a character eminently to be "used" and not displayed.

[. . .]

We neither dislike nor fear Hedda. We merely assent. Yes, the traits are recognizable. This feeling of *recognition of the species* belongs to comedy rather than to tragedy, and *Hedda Gabler* has a strong taste of that bitter comedy, the comedy of *Tartuffe* and *Volpone*, which is more purely pessimistic than tragedy. The basis of sardonic comedy is the theme of the biter bit. Fate is cleverer than Hedda at playing tricks, and she herself is outplayed at her own game. The story of her pretended enthusiasm for the Minister's villa is the first example of it. From sheer boredom and to find a subject for conversation, she feigned admiration for the house, as a result of which she finds herself living in it. The final example is the absurd promptitude with which Thea produces the rough notes of Løvborg's book, and sets to work on reconstruction. Archer felt this incident to be shockingly improbable and so it is. But Thea breathing fervent prayers that she may inspire Tesman and Tesman hopefully declaring: "Yes, Hedda, believe it or not – I really think I'm beginning to feel something like it, now . . .", are not meant to be probable. They are acidly comic. Even Hedda's last act, when she finds the courage she has always lacked and shoots herself, "beautifully", is completely wasted, for no one grasps its significance.

> TESMAN: Shot herself! Shot herself in the head! Think of that!
> BRACK: But, God bless my soul! People don't *do* such things!

Hedda Gabler is such very strong meat that, in an age when the tragic had to be the solemn, its savage comedy was not appreciated. [. . .] Normally, of course, this attitude goes with a heroic vitality; the peculiar and appalling effect in *Hedda Gabler* is that it accompanies a negative attitude.

From **G. Wilson Knight, "Imprisoned Souls"** in *Henrik Ibsen*, New York: Grove Press Inc., 1962, pp. 65–7

Singling out Hedda as the only active person, as Bradbrook does (see above), cleared the way for Ibsen's character to be treated as a traditional "heroine," and as a conventional tragic figure. The following excerpt marks the high point in the valorization of Hedda as a "positive" and "spiritual" figure. Wilson Knight, who dominated Shakespearean studies in the mid-century with over twenty books on Shakespeare, most notably on the tragedies, portrays the play in traditional terms by emphasizing the symbolic elements in the text. Reprinted in 1966, *Ibsen* (Knight's only study of a modern writer) was instrumental in shaping the critical view of *Hedda Gabler* for over a decade.

Intoxication is a power in *Peer Gynt* and *Ghosts*, and mystically honoured in *Emperor and Galilean*; and in recalling Løvborg from literary brilliance to drink Hedda may be seen as drawing him from a limited intellectual achievement to all the fiery vitalities defined by Shakespeare in Falstaff's speech on sherris-sack.[1] [. . .] That is why she takes such keen pleasure in envisaging Løvborg "with vine-leaves in his hair." In submitting himself to temptation she believes that he will regain his whole, Dionysian, self and be henceforth "a free man for all his days;" and she claims that her trust is greater than Mrs. Elvsted's, whose surface reformation has left him no better than a half-man and unfree. When Hedda hears of the miserable result, all she can say, quietly, "gazing straight before her," is, "Then he had no vine-leaves in his hair." Løvborg's failure repeats Julian's: searching for Dionysus [in Ibsen's 1873 trilogy *The Emperor and Galilean*], he finds himself in a police-station.

Ostensibly Hedda burns his manuscript in a paroxysm of jealousy because it has been the "child" of the supposedly reformed Løvborg and the trivial, mouse-like, Mrs. Elvsted. But if we remember Ibsen's cauterising satire on writing – Falk's burning of his books in *Love's Comedy*, Julian's comic pamphlets, and the philosopher on the battle-field anxious for his own safety in order to complete his great work "On Equanimity in Affliction" (*The Emperor Julian*, v. iii. 460) – we may again see Hedda's action as motivated from the very depths of her being. She had wanted to make Løvborg great; action to further that greatness has failed; action can yet define what that greatness was not. Whatever it might have been, and neither she nor Ibsen clearly knows, it was not a matter of pen and ink. Therefore the manuscript must be burned.

As in *Rosmersholm*, realization in life has been proved impossible. Hedda, functioning as a Sibylline authority, formulates what *Rosmersholm* left dark. Løvborg has hinted at suicide:

1 [Wilson Knight's note.] In *Henrik Ibsen: A Critical Study* (1912: 156), R. Ellis Roberts observes that Hedda here associates with drink a "beauty" not to be found in "asceticism."

HEDDA: Eilert Løvborg – listen to me. – Will you not try to – to do it beautifully?

LØVBORG: Beautifully? [*Smiling*] With vine-leaves in my hair, as you used to dream in the old days?

HEDDA: No, no. I have lost my faith in the vine-leaves. But beautifully nevertheless! For once in a way!

She gives him one of General Gabler's pistols. Here, faced by the ultimate negation, the positive drive within Hedda's actions is rendered explicit. And when she hears of Løvborg's death, shot in the "breast," she is sorry that it was not "in the temple," but content. At last she has found "a deed worth doing," "the one right thing"; and it gives her a sense of "freedom" to know that such "deliberate courage" and "spontaneous beauty" is still "possible." He has dared to live his life after his own fashion and pay the price.

When Hedda discovers that his dying was in fact neither voluntary nor beautiful and that he was shot in the bowels, it seems to her that whatever she touches turns "ludicrous and mean." Judge Brack, whose attentions had formerly served as an acceptable diversion, now increases his hold over her; he warns her that she may be implicated in Løvborg's death and arouses her deep-seated fears of scandal. As a composite and ambivalent personification of both sexual intrigue and social judgment he stands for all that Hedda most hates and fears in the society around her. She is trapped. While Tesman and Mrs. Elvsted are piecing together the notes of Løvborg's manuscript, Hedda plays wild, exultantly Dionysian, Tarantella[2] dance-music; a shot sounds from General Gabler's other pistol; and she lies dead. The prophetic work has, it is true, in part survived, but in death Hedda succeeds where Løvborg failed:

TESMAN: Shot herself! Shot herself in the temple! Fancy that!

BRACK: Good God! – people don't do such things.

Or if they do, they do not do it so exquisitely, showing such pride, scorn, and indomitable spirit. "In the temple." The mind is both man's highest possession and worst foe, and consequently the spirit's right antagonist and target. With a fine austerity of purpose Ibsen refuses his heroine any softening that might prevent her spiritual stature from asserting itself in independence of moral value. Probably in no other drama in existence is the positive essence within the apparent negations of a criminal temperament so exactly exposed, accepted, and driven to an honoured conclusion, as in this story of a general's daughter. In *Hedda Gabler*, in its sun-fire wine, its pistols, and its burning, the fiery veins of Ibsen's fearful quest are nakedly apparent.

2 A comparison to *A Doll's House*, the tarantella being the Spanish folk dance with which Nora signals her liberation before leaving her husband.

Hedda Gabler and Theories of Tragedy

The next series of selections illustrate the developing attempt through the 1960s to justify the "classic" nature of Ibsen's plays by accommodating them to theories of tragedy. This line of criticism was first suggested by Eric Bentley, one of America's leading scholars of modern drama, as far back as 1948; and subsequently confirmed by Joan Greenwood's 1960 performance – first tried out in Oxford as a personal vehicle for her, then four years later staged at a "vanity" theatre in London before transferring to the West End. As described by the critic and playwright Nigel Dennis, this may have authorized or perhaps inspired the comparisons between *Hedda Gabler* and Shakespearean tragedy (George Steiner, whose 1961 *The Death of Tragedy* is still a standard critical text), or between Ibsen and Aeschylus (Geoffrey Brereton, a specialist on Racine and French tragedy).

From **Eric Bentley, *The Modern Theatre: A Study of Dramatists and the Drama***, London: Ebenezer Baylis & Son Ltd., 1948, p. 31

Philosophically, Ibsen is a pragmatist denouncing fixed dogma, a vitalist denouncing the bodiless idea. But his work is more tragical than polemical, and the new life according to Ibsen comes only after conflagration.

Ibsen is not a Sophocles (though he is in many respects a Euripides). He does not hew out the positive and sublime sculptures which are what one usually thinks of as tragic portraiture. Like most other great men of the period, he felt that modernity did not permit grandeur and so after his bold beginnings, he progressively narrowed down his art till it was about almost nothing but himself. He perfected a 'bourgeois tragedy' but it was an uneasy perfection, and the longer Ibsen lived the further he retreated. The work of his last period, from *The Wild Duck* (1884) at the earliest or from *The Master Builder* (1892) at the latest, is the tragedy of his retreat, the tragedy of a repentant Axel.[1] The thesis and antithesis of his tragic dialectic are life and death, the meaning of which, as later in *The Waste Land*, is ironically and tragically reversed. T. S. Eliot's use of an heroic past contrasted with an ignoble present is a theme of only one Ibsen play (*Hedda Gabler*), but as in Flaubert, it is implied as between one work and another. Such early works as *The Warriors at Helgeland* are not the most important Ibsen, but they should co-exist in one's mind with the plays of modern life. The Viking plays are related to the modern plays as Flaubert's ancient and medieval studies are related to *Madame Bovary*[2]: Emma Bovary and Hedda Gabler would have had scope for their energies and their dreams in those earlier worlds.

1 The title figure of an 1890 Symbolist play by Guy de l'Isle-Adam.
2 Flaubert's scandalous 1857 novel, whose heroine's fantasies of romantic idealism and boredom with provincial life lead her to adultery, stealing money from her husband to pursue the lover who has abandoned her. Realizing she will be found out, Emma commits suicide by taking arsenic.

From **Nigel Dennis, *Dramatic Essays***, London: Cox & Wyman Ltd., 1962, pp. 38–40

If we are forever fitting Ibsen into our own contexts, are we not bound to limit his range proportionately and deny him any sort of timelessness? Can we not take for granted, for example, that Hedda will still be at pistol-practice when everyone has forgotten the Oedipus complex? Or, when Shaw gives us a chapter on 'The Technical Novelty in Ibsen's Plays'[1] and defines this novelty as 'making discussion . . . the real centre of [a] play's interest', may we not sympathize with the young enthusiast of 1891 but wish that he might have seen the discussion-play as something harking back to Aeschylus rather than immediately revolutionary?

Certainly, when the curtain rises on Minos Volanakis's production of *Hedda Gabler*, the mere sight of Michael Richardson's clean handsome set inspires us to look and listen as if Ibsen had never been produced before. The 'gloomy sort of ghoul, bent on groping for horrors by night' (as '*The Gentlewoman*' described Ibsen after seeing *Ghosts*) appears suddenly in a hard Greek light which shows brilliantly the artifices, the roots and the relationships of Ibsen's art. How stultifying and uninteresting in this hard light is the matter of late-Victorian rebellion compared with Hedda's splendid lineage, running back, as it here we see it does, first to *Macbeth* and *Arden of Feversham* and then right on to the cannibal ladies of *Medea* and *The Bacchae*! How dreary even to ponder the social strictures of nineteenth-century Christiania when there, before out eyes, is Miss Joan Greenwood carrying malice and vindictiveness as dashingly as she carries her clothes and fully capable, in a Greek moment, of popping *real* children into the domestic stove instead of paper ones! Surely it is a pity even to analyse her motives too much, let alone pin them down dead-in-time, when two-and-a-half thousand years of monstrous females are on the boil in her again? How strongly rooted in the feminine world of any age is a Hedda who, brave or coward, demands vine-leaves in a man's hair! And how much more spacious and splendid Ibsen himself; when he is allowed to stand in the company of his Greek and Elizabethan peers, instead of alone in his corner of time!

The brightness of Mr Volanakis's production also shows the Ibsen machinery at its starkest – which is far better than seeing it in its usual tureen of Brown Windsor. It is not of first importance, this machinery, but its cogs and leads are so lacking in style that one wishes the old maid [Ibsen] had been either more, or less, fussy. Except in the plays of China and Japan, we like to see visitors drop in and out naturally, instead of being summoned to the stage and dismissed on weak pretexts by the author; we dislike being shown two pistols so as to be sure that both will be fired; and we can grasp the burning significance of a stove without a domestic opening the fire-box door and showing us the electric light inside it. Geniuses, we think, do *not* carry their priceless MSS about in their pockets; and when they have lost these in whore-houses, as so few do, the rough drafts do not appear spontaneously from lady-helpers' petticoats. We think, too, that when a woman hears her beloved genius has been shot, she should be allowed at least a

1 In *The Quintessence of Ibsenism*: see above, pp. 56–7.

few days to keen properly in, and not selfishly sat down immediately to the assembling of his literary remains, solely in order that the author may finish his play. The pedant's Ibsen, in short – the methodical meticulous, master-building Ibsen – is, in truth, the weakest of Ibsen as well as the strongest, and if we admire the virtues of his method, let us confess as readily to its shockers. Coincidence and contrivance – the shotgun weddings of the theatre – do little harm to comedy and are prime necessity of farce. But this is precisely why they make tragedy look silly.

If Hedda Gabler helps us to see the line that runs from Ibsen back to Euripides, *Rosmersholm* surely connects us with Sophocles and Aeschylus [. . .]

From **George Steiner, *The Death of Tragedy***, New York: Alfred A. Knopf Inc., 1961, pp. 292–5

Steiner's path-breaking argument is that the tragic vision in European culture is rooted in Greek mythology, where the catastrophes that befall heroes are intrinsically unfair and unpredictable as well as inevitable. This is distinct from Judaic principles of justice, however severe, in which acts are rewarded or punished depending on the degree to which God's will is observed; and this rationalism, spreading through the eighteenth and nineteenth centuries, rules out tragedy. Hence the "vacuum" that forces a search for new terms of tragic reference. Steiner also noted that Freudian psychology refers back to Greek myths, and so offers a new basis for tragedy.

The decline of tragedy is inseparably related to the decline of the organic world-view and of its attendant context of mythological, symbolic, and ritual reference. It was on this context that Greek drama was founded, and the Elizabethans were still able to give it imaginative adherence. This ordered and stylized vision of life, with its bent toward allegory and emblematic action, was already in decline at the time of Racine [. . .] But after Racine the ancient habits of awareness and immediate recognition which gave to tragic drama its frame of reference were no longer prevalent. Ibsen, therefore, faced a real vacuum. He had to create for his plays a context of ideological meaning (an effective mythology), and he had to devise the symbols and theatrical conventions whereby to communicate his meaning to an audience corrupted by the easy virtues of the realistic stage. He was in the position of a writer who invents a new language and must then teach it to his readers.

Being a consummate fighter, Ibsen turned his deprivations to advantage. He made the precariousness of modern beliefs and the absence of an imaginative world-order his starting point. Man moves naked in a world bereft of explanatory or conciliating myth. Ibsen's dramas presuppose the withdrawal of God from human affairs, and that withdrawal has left the door open to cold gusts blowing in from a malevolent though inanimate creation. But the most dangerous assaults upon reason and life come not from without, as they do in Greek and Elizabethan tragedy. They arise in the unstable soul. Ibsen proceeds from the modern awareness that there is rivalry and unbalance in the individual psyche. The ghosts that haunt his characters are not the palpable heralds of damnation whom we find in *Hamlet* and *Macbeth*. They are forces of disruption that have broken loose from the core of the spirit. Or, more precisely, they are cancers growing in the soul. In Ibsen's vocabulary, the most deadly of these cancers is 'idealism', the mask of hypocrisy and self-deception with which men seek to guard against the realities of social and personal life. When ideals seize upon an Ibsen character, they drive him to psychological and material ruin as the Weird Sisters drive Macbeth. Once the mask has grown close to the skin, it can be removed only at suicidal cost. When [in *Rosmersholm*] Rosmer and Rebecca West have attained the ability to confront life, they are on the verge of death. When the mask no longer shields her against the light, Hedda Gabler kills herself.

To articulate this vision of a God-abandoned world and of man's splintered and vulnerable consciousness, Ibsen contrived an astounding series of symbols and figurative gestures. [. . .] From the start, Ibsen uses certain material objects to concentrate symbolic values (the wild duck, General Gabler's pistols, the flagpole standing in front of the house in *The Lady from the Sea*). And it is the association of an explicit, responsible image of life with the material setting and objects best able to denote and dramatize this image that is the source of Ibsen's power. It allows him to organize his plays into shapes of action richer and more expressive than any the theatre had known since Shakespeare. Consider the stress of dramatic feeling and the complexity of meaning conveyed by the tarantella which Nora dances in *A Doll's House*; by Hedda Gabler's proposal to crown Løvborg with vine leaves [. . .] Each is in itself a coherent episode in the play, yet it is at the same time a symbolic act which argues a specific vision of life.

From **Geoffrey Brereton, *Principles of Tragedy: A Rational Examination of the Tragic Concept in Life and Literature***, Coral Gables, Fla.: University of Miami Press, 1968, pp. 210–11, 212–13

Society for Ibsen is not monolithic. It is not conceived as some anonymous or unanimist force against which the individual must struggle in order to affirm himself. It is a collection of people holding certain views and convictions and is amenable or reformable through its component members. Among other consequences, it cannot therefore be a substitute for God who, being absolute, is beyond reform. Neither is there a metaphysical God in Ibsen's works, at least after *Peer Gynt*. There are fugitive references to the supernatural – the God of churches and the ministering spirits of the Master Builder, the earth spirits of John Gabriel Borkman, even the white horses of Rosmersholm – but all these are represented as the subjective emanations of individual characters and not the manifestations of some cosmic force. There is no supernatural power in Ibsen, while the community, though it can sometimes be formidable, possesses no particular mystique. The whole power, to use Blake's language, resides in the human breast. The whole interest of the plays consists in the exploration of what lies *there*, but – and this seems to be the chief difference – with no desire to give it a transcendent significance.

Is this a tragic exploration? [. . .] The fact that it deals with the domestic and the familiar, as these figured in contemporary life, cannot be allowed to disqualify it on any reasonable view. In that context the issues are by no means trivial. In fact on the modern stage they and the characters involved in them sometimes appear a little larger than life. Why should there be any hesitation in describing Ibsen as a tragic dramatist and his plays as tragedies of the only type which could authentically express the spirit of his time?

The present writer accepts them as such – some of them – and subscribes to the view that any general account of tragic drama must include Ibsen alongside the major names from Aeschylus onward.

[. . .]

The effect of holding that 'all deities reside in the human breast' and so of siting all power within the human psyche, while also rejecting the mystique of a collective power vested in the community, is to destroy the notion of an external authority, and with it that of any general law or sanction. Each man, as Rosmer said, judges himself – or else he submits consciously to the judgment of other individuals.

In this predominantly 'psychological' drama, in which the characters are engaged in examinations of their actions and motives which the situation invented by the playwright (the 'plot' in the simplest sense) has made it vital for them to try to understand, the only moral values consistently invoked are 'truth' and 'freedom'. It is all very well to say that we know what is meant by these, and even broadly what Ibsen meant by them, yet even in the context of his plays they are not presented as norms. 'Freedom' for Hedda Gabler is something quite different from the 'freedom' of Lona Hessel.[1] While it is true that the postulated existence of a fixed moral law based upon absolutes and merely awaiting discovery would be untragic, it is also true that the denial of any such law almost removes the possibility of a tragic recognition, or makes it relative and personal in each separate case. Ibsen tends to avoid the recognition altogether, particularly in those cases in which, if we harbour moral preoccupations, we most feel its necessity. The only significant verdict would be that which the character pronounces upon himself, but we are left to guess what it is.

In the world which Ibsen's characters inhabit, this omission is not wanton but realistic. Who, working without external terms of reference, will condemn himself absolutely? Who will be absolutely sure of his own rightness? We thus have an undoubtedly tragic exploration, bearing on matters of spiritual life and death, which does not lead to the tragic discovery to which earlier dramatists had accustomed us. In that case Ibsen would be incompletely tragic by universal standards, though as tragic as was possible in the context of nineteenth century realism.

1 The most important female character in Ibsen's first Naturalistic drama, *The Pillars of Society* (1877), who revolts against imposed gender roles and successfully asserts her independence.

Hedda Gabler and Poetic Drama

Traditionally tragedy is associated with verse drama, and another aspect of the search for a rationale to justify Ibsen's status as a "classic" was to bring out the poetry in his writing. His early historical plays had indeed been written in verse, and the overt symbolism of his last plays could also be fitted into this form. However, in analyzing his Naturalistic plays – where the dialogue was specifically in prose and the characters everyday or unexceptional figures – as a form of poetic drama, the critics of the 1950s and 1960s had to make a special case, redefining "poetry" as subtext. This led to the conclusion that the realism developed by Ibsen was an aberration in his career, as implied in the first example below by the Ibsen scholar John Northam, who defines the psychology as poetic. In the following extract Eric Bentley explores locating the poetic element in the subtext to the dialogue.

From **John Northam, *Ibsen's Dramatic Method: A Study of the Prose Dramas***, London: Faber & Faber Ltd., 1953, pp. 218–19

To force home on an unwilling public the immediacy of the questions which he asked, Ibsen abandoned poetry for prose and the conventions of romantic historical drama for contemporary realism which seemed to strip every veil from the unpleasant nakedness of social abuses. This surface realism, however, this verisimilitude of detail in settings, costume and language, was not enough; Ibsen wanted to persuade his public that these real problems involved real people in real suffering. He sought psychological realism as well.

Poetry, and the conventions of poetic drama, could have helped him in this, but only at the cost of restoring that comfortable remoteness which he wanted to destroy. When he set aside these aids, he produced in *The League of Youth* a play of mere surface realism. Then he found himself. Surface realism could be manipulated so delicately that the illusion of reality remained while the depths of personality were explored. Thereafter each play was a struggle to reconcile the two kinds of reality, a struggle which became harder as Ibsen's insight into human nature grew deeper. Perhaps the tension was highest, and the reconciliation most triumphant, in *Hedda Gabler*.

From **Eric Bentley, *The Life of the Drama***, New York: Atheneum, 1970 [1964], pp. 96–8

A person may open a volume of Ibsen and conclude: 'Well, this *is* just ordinary conversation.' There is nothing in the individual sentence, or sometimes on the individual page, to give him the lie. The dialogue of Ibsen, Strindberg, Chekhov and Pirandello does start both from ordinary conversation and from the kind of dialogue most closely related to it. The unit remains the actual uttered remark, but the units are then related to each other with extreme sophistication. Actors who till then had noticed only the banality of each sentence in a Chekhov scene are suddenly amazed to find that the scene as a whole is a poem. Ibsen should be credited with the invention of an anti-poetry. He made a fine art of the understatement, the evasion, the unfinished sentence. In a sense his writing undercuts poetry – and reduces it to triviality. This happens with Hedda Gabler's poetic phrase 'vine leaves in his hair', and with Hilde Wangel' s 'harps in the air' [in *The Master Builder*]. How little the literati of Ibsen's day were wise to this rhetoric of his is shown in Arthur Symons's dismissal of just these phrases on the grounds of their inadequacy as poetry.[1]

Nietzsche speaks of the really deep calm being one like that of sea, under which turbulence and power can be sensed, and the work of Ibsen suggests that the really effective prose in drama is that under which poetry can be sensed. The ordinary Naturalist achieves mere eloquence and therefore *non-art*. Ibsen contrives anti-eloquence and makes *another kind of art* from it. [. . .] In a sense there is now no 'writing' at all. The Aristotelian idea of the primacy of the Action takes on a new meaning. The Ibsenite Action is so all-embracing that people can hardly get a word in edgewise. Words are spoken only when they are pried loose by the situation, and the situation is one that will not let many words be pried loose. The greater the pressure the less people can say. Still, a hundred pages of words – much the usual amount for a play – do finally get down on Ibsen's writing paper, and it is fair to ask: how have they been chosen? I think Pirandello found the best phrase to answer this question with, and since he regarded Ibsen as second only to Shakespeare, it is fitting that he should have. His phrase is: *l'azione parlata* – the Action spoken, the Action in words.

Postmodern Interpretations

From **Frederick and Lise Lone Marker, "The Airless World of Hedda Gabler"**, *Ingmar Bergman: A Life in the Theatre*, 1992

Ingmar Bergman's 1964 production of *Hedda Gabler*, presented in London in 1968, and remounted in an English version at the National Theatre (with Maggie Smith) in 1970, stands in complete contrast to the kind of heroic reading illustrated by Knight and to the poetic/tragic line of interpretation. Bergman's pathbreaking interpretation set the tone for productions and much of the critical commentary through the 1970s.

As he had done in *Peer Gynt*, Bergman resolutely swept aside the dusty impedimenta of accumulated tradition – in this case the assumptions acquired through three-quarters of a century of naturalistic performances. In his hands *Hedda Gabler* emerged, with almost hypnotic intensity, as a work whose vision extends

1 Symons was the first to analyze the Symbolist aesthetic in the poetry of Stéphane Mallarmé, Arthur Rimbaud, and Paul Verlaine in his highly influential book on *The Symbolist Movement in Literature* (1899).

far beyond the realistic or the social plane. His starkly simplified and stylized interpretation created a tightly controlled distillation in which nothing was permitted to distract from the ruling image of the play as a drama of destiny, a cold fable of characters buried alive in a deadly vacuum. [. . .]

To articulate this vision, Bergman relentlessly stripped away the heavy mosaic of realistic details present in Ibsen's "handsomely and tastefully furnished drawing room" – the thick carpets, the dark porcelain stove, the curtained French windows, and, not least, the portentous portrait of Hedda's father, General Gabler, were all eliminated, for much the same reason that the symbolic allusions to the Dionysian vine leaves in Løvborg's hair (pointers so dear to the hearts of literary scholars) were ruthlessly expunged by him. [. . .] The entire stage space was transformed by Bergman and his designer (Mago) into an immense, non-representational box that reflected and contributed to the prevailing atmosphere of claustrophobia, rather than illustrating it in a photographic manner. Uniformly lined with a dark red, velvet-like fabric, this mausoleum-stage radiated an oppressive sense of enclosure and lifelessness. "One looks into this strange locale and wonders how human beings can breathe there. It is as though there is no air in this red chamber of horrors," wrote Nils Beyer (*Stockholms-Tidningen*) of this "ghostly vision." There were neither actual windows nor walls, only a succession of simple screens, all covered in the same dark-red velvet, which demarcated a shallow playing area within the empty space.

A smaller, movable screen – sometimes a door, sometimes a barrier in the central character's mind – bisected the stage vertically into two separate spheres of simultaneous action. "A red screen divides life into two compartments," remarked *Dagens Nyheter*. "In one of them the dull routine of living drags on, in the other Hedda Gabler writhes in desperation and frustration." This was the "inner room" of Ibsen's stage directions, the physical and psychic retreat where Hedda keeps her piano and the General's pistols, which Bergman now laid bare to view.

[. . .]

The characters in the drama appeared like figures suspended in a void. Each was dressed in a muted, unrelieved monotone – Hedda in dark green, the others in yet more subdued color values that ranged from pale gray and olive to black. A hint of period flavor in the costumes – pointedly simplified and stylized – completed the impression of characters that existed, independent of any material surroundings, in an atmosphere in which reality had no place. [. . .] Inevitably, perhaps, the impact created by these isolated human figures, seen against a ground of strangely menacing vacancy, evoked allusions to Bergman's own austere vision as a film maker and, in particular, to Edvard Munch's brooding studies of a mood of spiritual desolation and paralysis.[1] "The memory of Munch's great canvas of

1 This association with the Norwegian artist Edvard Munch (1863–1944) reflects part of the cultural background of *Hedda Gabler*. In 1891, the year the play was produced, Munch held a major exhibition of his highly personal and atmospheric pictures in Christiana, including "Melancholy," and started work on "The Scream," his best-known image, as well as his "Frieze of Life": a cycle of paintings obsessed by death and the dark side of sexuality. Influenced by the Symbolists, Munch was also attuned to Ibsen, designing placards and scenery for productions of Ibsen's plays by Lugné-Poe in Paris and by Max Reinhardt in Berlin between 1896 and 1906.

humanity haunts one's inner eye: those swaying figures of women in monochrome, suffused in the color of blood ... It is oppressive, subdued, and enclosed," remarked one critic.[2]

[. . .]

Ultimately, however, the real impact of Bergman's interpretation of *Hedda Gabler* derived not so much from his revolutionary dematerialization of the physical setting as from his analytical, almost surgical dissection of the enigma of Hedda herself. In Bergman's version Hedda was never allowed to disappear from sight. She stood trapped before us on the stage, caught in a Pirandellian situation of having to watch her innermost spiritual agony dragged into the spotlight of public scrutiny. Even when she was not directly involved in the action, she remained a visible, restless, solitary presence isolated on her own side of the stylized dividing screen.

[. . .]

From the outset, in the dreamlike opening pantomime with which Bergman prefaced and defined the play proper, Hedda's entrapment was boldly underscored. Silently, like a sleep-walker, she came on to the empty stage, her features locked in a death mask of despair and frustration. "We do not experience her as a human being of flesh and blood," wrote Nils Beyer ... "It is a damned soul who is stirring in this strange abode, before Ibsen himself starts to speak and the intricate clockwork mechanism begins to operate." As the light focused on Hedda and the auditorium gradually darkened, she moved noiselessly towards the audience. At the very front of the stage she stopped and, for a frozen moment, she stood, utterly immobile and expressionless, staring with wide open eyes into vacant space. [. . .] Turning away, she walked over to the (empty) mirror and began a critical examination of her person – first of her face, then her figure, letting her hands run slowly down her body to her stomach. Then, in a violent reaction of revulsion and despair, she suddenly bent double and pressed her hands to her abdomen, pounding it several times with the full force of her clenched fists. At last, in an effort to regain control over herself, she walked to the piano, lit a cigarette, stubbed it out at once, and then settled herself in an armchair. Meanwhile, the intrusion of the outside world, in the persons of Aunt Julle and the maid, began, as their expository small talk broke the silence for the first time.

Hence, the outcome was inevitable from the start. This preliminary, oneiric movement in Bergman's production proclaimed a relentlessly closed framework of doom from which there was clearly no escape. "She is forced into a corner because she is a woman who, when she is pregnant, is left with no choice. She is in a blind alley. Whether she likes it or doesn't like it, there it is. It says so in the score," Bergman himself has declared.

[. . .]

Once established, the pattern of Hedda's alienation and spiritual nausea proceeded to grow and develop through a continuous sequence of peripheral actions, performed as she listened – or pointedly refused to listen – to the conversation taking place on the other side of the dividing screen. The spasmodic movements of

2 [Markers' note.] Tord Baeckström, *Göteborgs Handels*, October 18, 1964.

Hedda in her cage – lighting and extinguishing cigarettes, biting her own hand in a sudden neurotic gesture of self-contempt, or ironically perusing a book in a parody of the manners of the well-educated nineteenth-century woman, only to let it fall to the floor a moment afterwards – were signposts marking her inexorable progress towards destruction. "One might have thought that Hedda was spying; but the impression produced was rather that the stage spied on Hedda, that she was being dissected by it against her will," observed Melchinger (*Theater heute*, 10. 1967). [. . .] Humiliated by the superimposed identity that Tesman's world has prepared for her, she searched in vain for some reliable evidence of her elusive self. Tormented by the thought of this incarceration in a role, she found herself drawn to the mirror – that most central of all props in Bergman's art – in which she could watch herself live and watch herself prepare to die. She was "continually shown before the imaginary mirror, striking poses, testing attitudes, examining her fading complexion, trying as it were to convince herself that she is truly real; now and then she stands so close to the mirror that it seems as if she wants to breathe away her human features," commented Wahlund. Much more important than as a device for reassuring Hedda of her reality, however, was the mirror's function as a glass in which *the actress* observes her own performance.

[. . .]

Eilert Løvborg, the third man in Hedda's life and, in Bergman's interpretation, so obviously her former lover, was from the beginning a man who had reached the end of his rope. This deromanticized Løvborg was no free-spirited Dionysian visionary. He possessed neither vine leaves nor a future any longer, and the "masterpiece" containing his prescription for the future of human civilization was nothing more than a pitifully few sheets of paper. (Questioned about this very suggestive detail of the strikingly thin manuscript, Bergman finds a characteristically concrete explanation, pointing out that had it been any thicker Løvborg would certainly have noticed his fatal loss of it once.)

[. . .]

As the scene between Hedda and Løvborg took on the character of a virtual reenactment of similar scenes between them in the past, Bergman's choreography and lighting established an eerie visual adumbration of unreality and déjà vu. [. . .] The struggle reached its climax when Løvborg, in a final and erotically charged gesture, impulsively embraced Hedda from his seated position, passionately pressing his face against her. For a single instant she seemed about to relax her steely self-control. Then, brutally reasserting her dominance, she thrust him away with both hands. Immediately afterwards Thea entered – "as in a dream," Bergman had observed during rehearsals, "because when you want something to happen in a dream, it does. And Hedda wants a showdown with Thea."

[. . .]

This final, destructive encounter between the two gained emotional intensity through pruning away the punctilious exposition and naturalistic "small talk" that link the play to the theatrical conventions of an older period – but that, in his terms, only serve to dissipate the potential emotional impact on a modern audience. Bergman's commitment to the view that cinematic or theatrical art must speak directly to the subconscious mind rather than to the conscious intellect has provoked its share of critical quarrels, to be sure. It is a view that necessarily resists the imposition of any closed framework of "meaning" – be it symbolic, Freudian, feminist, political, or whatever – that will point the spectator in a single predetermined direction and deny him imaginative alternatives, thereby voiding his truly creative participation in the dramatic event.

[. . .]

Nothing was permitted to mitigate the harshness or obscure the clarity of this final scene. The "frenzied dance melody" that Hedda plays on the piano in Ibsen's text was reduced to a few dissonant, nonmusical chords hammered out in frustration. As she stood before the mirror and quietly prepared to put a bullet through her head, her husband and the self-possessed Thea Elvsted sat motionlessly at the other end of the stage, totally absorbed in their absurd task of reassembling the dead Løvborg's notes – a deadly picture of hollow people trying to paste together a vision whose spirit they do not comprehend, clinging to a meaningless past that completely overshadows both the present and the future. Hedda's last act before withdrawing into the ultimate isolation of death was to remove her high-heeled shoes carefully, in a final irrational attempt to control and transcend a reality that had become a nightmare. "The only thing she wants is to die a beautiful death," Bergman has been prompted to explain. "She has rehearsed the last gesture before the mirror. She knows how to use the pistol so that it becomes aesthetic. Perhaps she also takes into consideration that she wants to fall nicely. It is an uncontrollable moment that she subconsciously tries to control by taking off her shoes."[3]

Judge Brack had the last word, as of course he does in Ibsen, in all three of Bergman's productions of the play. In Munich, however, his line was reinforced by an astonishing gesture of sheer brutality. Standing nonchalantly over Hedda's out-stretched corpse, Brack seized her roughly by the hair and lifted her head, as though to assure himself that she was dead, before pronouncing his cynical verdict that "people don't do such things!" Like Eilert, Hedda had found only a harsh and unlovely end. "The irony in all this" Bergman remarks, "is that she dies such an ugly death anyway – that she ends up lying there with her rump in the air."

Feminist Readings

From **Elenore Lester, "Hedda – Frigid Woman or Life Bearer?"**, in the *New York Sunday Times*, March 7, 1971, section 2, pp. 3, 29

During the 1970s, in America, feminist readings of *Hedda Gabler* began to appear. This 1971 extract by Elenore Lester has been selected since it was the first such interpretation, and is clearly distinct from the (Freudian) view of the

3 [Markers' note.] Quoted in *Kvällsposten* (Malmo), October 18, 1964.

play that dominated American criticism over the previous two decades. It also brings out the main points expanded on by subsequent feminist critics. Thus a 1990 essay also refers to Kate Millett's *Sexual Politics* (1970), as Lester does, and gives the same view of the play as an "illustration of the effects of living in a patriarchal society where freedom and power are relegated to men, while even the brightest and most competent of women is firmly placed in the drawing-room" so that "in a society where men have the only real power, Hedda's need to control becomes perverted into physical violence" – asserting Hedda (and even Thea) as feminist icons.[1]

Hedda Gabler – castrator, penis-envy (pistols), frigid, unresolved Electra complex (father's portrait), lesbian tendencies (obsession with Thea's hair).

In terms like these the case of Hedda Gabler went into the Contemporary Drama notebooks of the Fifties. Ibsen was a breeze in those days of find-the-phallic-symbols-and-you-have-the key. The American "adjustment" version of Freudian psychology dominated not only the personal lives of a large percentage of the middle class, but the study of literature as well. Each literary character worthy of "analysis" was laid out like a patient on the couch [. . .]

Hedda had shocked and baffled earlier generations. Cruel, perverse and fiendish were the adjectives pre-Freudian critics usually applied to her. We knew better – Hedda was simply sick.

But even back then one closed the casebook on Hedda with some misgivings. We were children of the romantic era. We loved a rebel. How could we condemn as sick Hedda's desperate thrashing inside the social straitjacket, her contempt for plodding, as opposed to inspired, work, and her hunger for power beauty, heroic achievement – even though her concept of such things was bourgeois-romantic? Such uncertainties were repressed. In those days it took courage to challenge the "Freudian interpretation."

Now, in the year of women's lib, one might reasonably hope that the clammy hand of the 1950's psychiatric sexist view of Hedda might be released from her neck. This would be reason enough to revive Hedda. Let us see that what Hedda envies is men's power and that, being a general's daughter, the penis-pistols give her a sense of that power. Let us see that her pitiful yearning for power over another's life comes out of a sense of powerlessness to control her own. Let us see that she is temperamentally unsuited to play her socially assigned role and that it is society, not biology, which traps her. An alternative life style was conceivable, even in the 1880s. Hedda's friend, Judge Brack, suggests that she think of a vocation for herself. But Hedda has been conditioned to believe she act only through men. Her answer to Brack: "I wonder whether I might put Tesman into politics."

1 Katherine Anne Ackley, "A Rage to Live: The Violent Life and Death of Hedda Gabler," in *Women and Violence in Literature: An Essay Collection*, New York: Garland Publishing Inc., 1990, p. 174.

A woman's lib emphasis would by no means bring out all the dramatic possibilities in Ibsen's play, but it would let in a bit of fresh air.

[. . .]

In Ibsen's play, Hedda is unfeminine by all traditional standards, but she is fire, not ice (firearms, threatened hair burnings, actual book burning, metaphorical baby-burning). Hedda is the bomb in the living room. She is terrified of scandal because she has much to hide, much to repress. All of her instincts would drive her outside of acceptable social channels. Her alter-ego in the play is an unseen woman, the flame-haired, pistol-packing whore who finally does Løvborg in with a shot in the groin. [. . .]

Thea, on the other hand, is a fine specimen of womanhood by the mental health standards of the Freudian Fifties. She has the guts to walk out on an obnoxious husband and three stepchildren to pursue the man she loves. But oddly enough in Ibsen's version, this golden goddess suggests cotton batting more than emotional release. She can afford to face small-town scandal because her instincts are basically socially acceptable. Løvborg, in speaking of the wild, esoteric pleasures he and Hedda enjoyed in their secret game of verbal exhibitionism and voyeurism, remarks that Thea is "stupid" about that kind of thing. Furthermore, he points out, Thea has domesticated him, broken not only his appetite for pure sensuality, but "my courage, my power of braving it out." It is right and inevitable that Thea should wind up with Tesman.

[. . .]

Yes Hedda must be seen as a bored, middle-class, unloving wife with foolish, dangerous fantasies about Freedom, Beauty, Nobility, but she must also be seen as a true outlaw of the spirit. Suffocated in corsets, smothered in silks and bustles and oppressively tasteful furniture, preyed on by a stuffy husband, a creepy admirer, a cloying auntie, Hedda is an unleasher of tabooed Dionysiac forces – forces which destroy the social structure, but without which life dries up. Hedda's comment about the withered leaves outside her door early in the play points to the withering of the society around her.

In this context, it is significant that the main instrument of Løvborg's destruction is alcohol. On the naturalistic level, Hedda is purely malicious to send Løvborg, the dry alcoholic, back to the bottle, but on the poetic level she is right. The spirit of Dionysus, god of drunken frenzy, ecstatic debauchery and unshaped creative energy is needed and Hedda wants to put Løvborg back in touch with those dark forces and see him, wearing "vine leaves in his hair" like the god himself, return triumphant to her claustrophobic Victorian parlour. [. . .]

It is possible to see Tesman as a contemporary debase representative of the Apollonian spirit of temperance, individuation, ethics – just as Løvborg is a debased representative of the Dionysiac spirit. It is the conflict between these which, according to Nietzsche in "The Birth of Tragedy" made for the greatness of Greek tragedy and the Greek world view.

The beauty of *Hedda Gabler* lies in its glimmering ironies and ambiguities and complex reverberations. It can also be seen as a play about emotional cannibalism. Hedda tries to use men and fails, but Thea succeeds. Brack and Aunt Julia feed off the lives of the vulnerable and try to insinuate themselves in another's marital bed. Tesman feeds off the work of others and Løvborg uses women for whatever they'll give.

They are unpleasant people, but also average, multifaceted, mysterious. Is there not love in Tesman's humble dedication to scholarly research? And doesn't even the sinister Brack show a vein of sensitivity in his understanding of Hedda? And what of Løvborg? Is he really a profound thinker? There is nothing to go on except his opinion and that of Thea and Tesman. From Løvborg's description of his book ("It is about the future") and Tesman's excitement over it, it appears Løvborg may be a flashy Book-of-the-Month-Club genius who has written *The Greening of America*.[2] In the current adaptation of the play by Christopher Hampton, Løvborg adds to his brief description of the book that it is also about "the underground revolution in women's thoughts." So the book may well incorporate *Sexual Politics*.[3]

Hedda Gabler may still be a live play for our time if it is released from the bonds of simplified psychology [. . .] It is ironic that Hedda has come to be a symbol of the frigid woman when, in the essential pattern of the play, she is a life-bearer. But she cannot be assimilated by society – she is too potent. It is only as a sacrificial victim that society can use her.

When Thea and Tesman pore over the notes to Løvborg's treatise about the future of mankind, they are feeding off Hedda's living spirit, for *she* is Løvborg's muse. From Ibsen's balanced and ironic point of view, this is closer to black comedy than tragedy. It is the way things are.

From **Irving Wardle, "Glenda Jackson Meets Hedda Gabler"**, Interview with Glenda Jackson, *Los Angeles Times*, April 6, 1975

Glenda Jackson's 1975 interpretation of Hedda Gabler for the Royal Shakespeare Company, which played in Australia, and in Los Angeles and Washington, D.C., as well as in London, was as much a landmark as Bergman's. Not only did it incorporate the feminist view of the play – focusing on the surrounding characters to show Hedda as the victim of a male-dominated society and as one type of feminist icon, with Thea as another – but also stressed the way, as the character says, Hedda's life was "a grotesque farce." The following extract is taken from an interview with Jackson during the run of the production in Los Angeles.

[Hedda] isn't simply a capricious, bad-hearted, interfering femme fatale. In her own mind, she does everything for the best, but she's committed to a very

2 *The Greening of America* by Charles Reich (published in 1970) was one of the earliest books to popularize ecology by linking it to the flower-power counter-culture of the time, as his subtitle makes clear: *how the youth revolution is trying to make America livable*.

3 Kate Millett's *Sexual Politics* (1971), analyzing gender roles in history and literature, became the bible of modern feminism.

old-fashioned set of principles and totally out of her depth with the other characters. She is not the motor of the play. They are.

Ibsen has written a set of incredibly self-centered people. Few of them have laudable human characteristics of any kind. As soon as you scrape the surface of the text it's jungle warfare underneath, and that has to come across because the whole action of the play is only 36 hours. She comes home after that disastrous six-month honeymoon, and 36 hours later she blows her brains out. That wouldn't happen if the other characters weren't so strong and hounding her.

They are all users. Judge Brack, obviously. Løvborg, too; you have to ask how much he's playing the part of a genius for his own advantage. Tesman isn't a vacillating, idiot husband; he wants his own way, he's on at her all the time. And Aunt Julie isn't a silly old lady. The way Constance Chapman plays her [in the RSC production], she brings an immense critical attitude towards Hedda. One gets the feeling that Hedda Gabler had better pull up her socks and become Hedda Tesman.

At the beginning of the play, the interesting thing is that they all think they've got Hedda where they want her. There's no need for Tesman to court her any more. Brack knows exactly how to play her. Julie's going to turn her into Mrs. Tesman before you can say knife. So all that glorious freedom she had as Miss Gabler, where is it? It's gone! Suddenly she's put into this house and there she is, battering herself against the walls.

They're all immensely energetic. They aren't gray, Nordic-gloom people. Hedda says she's bored because there is nothing she can pour all that energy into that she would regard as worth spending time on. She finds it all totally banal. That is not a problem that the others have. She can't cope with bourgeois life or with modern feminism. That's why I say she's the old-fashioned character and the others are all forward-looking. Thea Elvsted's a feminist, but for Hedda it's a question of wanting to be a man herself, rather than wanting women to have equal rights.

That's one reason why she finds her pregnancy intolerable. She wasn't a son, and as old General Gabler was a god to her, then it's her fault that she wasn't. So she becomes an excellent shot and pretty good on horseback and she can't stand being touched. It's all mental excitement for her. She's terrific in the early stages of flirtation. It all goes bubbling along, with Brack. Then, when it comes to the crunch, she can't handle him. She's always overconfident, and these terrible things keep on happening to her.

Then remember how she gets pregnant? The knight in shining armor failed to arrive, so she got married, still a virgin, to George Tesman and they have this honeymoon. First she discovers that she isn't very good at sex and for Hedda Gabler to discover that she isn't very good at anything is a terrible shock. All these years men have been saying, "You're the greatest; if only we had the opportunity, wouldn't it be wonderful." Somebody then gets the opportunity and it is not so wonderful. When she says the honeymoon was boring, what she's actually been is a total failure. Out of this singular loss and emptiness she's suddenly stuck with a baby, and she finds the whole physical process absolutely repellent.

Those are my thoughts on the part. The difficulty is finding ways of showing

Figure 4 **Glenda Jackson as Hedda Gabler (Act 2) in the 1976 film. (Billy Rose Theater Collection, The New York Public Library.)**

them. Hedda is a steely character and many emotional areas one would normally use are not available for her. She would never cry. She's shown three times alone on stage and each time it's very specific that she's pacing up and down. She is not a lady who would stand and quietly shake in a corner. It would be very easy to let her bury her head in her hands but that isn't what she's about. She suggests a big cat, but that may come out of being caged; if she was asked what she'd like to be it would probably be an eagle. It's easy to stay on the prickly level of aggression and wit; it is most difficult to let the audience see into her fears. She cannot openly say, "I am afraid," so all the area has to be transmitted into something other. I don't think I've cracked that yet. [. . .]

I don't think we shall ever be really comfortable with the play because it moves over so much ground so quickly. You have to turn on a sixpence. One minute it's genuinely tragic; the next it's rip-roaring farce. For actors, the difficulty is to be sufficiently poised to do a full 90-degree turn with a snap of the fingers. You cannot save yourself for big moments. You've got to commit yourself totally to the left and immediately switch to the right.

Take that scene with Mrs. Elvsted. Hedda says, "I'm going to burn your hair off." Then the maid comes in to say tea's ready, and she becomes the polite hostess again. Not that Hedda ever does anything violent to anyone else. From her point of view, all she does is to burn paper. No matter how it looks to the audience when she puts Løvborg's manuscript in the stove, that's all it is to her. She establishes this earlier on when Løvborg tells Mrs. Elvsted that he's lost their child. Hedda says, "It's all very well talking about losing children, but what you're really talking about is a book." Hedda's actually carrying a baby, and for somebody to say that paper with words written on it is the same is for her a monstrous absurdity. When she destroys it she's simply putting Thea Elvsted in her place. I don't want a great big paper-burning scene.

Recent Approaches to *Hedda Gabler*

From **Janet Suzman, "*Hedda Gabler*: The Play in Performance"** in Errol Durbach (ed.) *Ibsen and the Theatre: The Dramatist in Production*, New York: New York University Press, 1980, pp. 84–5, 86–7, 89, 90

The most balanced, and in some ways most sensitive, portrayal of Hedda Gabler came in Janet Suzman's performance, originally an American public television production broadcast in the same year as the Glenda Jackson staging (1975) and remounted for the London theatre in 1977. She was described by a London reviewer as "a Hedda for whom the bell has long tolled, an intelligent and suicidal bird trapped in a rather shabby and . . . overcrowded cage" (Steve Grant, *Plays and Players*, 24(11), August 1977, p. 22). In preparing the role, which she had seen Joan Greenwood perform, Suzman took into account the notes Mrs. Patrick Campbell made in her acting copy of the play (during rehearsals for her 1908 and 1922 performances) as well as discussing the characterization with Peggy Ashcroft (who had performed Hedda in 1954). However, the basis for her performance was Ibsen's remark that "Hedda as a personality, is to be regarded rather as her father's daughter than as her husband's wife" (see **p. 32**: letter to Moritz Prozor, December 4, 1890), and like Glenda Jackson, she brought out the comic elements in the play, as well as emphasizing – in deliberate contrast to the picture of Hedda as "frigid" – the emotion beneath the "seemingly cold beauty" (see **p. 33**: Ibsen, working notes).

I had scribbled on the front of my script a fraction of a poem, by Verlaine I think it is. . . . Where I came across it I don't remember but it went straight to my heart. It was Hedda's epitaph. "I go/with the evil wind/carried here/carried there/as a dead leaf is."[1] It went to my heart because I knew that the one thing I understood about Hedda [. . .] was that she was a prey to hers. Her strong heart, pumping away inside her healthy body. I get no . . . feeling of illness from her. Rather too much life. But I knew she suffered from an ancient disease. [. . .] Accidie.[2] Rendering the world black. Making even the autumn leaves outside the window not melancholy, not autumnal, not exquisite, but withered.

A prisoner of her heart? Impulsive then? Not an adjective easily ascribed to Hedda, but I knew that it was the one for me. . . .

Reading as I did the Norwegian original, I was struck . . . by its verve and simplicity. No long words. Banal everyday phrases. A proliferation of expletives like 'Good God.' No French in the conversations with Brack. Just one or two words of Danish, I'm told, to denote sophistication or 'in talk.' So, after all, small-town Hedda and small-town Brack were a bit less adept at witty small-talk than I had realized. [. . .] In this play we discovered that every word that a character utters springs directly out of what another has said. There are no apparent non-sequiturs as there are in, say, Chekhov. Despised domesticity . . . and despised motherhood. Do you know, I have actually heard it said that Hedda's pregnancy is in dispute! How odd. . . . Discounting Auntie's broad hints there are *at least a dozen* references to it, made by Hedda, during the play, starting with "God yes, September already!" in Act One. [. . .]

I believe that she cannot equate compromise with living, and in that sense is more true to herself than anyone else in the play. Tesman will adapt. Bertha will adapt. Auntie will adapt. The Judge will adapt. Thea will do anything to adapt. Eilert tried and failed. Hedda cannot try and must not fail.

Paralyzed by her own perfectionism, tied down by the lack of alternatives, devoured by the unquestioning greedy lives around her and inside her, where is she to direct that nervous animal energy of hers? She must be central to everyone's attention and not peripheral. She must know everything and commit herself to

1 Paul Verlaine (1844–96) was one of the poets who defined the Symbolist movement, and it is significant that Eva le Gallienne also makes the same link as Suzman: see **p. 74** above.

2 "Accidie" (sloth – one of the Seven Deadly Sins) was the medieval medical term for listlessness, and has become used to signify a state where all activity seems pointless since life has no purpose.

nothing. The baby forbids that. And what a committal to the future it is! Her final act is a combination of expertise and taste. But it is also an absolute necessity and in that sense it is an act of passion and commitment.

From **Richard J. Beckley, "Interview with Janet Suzman"**, June 30, 1982 in Robert Schanke, *Ibsen in America: A Century of Change*, Metuchen, N.J.: The Scarecrow Press, 1988, pp. 256–60

SUZMAN: Hedda must not be played as a cold, passionless, unvulnerable creature who is superior to the situation in which she finds herself. It is true she is bored with everything around her, and contemptuous too, and this may appear to give her an air of superiority in relation to the other characters, but this boredom is not a passive emotion, and in its depth and intensity it [. . .] results in an intense inner frustration that threatens to paralyze her.

BECKLEY: That makes her akin to most naturalist heroines, doesn't it, who are threatened and eventually fall prey to the stifling restrictions of their environment, like Emma Bovary?[1]

SUZMAN: Yes. She is very provincial as well as being the proud daughter of her father, General Gabler. [. . .] She has failed to make her escape into the romantic world she imagines Eilert Løvborg inhabiting. [. . .] There will be no horse, no new piano, no butler, no entertaining – only her guns to afford her some relief from her frustration. And the greatest threat of all is the expected baby, which will destroy all her dreams of freedom and reduce her status to that of a provincial housewife and mother, and it is Tesman's. When the play opens she is spoiling for a fight [. . .] The way I dealt with the tearing-up of the manuscript may serve as an example of how I tried to convey this intense inner frustration in Hedda. In the early TV production I tore up the manuscript slowly, and with delectation, savouring the destructive act, and rejoicing in the feeling of danger and the release from pent-up anguish it gave me. In the stage production I thrust the manuscript in one piece into the stove, then tried to withdraw it again, horrified at my own temerity, perhaps aware of the fleeting nature of the feeling of freedom which the act had afforded me.

BECKLEY: Why are these drives so strong in Hedda?

SUZMAN: Because she feels trapped. Everything aggravates her situation, and when she fails to triumph over it vicariously through the suicide she encourages Eilert to commit, she has no alternative but to destroy herself. She sets up the scenario for her own death. Eva le Gallienne has mentioned in this respect the curtains she draws, as if they were stage curtains, before shooting herself. Hedda is a weak character in the sense that she hasn't the courage to face her mundane life of day-to-day existence, yet she has the courage to shoot herself. This shooting is adumbrated by all the unusual, "shocking," and unexpected things she does

1 Comparisons between Emma Bovary and Hedda are frequent (see, for example, Eric Bentley, p. 82 above), both figures having been adopted as symbols by the feminist movement.

time and again in the play. Her weakness as an ordinary mortal and her struggle as an extraordinary one give her her tragic stature, and make of her an enigmatic, awesome creature.

[. . .]

BECKLEY: Do you find the play particularly relevant for our day and age?

SUZMAN: I do indeed. It gives an all too faithful picture of the kind of frustration, masquerading as plain boredom, which so many people still experience, especially women. The various modern liberation movements have probably not done much to change this situation. Perhaps it is fundamental to the nature of existence.

BECKLEY: That would seem to confirm the universality of Ibsen's play?

SUZMAN: Yes.

BECKLEY: Is that perhaps why some moments in the play should be played for comedy as well as tragedy?

SUZMAN: Yes. There is quite a lot of comedy in *Hedda Gabler*, and it's as essential to it as it is, say, in Shakespeare. [. . .] Cleopatra's ill-usage of the messenger who brings her news of Antony is a good example. We dislike her for her ill-usage of the messenger – one should not treat a servant like that – but there is also something laughable about her loss of self-control and the shocked surprise of the messenger which makes us warm to Cleopatra because it reveals her as human and fallible. The scene with the aunt's hat in *Hedda Gabler* is like that, both when she mistakes it for the servant's, and when she tells Brack later with disarming candour that the mistake was calculated. We dislike her for her spitefulness, laugh at the discomfiture of the fussy aunt, and appreciate Hedda's irritability as all-too-human.

BECKLEY: In spite of these moments don't you think she comes across as a pretty unsympathetic character?

SUZMAN: She might do so if she were not surrounded by such very unsympathetic people – the foolish pedantic husband, the smotheringly affectionate aunt with her unwelcome and arch allusions to her pregnancy, the predatory insinuating judge, the mouse-like Thea. Hedda is no saint.

BECKLEY: What would be the advantages and disadvantages of producing the play in modern dress?

SUZMAN: Few advantages, if any, but a lot of disadvantages, mainly because women are rather more socially emancipated today than in the late nineteenth century. To perform the play in modern dress would make much of the action appear anachronistic or unbelievable without making it seem more significant or true-to-life in any way. It would create far more problems than it solved.

From **James McFarlane, "Drama and the Mind: *Hedda Gabler*"** in *Ibsen and Meaning: Studies, Essays and Prefaces* 1953–87, Norwich: Norvik Press, 1989, pp. 286–7, 288, 289, 290–2

The final critical extract represents the contemporary, more balanced interpretation of the play. It is an example of one way in which Ibsen's working notes may be used to provide insight into the theme of the play. While analyzing Hedda in terms of a "polarity of domination and dependence," it rejects the Bradbrook/le Gallienne notion of a "portrait play" in which the title figure is the exclusive focus, to suggest that the subject is society – though in very different terms to the feminist criticism of *Hedda Gabler* – and emphasizes that the same theme is demonstrated in all the characters.

But what, then, if the *character* of Hedda, highly individualized though she might be, is not the real business of the play, not the thing it is chiefly concerned to communicate? A provisional and rather bleak suggestion is that one regards the central character of Hedda not as an end but as a means – a means serving a much more general and characteristically Ibsenist idea. And that consequently the other characters in the play, far from being merely 'feeds' or foils to Hedda, are themselves essential and integral to a full articulation of the statement the play is concerned to make.

There is, in among the draft material of the play, a clear hint of where to look for this 'general idea', the kind of idea which Gosse and Archer and others have found it impossible to detect. The draft material in this instance is very extensive, including a complete draft version of the play, a number of revisions to that draft, together with two notebooks of notes and jottings and trial dialogue. One of the entries in the notebooks (as others before have remarked) leaps at once to the eye; it reads: 'The demonic thing about Hedda is that she wants to exert an influence over another person.' This immediately suggests a rather different way possibly of defining what the play is 'about'. Instead of drawing a portrait, the study of a bored and frustrated and mischievous society beauty, the play documents a campaign. When Hedda discovers early in the play that Thea Elvsted, a silly girl whom she used to despise at school, has been a great constructive influence in the life of Eilert Løvborg, this dissipated, unstable, but highly talented young man, she decides to break Thea's hold and exert the influence herself. If the focal point of the play is here, it then invites consideration not as the record of an '*etat d'âme*', nor as 'a character study in a vacuum',[1] but rather as the dramatic account of certain proceedings: the history of Hedda's bid for control of Løvborg, of the savagery of her failure, and of its consequences.

Pause in the analysis at this point, and it is possible to recognize in this an aspect of existence that had always roused Ibsen to fury: any interference of this order in other people's lives, any tampering with their liberties or their efforts at

1 Quoting Henry James and William Archer – see **pp. 63–4** and **64–6** above.

self-realization, particularly if done under the guise of altruism or in the name of righteousness, at once drew his anger. Hedda's interference is *personal*, of course; whereas in earlier plays the interference was often impersonal, social, institutional: the pressures of convention, the compulsion to do the done thing, the fear of what people will think, the often inauthentic calls of duty or loyalty or of outdated moral obligation.

[. . .]

This is of course not the only element in what is always admitted to be a very complex pattern of behaviour on the part of Hedda: this baleful influence upon the life of Løvborg. A very similar configuration can also be seen in her relationship with her husband, Tesman; only that in his case one can see how, once the domination is asserted and assured, there is only contempt for the victim. Possible even more interesting than this is the threat she represents to herself. In Ibsen, the Self in its dealing with others is commonly exposed to a double hazard: one from without, the other from within. There is not only the danger of imposed domination from without; there is also the inner threat to the Self that comes from being dependent, of having to live by some essentially humiliating reliance on others, and of having to look to them to provide what the individual Self should supply from within, but cannot.

[. . .]

Of even greater fascination is to observe Ibsen probing the kind of situation that emerges when these two related phenomena coalesce: when these two threats to independent and authentic Selfhood combine to assault the one individual, when the urge to dominate and the necessity to depend are simply two facets of the same thing. This is what it is tempting to select as the main characteristic of the Hedda syndrome. The demonic in Hedda's character – one reminds oneself of Ibsen's jotted note – is that she wants to control another's destiny. But her mischief is not mere villainy; in the last analysis, she does it in an effort to make good some inner deficiency in her own self, to give a kind of borrowed significance to her own life, or to achieve something she was by herself incapable of achieving.

Indeed, it is here that a lot of what used to be thought of as Ibsen's propaganda for Women's Rights now falls into a more meaningful perspective. In a world dominated by the male (which was how Ibsen saw his own age), Woman was often unnaturally deprived by social convention of an adequate opportunity to realize herself; the most she could hope to do, very often, was to make her achievements through the intermediacy, or in the company of some man.

[. . .]

This polarity of domination and dependence, this living upon others, does not in the play stop at the character of Hedda. Indeed, it has been persuasively suggested that in some form or another it pervades the whole action of the play and informs the conduct of many of the other characters.[2] The urge to control and exploit others is never far below the surface of any of their motives. The

2 [McFarlane's note.] The discussion of *Hedda Gabler* here is indebted at a number of points to Jens Arup, 'On *Hedda Gabler*', *Orbis Litterarum*, Copenhagen, xii, 1957, pp. 3–37.

significance of the part played by these other characters is then seen to be not the negative one of acting as foils to Hedda, but the positive one of functioning as essential elements in the fuller articulation of a very richly developed dramatic statement. The most blatant, and yet in one sense the most honest, example of this is the behaviour of Brack. 'His passion in life', it has been said by Eva le Gallienne, 'is discovering other people's secrets; this gives him a sense of power. He will go to infinite trouble, to any lengths, to be the one who knows . . . He is obviously a sensualist . . . but one has the feeling that . . . his sensuality has become perverted, impotent . . . and now finds an outlet in watching others, in spying on their lives, on their emotions, in worming his way into the heart of their mysteries, in manoeuvring himself into a position of control over their fate.' [. . .] Brack tries to win sexual domination over Hedda, ruthlessly, by blackmailing methods; the one saving thing is that he at least does not pretend he is moved by altruism.

Thea Elvsted is Hedda's rival at her own game. True, she appears genuinely convinced of the altruism of her motives in seeking to help Løvborg; and one might also argue that in the past Løvborg has derived positive benefit from her attentions. But it does not escape notice that she abandons husband and stepchildren with almost indecent haste to run after Løvborg; and that when Løvborg himself is beyond her attentions, she very promptly finds a substitute in Tesman himself, Hedda's husband. If Hedda can take away her man, she can take Hedda's.

What of Løvborg? Is he simply the victim of the interference of others? Not entirely, if we attend again to Ibsen's notes. Here the emphasis once more is on control and on the Self: 'the despairing thing about [Løvborg] is that he wants to control the world, but cannot control himself.' The relevance to the present argument – the interplay of domination and dependence – could hardly be more apposite. In the case of Tesman, the thing is given a delightful academic twist . . . Tesman takes possession of the manuscripts of his rival: an act of seemingly benevolent usurpation. Yet how devastatingly Tesman betrays himself when, as he and Thea settle down to arrange Løvborg's surviving papers, he cries gleefully: 'This business of getting another man's papers in order – this is exactly in my line.' The words profess altruism; but they are born of a profound sense of inadequacy. Even Aunt Julie is not exempt; however saintly she may wish to appear, she too is not altogether free of the suspicion of living by this now recognizable compound of domination and dependence: no sooner has she been deprived of the opportunity of looking after her nephew and her ailing sister than her altruism reaches out after somebody else to make beholden to her, announcing that 'there's always some poor invalid or other who needs a bit of care and attention, unfortunately'.

Everywhere one finds a complex interrelationship between domination and dependence, the inauthenticities of an individual's search for self-fulfilment at another's expense, the frustrations of an impotent's will to power. It is in the generality of this idea that one must surely seek the meaning of the particularity that is Hedda's character. When one looks for 'antecedents and explanations' of what happens in the play, it is not sufficient to rummage in some extraordinary rag-bag of qualities called 'Hedda's character'. But it is equally unsatisfactory to think of the particular, i.e. Hedda's character and fate, as merely exemplifying some general idea. Rather one must think of the two things as being fused and compounded into an elaborately developed dramatic image [. . .]

Familiar and recognizable now in many of its features, the world of *Hedda Gabler* is a thing of characteristically Ibsenist construction, populated by recognizable Ibsenist creatures: not a loose assemblage of characters that *are*, but a tightly woven mesh of things done or intended, a shifting pattern of event, a series of encounters and conflicts and defeats in a world where life is a relentless living on or living off others. It is an extra-ordinarily predatory world, a world of wolves, of parasites, of vampires even. Merely to describe the events of the play as strange or complicated or irreconcilable, and to ascribe the oddity to the inexplicable character of Hedda herself, is no explanation at all – or at least not the one that commends itself to anybody familiar with the rest of Ibsen's precisely drawn and rigorously integrated imaginative world.

3

Key Passages

Introduction

Note on the Text

There are various modern translations of the play (discussed in Further Reading) but I have chosen to follow the earliest English version by Edmund Gosse from 1890. The extraordinarily modern-sounding language developed by Ibsen in *Hedda Gabler*, with its extremely short speeches, broken sentences, and use of simple words punctuated by clichéd exclamations, means that the language itself actually requires very little updating. Even if new translations may have been a real advantage in understanding Ibsen's other plays, in the case of *Hedda Gabler* there is very little significant difference between the wording in the different translations, as can be seen in the various renditions of the play's final line:

> Ellis-Fermor (1950) "But merciful God! One doesn't *do* that kind of thing!"
> McFarlane (1966) "But, good God almighty . . . People don't do such things!"
> Beissel (1983) "But, good God! That sort of thing just isn't done!"
> Rudall (1992) "God – people – people don't do things like that."

Gosse's "Good *God* – people don't do such things" is stylistically closer to Ibsen in being the simplest and shortest. Gosse also knew Ibsen well and was familiar with Christiana and Norwegian society of the time, as well as being attuned to the *fin-de-siècle* ambience of the closing decade of the nineteenth century. Indeed, as he points out in his brief Introductory Note, Gosse's text was "issued simultaneously with the publication of the original in Copenhagen." That may occasionally give it the tone of a period piece, but this is not inappropriate, however contemporary the play's theme.

Synopsis

Hedda Gabler revolves around relationships. The seven characters are a tight-knit group: Hedda and her newly married husband, George Tesman, his Aunt Julia (and off-stage Julia's bedridden sister, Aunt Rina), and the old family maidservant Berta; Thea, a school fellow of Hedda's and "old flame" of George's, his former companion and fellow historian Eilert Løvborg who has ruined his reputation through drink, and Judge Brack, a family friend. And more than in almost any other play, the action consists of revelations about past relationships: that Hedda, the daughter of a General, has married beneath her social station, and that on their honeymoon George neglected her for academic research; that they cannot afford the grand house he has bought for her, which his aunt has mortgaged her annuity to Brack in order to pay for; that Løvborg once had an intense relationship with Hedda, took to drink when she rejected him, and has been reformed by the love of Thea, who has left her husband and children to be with Løvborg and is the inspiration, indeed the real author, of a brilliant new book that is to make his reputation.

In comparison to this extensive retrospective, the time frame of the play, from the first morning Hedda and her husband wake up in their new home, to the final moment when she kills herself, is extremely compressed. It takes just two days; and there are three interlinked motifs running through the action. There is Løvborg's unpublished manuscript – which will win him the professorship that Tesman believes he has earned with his competing but dully academic book. Drunkenly dropped in a gutter, but picked up by Tesman, it is the cause of Løvborg's disgrace when he accuses a prostitute of stealing it, and gets arrested for causing a public disturbance. Hidden and then burnt by Hedda, it brings Tesman and Thea together after Løvborg's death as they rewrite it. Paralleling this is Hedda's competition with Thea over Løvborg that motivates her: first to provoke the reformed alcoholic into drinking and accompanying Tesman and Brack to a dinner party that leads to his fatal visit to the brothel; then to burn the manuscript. And this jealousy ultimately becomes a factor in her suicide, when Thea wins over Tesman with the offer of remaking Løvborg's masterwork, leaving her isolated. Thirdly, there is the pair of pistols, inherited from her father, which Hedda threatens to use as an antidote to boredom in Act 1, and uses to shoot (semi-playfully) at Brack in Act 2. She gives one to the ruined Løvborg in Act 3, when she sends him out to commit suicide as the only way of redeeming himself – urging him to "do it beautifully" – only to trap herself in Brack's sexual clutches because, recognizing the gun, he can blackmail her for complicity in Løvborg's death. And, cut off from any way of escaping Brack's power, disgusted by the ignominious manner of Løvborg's dying (shot in the bowels during a scuffle), in Act 4 she uses the companion gun to shoot herself in the temple.

There is relatively little plot of a conventional sort; instead the progress of the play is structured by underlying patterns: as with the descent from early morning sunlight at the opening into night. Two morning scenes (Acts 1 and 3) are followed by evening (Acts 2 and 4), but Act 2 ends with dusk, while at the beginning of Act 3 the curtains are drawn even though it is full daylight outside, then the ending takes place late at night, corresponding to the blackness of death. In addition all the dialogue is highly colloquial, composed mainly of single sentences – no internalized soliloquies; no big, rhetorical speeches – while the whole play is structured to allow an almost continual series of private two-person conversations. Even the Act divisions simply indicate gaps of time in a single unbroken sequence of apparently insignificant events that together culminate in tragedy. The play forms a seamless whole, where all the incidents are interdependent. As a result it is extremely difficult to select "key passages." To illustrate the essential qualities of the play, fairly long sequences are necessary; but this has meant restricting them to just seven excerpts. Those chosen are:

1. (**pp. 114–27**) The opening section of Act 1;
2. (**pp. 128–33**) Hedda's interrogation of Thea, revealing her relationship with Løvborg;
3. (**pp. 134–9**) The arrival of Brack in Act 2, and his first attempt to draw Hedda into his web;
4. (**pp. 141–50**) Løvborg's conversation with Hedda, and her manipulation of him into drinking;
5. (**pp. 151–4**) Hedda's persuading Tesman to hand Løvborg's manuscript to her for hiding;
6. (**pp. 155–9**) Hedda's urging Løvborg to suicide, and her burning of his manuscript;
7. (**pp. 160–9**) The final section of the play leading up to Hedda shooting herself.

At the same time the apparent simplicity and extreme brevity of the dialogue means that it is all too easy for a reader to miss the true significance of the words. Gosse singled out the uniqueness of the style, as being so compressed in its rapidity and concision that it made this the most difficult of Ibsen's plays to understand. In his view these "fragments of sentences without verbs, clauses that come to nothing, adverbial exclamations and cryptic interrogatories" served to give an extraordinary sense of reality – but they also convey an image of a society on the verge of breakdown, where relationships have become distorted and communication is only barely possible, while the linguistic concision can be seen as representing the intensity of the pressures on the characters. (See Gosse, **pp. 53–6**; and Bentley, **pp. 87–8**.)

So it has been necessary to provide extensive notes, although these glosses are not intended to close off other possible readings. Nor, even if they are at times far longer than the text they accompany, are such notes by any means exhaustive. What they indicate is simply the nature of the play, the extent of the subtext, and the way its form mirrors the content, where the apparently normal social surface covers hidden depths and the title-figure is a frustrated woman prevented from expressing or realizing her own potential.

Key Passages

From Act 1: The Family Versus Hedda

The whole opening section of the scene serves as a build-up to Hedda's deliberately delayed entry (which occurs twelve pages into Gosse's text), and shows the importance this sort of exposition has for Ibsen (see his letter to Reimers, **pp. 31–2**). It demonstrates the way Ibsen conveys his themes through detail, even in the title of the play itself – while all of Ibsen's previous Naturalistic dramas had highlighted female experience, this is the first titled by a woman's name – and in the length of the scene description. So, although the furnishings could be from any decade of the nineteenth century, and Ibsen specified to his German translator that the characters were depicted against "present day" (i.e. 1890–1) social conditions (see **p. 32**), details like the exchange of letters or the fact that the town is small enough for the characters to walk everywhere, suggest that the play is actually set some thirty years earlier, in the 1860s, when Ibsen was living in Christiana and before its expansion into a sizable city with trams and telephones (see Archer's Preface, **pp. 64–6**). His intention may have been to depict the problematic status of women more clearly by showing the situation over a generation earlier, or to make the melodramatic aspects of the action more credible by distancing in time. There is no mention of any Women's Movement – already firmly established by 1888 (see Ibsen's speech, **p. 26**) – which might have provided Hedda with psychological support. This omission underlines that his aim, as he explicitly told his German translator, was to deal with people in a contemporary social context, but not with "problems" (see **p. 32**). Beyond that, the effect of leaving the Women's Movement unmentioned, which implies that this particular group are not aware of its existence, is to heighten the provincialism that Hedda finds so constricting (see note to James, **pp. 63–4**).

Even the way Ibsen designates the speakers in the text has wider significance: only Berta (who as a servant is not accorded "adult" status) and Hedda are listed by their "personal" first names. In Hedda's case the implications are ambiguous. It might signify that she is being treated as a child or a possession, or that in spite of her marriage her character is unchanged and she remains the daughter of General Gabler; alternatively it could be read as underlining that her personality is unique, or that one of Hedda's most deep-seated drives is asserting her individuality. Without exception all the other speakers are listed by family name and (if female) by prefix denoting marital or (in the case of one male) official status: MISS TESMAN, MRS. ELVSTED, JUDGE BRACK. These distinctions are carried through in the way the characters address each other, with Hedda even, significantly, objectifying her husband and distancing herself from him by speaking to him as "Tesman", right up until the last Act, where she is attempting to protect herself by persuading him that she burned Løvborg's manuscript out of love for him. Even then she speaks George's personal name "*coldly*" and couples it with a rejection of her whole situation – including her marriage and pregnancy – as "absurdity."

Several important themes surface in this opening section, apparently passed over as incidental, but to be picked up later in the play: the professorship, and Tesman's hopes; the financial debts incurred by his marriage to Hedda, which in different ways give Aunt Julia and Brack a hold over Hedda; her pregnancy (extremely obliquely mentioned, corresponding to the social customs of the time) and Hedda's rejection of it; the Tesman family as a group versus Hedda as an individual forced to stand out against them. The first of the objects in the play that gain symbolic resonance, the portrait of Hedda's father and Tesman's homely slippers, are also introduced; and we get the first reference to Hedda dressed in black. (While Ibsen's stage directions specify that Hedda – as here – wears different, fashionable dresses for each Act, in the final Act she reverts to the black that characterized her earlier life.) This image of Hedda, in a floor-length black gown and holding a pistol, a composite of her firing at Judge Brack when he enters the garden at the beginning of Act 2 and her dress at the end of the play (epitomized by the pictures of Glenda Jackson, **p. 97** and Christine Buchegger, Frontispiece), has come to stand as a symbol for the play and for Ibsen's Naturalistic drama as a whole.

Particularly in the opening Act, Ibsen injects elements of comedy, both to create a light atmosphere (going along with the hopeful "morning light") and in order to deepen the increasingly tragic impression of the rest of the play by contrast: a traditional technique that goes back at least as far as Shakespeare. However, as with the incident of Aunt Julia's bonnet – the major "event" in the whole opening section, and a prime example of the way Ibsen uses a trivial occasion to reveal complex ambiguities of the situation and the characters' psychology – even at this point such comedy contains a darker side, displaying Tesman's naivety or Hedda's malice.

HEDDA GABLER[1]

The scene of the action is Tesman's villa, in the west end of Christiana.[2]

A spacious, handsome, and tastefully furnished drawing-room, decorated in dark colours. In the back, a wide doorway with curtains drawn back, leading into a smaller room decorated in the same style as the drawing-room. In the right-hand wall of the front room, a folding door leading out to the hall. In the opposite wall, on the left, a glass door, also with curtains drawn back. Through the panes can be seen part of a veranda outside, and trees covered with autumn[3] *foliage. An oval table, with a cover on it, and surrounded by chairs, stands well forward. In front, by the wall on the right, a wide stove of dark porcelain, a high-backed arm-chair, a cushioned foot-rest, and two footstools. A settee, with a small round table in front of it, fills the upper right-hand corner. In front, on the left, a little way from the wall, a sofa. Further back than the glass door, a piano. On either side of the doorway at the back a what-not with terra-cotta and majolica ornaments.*[4] *– Against the back wall of the inner room a sofa, with a table, and one or two chairs. Over the sofa hangs the portrait*[5] *of a handsome elderly man in a General's*

1 Properly speaking, the name of the heroine should be "Hedda Tesman" since at the date of the play women automatically took their husband's surname on marriage. Ibsen pointed out to his German translator that the title is intended to emphasize that she is "her father's daughter" (**p. 32**). The title also signals Hedda's unconventional nature and her assertion of her own individuality in opposition to social convention – in contrast to Thea, who insists on being called Mrs. Elvsted in spite of having left her husband. It is also possible to deduce from the title that this is "a character-study pure and simple" (see Archer's Preface, **p. 66**), which goes along with Ibsen's principle of dramatic composition, that the play "proceed[s] from the individual" (see letter to Lothar, **p. 29**).

2 Christiana (Kristiana) – the modern-day Oslo. Although the political capital, and focus for national independence (see Seip, **pp. 6–7**), the cultural center of Norway in the mid-nineteenth century was Bergen. Ibsen is generally assumed to have set the play around 1860, when he was having difficulties in Kristiana which led to self-exile in Rome. It is possible that the choice of location is designed to reflect a parochial society, where Hedda has no outlet for her energies, as well as representing Norway as a whole.

3 As Ibsen's comments about the staging of *The Wild Duck* show (see his letter to Lindberg, **p. 31**), he places particular emphasis on the lighting as a means of establishing the different emotional tone in each section of a play's developing action. Every detail is designed to contribute to the overall effect. On a Naturalistic level, summer is the season for extended European travel, so it is logical that the Tesmans would have returned at this point in the year. However, the autumnal details are carefully chosen to set a particular emotional tone for the play. In Scandinavia the autumn is precursor to a long northern winter where days shorten until at the solstice the nights last for the whole twenty-four hours. It therefore evokes a sense of melancholy and approaching loss; and Ibsen uses this as a subliminal correlation to Hedda's character and to the action.

4 These are the standard furnishings of a middle-class household of the period, including the typical clutter of ornaments on the "what-not" (the 1808 usage being "an open stand with shelves one above the other, for keeping or displaying various objects," *Shorter Oxford Dictionary*, Oxford: Oxford University Press, 1973, p. 2533), presumably souvenirs from the Tesmans' trip, terra cotta and majolica being associated with the Mediterranean.

5 As the only completely personal object on display, this portrait takes on particular importance for a viewer. Conventionally such a portrait would represent the present owner of the house, or his ancestor, but as the context gets filled in it comes to represent both Hedda's upbringing and the biological influence on her personality (the twin bases of Naturalistic characterization: see Strindberg on "physiological and psychological" elements of character, **p. 29**) as well as explaining her "unfeminine" desires and acts. Its presence in the inner room also marks this as specifically Hedda's space, private, even interior in the sense of being inside her psyche.

The uniform in the portrait is also a visual clue to the values Hedda has derived from her father: in the nineteenth century most generals were aristocrats, who commanded men (which Hedda also aspires to do).

uniform. Over the table a hanging lamp, with an opal glass shade. – A number of bouquets are arranged about the drawing-room, in vases and glasses. Others lie upon the tables. The floors in both rooms are covered with thick carpets. – Morning[6] *light. The sun shines in through the glass door.*

[MISS JULIANA TESMAN, *with her bonnet on and carrying a parasol, comes in from the hall, followed by* BERTA, *who carries a bouquet wrapped in paper.* MISS TESMAN *is a comely and pleasant-looking lady of about sixty-five. She is nicely but simply dressed in a grey walking-costume.* BERTA[7] *is a middle-aged woman of plain and rather countrified appearance.*

MISS TESMAN. [*Stops close to the door, listens, and says softly*:] Upon my word, I don't believe they are stirring yet!

BERTA. [*Also softly:*] I told you so, Miss. Remember how late the steamboat got in last night. And then, when they got home! – good Lord, what a lot the young mistress had to unpack before she could get to bed.

MISS TESMAN. Well, well – let them have their sleep out. But let us see that they get a good breath of the fresh morning air when they do appear.

[*She goes to the glass door and throws it open.*

BERTA. [*Beside the table, at a loss what to do with the bouquet*[8] *in her hand.*] I declare there isn't a bit of room left. I think I'll put it down here, Miss.

[*She places it on the piano.*

MISS TESMAN. So you've got a new mistress now, my dear Berta. Heaven knows it was a wrench to me to part with you.

BERTA. [*On the point of weeping.*] And do you think it wasn't hard for me too, Miss? After all the blessed years I've been with you and Miss Rina!

MISS TESMAN. We must make the best of it, Berta. There was nothing

6 The early morning sunshine has implicit symbolic significance: the bright beginning of a new marriage and promise of new life, which is then denied by the progress into night in the following Acts.

7 The physical descriptions of these two women subtly emphasize differences of class and education, elements that will emerge as significant in determining the relationship of the main characters. Even though Berta's minor role, subservient position, and plainness may lead her to be overlooked, she is an integral part of the group that surrounds and constricts Hedda, the singular individual (see Ibsen's letter to Stern, p. 32).

8 The superfluity of bouquets suggests a wide circle of friends – another misleading indication of promise and happiness. In fact Hedda will find the scent of the flowers cloying and overwhelming and an early signal of her isolation, which increases until by the end of the play she is completely and painfully alone.

else to be done. George can't do without you, you see – he absolutely can't. He has had you to look after him ever since he was a little boy.

BERTA. Ah but, Miss Julia, I can't help thinking of Miss Rina lying helpless at home there, poor thing. And with only that new girl too! She'll never learn to take proper care of an invalid.

MISS TESMAN. Oh, I shall manage to train her. And of course, you know, I shall take most of it upon myself. You needn't be uneasy about my poor sister, my dear Berta.

BERTA. Well, but there's another thing, Miss. I'm so mortally afraid I shan't be able to suit the young mistress.

MISS TESMAN. Oh well – just at first there may be one or two, things –

BERTA. Most like she'll be terrible grand in her ways.

MISS TESMAN. Well, you can't wonder at that – General Gabler's daughter![9] Think of the sort of life she was accustomed to in her father's time. Don't you remember how we used to see her riding down the road along with the General? In that long black habit – and with feathers in her hat?[10]

BERTA. Yes indeed – I remember well enough! – But, good Lord, I should never have dreamt in those days that she and Master George would make a match of it.

MISS TESMAN. Nor I. – But by-the-bye, Berta – while I think of it: in future you mustn't say Master George. You must say Dr.[11] Tesman.

BERTA. Yes, the young mistress spoke of that too – last night – the moment they set foot in the house. Is it true then, Miss?

MISS TESMAN. Yes, indeed it is. Only think, Berta – some foreign university has made him a doctor – while he has been abroad, you understand. I hadn't heard a word about it until he told me himself upon the pier.

BERTA. Well, well, he's clever enough for anything, he is. But I didn't think he'd have gone in for doctoring people too.

MISS TESMAN. No, no, it's not that sort of doctor he is. [*Nods signifi-*

9 As Blanche Yurka and others have pointed out (see **p. 71**), Hedda's mother is nowhere mentioned. She is consistently identified as her father's daughter, with all that implies about aristocratic background at odds with her middle-class marriage and the dominant influence on her personality. This is set in sharp contrast to her husband, who as an orphan was brought up solely by females: his maiden aunts and the maid Berta, who has implicitly spoiled him by catering to his every whim.

10 Feathers on women's hats would have been somewhat unusual in the mid-nineteenth century, worn only by the highest society and out-of-place in a provincial town like Christiana, so this perhaps implies an assertion of difference to the bourgeois townspeople. There may also be a suggested comparison to military plumes, reinforcing Hedda's identification with her father, or as substitutes for her thin hair – thick, luxuriant tresses generally representing feminine sexuality and maternal capacity in Ibsen's women.

11 The characters' continual insistence on correct modes of address is a way of representing the hierarchical nature and formality of this society and the degree to which it subsumes individuality into standard categories. It is worth noting that this doctorate is an unearned honorary degree. In the list of characters in the original he is described as "stipendiat i kulturhistorie" (holder of a research scholarship in the history of civilization).

cantly.] But let me tell you, we may have to call him something still grander[12] before long.

BERTA. You don't say so! What can that be, Miss?

MISS TESMAN. [*Smiling.*] H'm – wouldn't you like to know! [*with emotion.*] Ah, dear, dear – if my poor brother could only look up from his grave now, and see what his little boy has grown into! [*Looks around.*] But bless me, Berta – why have you done this? Taken the chintz covers[13] off all the furniture?

BERTA. The mistress told me to. She can't abide covers on the chairs, she says.

MISS TESMAN. Are they going to make this their everyday sitting-room then?

BERTA. Yes, that's what I understood – from the mistress. Master George – the doctor – he said nothing.

[GEORGE TESMAN *comes from the right into the inner room, humming to himself; and carrying an unstrapped empty portmanteau. He is a middle-sized, young-looking man of thirty-three, rather stout, with a round, open, cheerful face, fair hair, and beard. He wears spectacles, and is some-what carelessly dressed in comfortable indoor clothes.*[14]

MISS TESMAN. Good morning, good morning, George.

TESMAN. [*In the doorway between the rooms.*] Aunt Julia! Dear Aunt Julia! [*Goes up to her and shakes hands warmly.*] Come all this way – so early! Eh?

MISS TESMAN. Why, of course I had to come and see how you were getting on.

TESMAN. In spite of your having had no proper night's rest?

MISS TESMAN. Oh, that makes no difference to me.

12 Typical of Ibsen's indirect way of introducing important information, this refers to Tesman's hopes for a professorship, which underlies much of the action (his ability to afford the lifestyle Hedda demands; his rivalry with Løvborg, willingness to conceal Løvborg's manuscript and misunderstanding of Hedda's motive for destroying it).

13 These are dust-covers to preserve upholstery in the most formal room in a house, carrying connotations of middle-class thriftiness. By having them removed Hedda is signaling her intention to lead a high-society existence and a rejection of conventional bourgeois mores. In addition, chintz is printed with brightly colored flowers, while the furniture beneath (as the opening stage direction specifies) is dark in color: a sombreness that expresses Hedda's mood and, since this is her way of setting her mark on the house, indicates that this will be the opposite of a "happy home" – suggested by the missing brightness.

14 The importance Ibsen places on precise exterior details in constructing his characters is clearly stated in "On the Primacy of Character" (see **p. 29**). Ibsen's working notes stress that although physically he may be a nonentity, Tesman has admirable qualities – "honourable," "gifted," "liberal-minded," which would help to explain why Hedda marries him (see **p. 34**) – and the description here corresponds with this. However, typical of Ibsen's working method, everything could be read in quite a different way: thus Tesman's appearance can also be seen as signaling his personality to be self-satisfied ("humming to himself"), excessively ordinary ("middle-sized" as well as approaching middle age), and somewhat immature ("young-looking") in addition to discounting his pretensions as an intellectual ("stout, with a round, open, cheerful face"). In every way he is the physical opposite of Løvborg, as we are expected to recognize when Løvborg enters in Act 2.

TESMAN. Well, I suppose you got home all right from the pier? Eh?[15]

MISS TESMAN. Yes, quite safely, thank goodness. Judge Brack was good enough to see me right to my door.

TESMAN. We were so sorry we couldn't give you a seat in the carriage. But you saw what a pile of boxes Hedda had to bring with her.

MISS TESMAN. Yes, she had certainly plenty of boxes.[16]

BERTA. [*To* TESMAN.] Shall I go in and see if there's anything I can do for the mistress?

TESMAN. No thank you, Berta – you needn't. She said she would ring if she wanted anything.

BERTA. [*Going towards the right.*] Very well.

TESMAN. But look here – take this portmanteau with you.

BERTA. [*Taking it.*] I'll put it in the attic.

[*She goes out by the hall door.*

TESMAN. Fancy, Auntie – I had the whole of that portmanteau chock full of copies of documents. You wouldn't believe how much I have picked up from all the archives I have been examining – curious old details that no one has had any idea of –

MISS TESMAN. Yes, you don't seem to have wasted[17] your time on your wedding trip, George.

TESMAN. No, that I haven't. But do take off your bonnet, Auntie. Look here! Let me untie the strings – eh?

MISS TESMAN. [*While he does so.*] Well, well – this is just as if you were still at home with us.

TESMAN. [*With the bonnet in his hand, looks at it from all sides.*] Why, what a gorgeous bonnet you've been investing in!

MISS TESMAN. I bought it on Hedda's account.

TESMAN. On Hedda's account? Eh?

MISS TESMAN. Yes, so that Hedda needn't be ashamed of me if we happened to go out together.

TESMAN. [*Patting her cheek.*] You always think of everything, Aunt Julia. [*Lays the bonnet on a chair beside the table.*] And now, look here – suppose we sit comfortably on the sofa and have a little chat, till Hedda comes.

15 This habitual – and deliberately irritating – verbal tic expresses the indecisiveness that will become crucial in later scenes, and suggests not only conventionality but also a certain insecurity beneath Tesman's self-satisfaction, both of which make him an unsuitable partner for Hedda.

16 The pile of boxes (presumably containing luxury clothes or hats) here forecasts Hedda's desire to set up barriers between herself and Tesman's family. The number of boxes also attests to Hedda's profligacy.

17 The incongruity between Tesman's archival activities and the bonding with Hedda that should have occupied a honeymoon is glaringly obvious though here left unstated since (corresponding to Ibsen's comment about the "unity" of the group in his letter to Kristina Stern, p. 32) Tesman's aunt is completely supportive, sidelining Hedda and subordinating her interests to Tesman's.

[*They seat themselves. She places her parasol in the corner of the sofa.*

MISS TESMAN. [*Takes both his hands and looks at him.*] What a delight it is to have you again, as large as life, before my very eyes, George! My George – my poor brother's own boy![18]

TESMAN. And it's a delight for me, too, to see you again, Aunt Julia! You, who have been father and mother in one to me.

MISS TESMAN. Oh yes, I know you will always keep a place in your heart for your old aunts.

TESMAN. And what about Aunt Rina? No improvement – eh?

MISS TESMAN. Oh no – we can scarcely look for any improvement in her case, poor thing. There she lies, helpless, as she has lain for all these years. But heaven grant I may not lose her yet awhile! For if I did, I don't know what I should make of my life, George – especially now that I haven't you to look after any more.[19]

TESMAN. [*Patting her back.*] There, there, there – !

MISS TESMAN. [*Suddenly changing her tone.*] And to think that here are you a married man, George! – And that you should be the one to carry off Hedda Gabler – the beautiful Hedda Gabler! Only think of it – she, that was so beset with admirers!

TESMAN. [*Hums a little and smiles complacently.*[20]] Yes, I fancy I have several good friends about town who would like to stand in my shoes – eh?

MISS TESMAN. And then this fine long wedding-tour you have had! More than five – nearly six months –

18 Ibsen's technique of intimating the larger issues that will emerge during the play in an apparently banal, everyday exchange is well illustrated in these short speeches depicting her relationship to her family. While Aunt Julia's devotion to serving others – her ailing sister, her brother's orphan (Tesman) – is entirely admirable, it also suggests the restricted opportunities open to women in this society: family care centered on the home is the only occupation she can conceive for herself (see Hovde, on women's lives, **p. 10**). It also represents the cloying enclosure that faces Hedda.

"My poor [. . .] boy" indicates the infantilization of Tesman, helping to explain his flawed character, while throwing her earlier interest in Hedda's pregnancy into a new light. There is little doubt that once Hedda's baby is born, it will absorb Aunt Julia's attention, substituting for Aunt Rina. Note her statement that if she should "lose" Rina, she wouldn't "know what [she] should do with her life," and her promise at the end of this scene to visit every day – her kindness is therefore a potential threat to Hedda on more than one level.

19 Beneath her pleasant appearance, even Aunt Julia can be seen as an emotional vampire – and some critics have emphasized the rapacious nature of all these characters (see McFarlane, **p. 105**). A great deal of the effectiveness of this play comes from the way perfectly normal and, on the surface, even admirable characters are all gradually revealed as unpleasantly egoistic or inherently vicious, making the action an implied attack on society in general (see Lester, **p. 94**). Ibsen wrote to his German translator that he found identification with such (universally negative) figures during the writing of *Hedda Gabler* psychologically draining (see **p. 32**).

20 When Ibsen's characters boast of good fortune, the qualities they pride themselves on are the things that will prove disastrous for them. In this case, Tesman's complacency blinds him to Hedda's reception of one earlier admirer and the sexual machinations of another – both of which are crucial contributions to the eventual tragedy. This complacency could also be seen as justifying Hedda's perception that rather than loving her, Tesman views her simply as a prize (see Ibsen's scenario, **p. 34**) although she never mentions this herself. This is characteristic of the subtle way in which motivations are handled in this play.

TESMAN. Well, for me it has been a sort of tour of research as well. I have had to do so much grubbing among old records – and to read no end of books too, Auntie.

MISS TESMAN. Oh yes, I suppose so. [*More confidentially, and lowering her voice a little.*] But listen now, George, – have you nothing – nothing special to tell me?

TESMAN. As to our journey?

MISS TESMAN. Yes.

TESMAN. No, I don't know of anything except what I have told you in my letters. I had a doctor's degree conferred on me – but that I told you yesterday.

MISS TESMAN. Yes, yes, you did. But what I mean is – haven't you any – any – expectations – ?

TESMAN. Expectations?[21]

MISS TESMAN. Why you know, George – I'm your old auntie!

TESMAN. Why, of course I have expectations.

MISS TESMAN. Ah!

TESMAN. I have every expectation of being a professor one of these days.

MISS TESMAN. Oh yes, a professor –

TESMAN. Indeed, I may say I am certain of it. But my dear Auntie – you know all about that already!

MISS TESMAN. [*Laughing to herself.*] Yes, of course I do. You are quite right there. [*Changing the subject.*] But we were talking about your journey. It must have cost a great deal of money, George?

TESMAN. Well, you see – my handsome travelling-scholarship[22] went a good way.

MISS TESMAN. But I can't understand how you can have made it go far enough for two.

TESMAN. No, that's not so easy to understand – eh?

MISS TESMAN. And especially travelling with a lady – they tell me that makes it ever so much more expensive.

TESMAN. Yes, of course – it makes it a little more expensive. But Hedda

21 Throughout this scene, Ibsen uses Tesman's utter incomprehension of his aunt's probing to discover if Hedda is pregnant to show his naivety and the egotistical self-absorption that, although presented as comic here, will cause the final tragedy. This exchange points to the way in which pampering by subservient females has pandered to this self-indulgence.

22 Possibly an autobiographical reference, linking the character of Tesman in a parodic way to Ibsen, who was given a parliamentary grant to travel to Rome in 1864 at the age of thirty-six with his young wife (see Archer's comments on autobiographical connections, **pp. 36–7**). However, it is the contrast between Ibsen and his character that helps to define Tesman. It highlights Tesman's inexperience (when Ibsen first left his country he had been married four years, and already had a young child); his material advantages (unlike Ibsen, who lived his early years in poverty and had no generous aunt to set him up in a middle-class home); as well as the pettiness of his work ("grubbing among old records" in libraries, while Ibsen wrote *Brand*, the poetic moral drama which first made his reputation).

had to have this trip,[23] Auntie! She really had to. Nothing else would have done.

MISS TESMAN. No, no, I suppose not. A wedding-tour seems to be quite indispensable nowadays. – But tell me now – have you gone thoroughly over the house yet?

TESMAN. Yes, you may be sure I have. I have been afoot ever since daylight.

MISS TESMAN. And what do you think of it all?

TESMAN. I'm delighted! Quite delighted! Only I can't think what we are to do with the two empty rooms between this inner parlour and Hedda's bedroom.

MISS TESMAN. [*Laughing.*] Oh my dear George, I daresay you may find some use for them – in the course of time.

TESMAN. Why of course you are quite right, Aunt Julia! You mean as my library increases – eh?[24]

MISS TESMAN. Yes, quite so, my dear boy. It was your library I was thinking of.

TESMAN. I am specially pleased on Hedda's account. Often and often, before we were engaged, she said that she would never care to live anywhere but in Secretary Falk's villa.[25]

MISS TESMAN. Yes, it was lucky that this very house should come into the market, just after you had started.

TESMAN. Yes, Aunt Julia, the luck was on our side, wasn't it – eh?

MISS TESMAN. But the expense, my dear George! You will find it very expensive, all this.

TESMAN. [*Looks at her, a little cast down.*] Yes, I suppose I shall, Aunt!

MISS TESMAN. Oh, frightfully!

TESMAN. How much do you think? In round numbers? – Eh?

23 Although on the surface all these references to Hedda are admiring – high-born (equestrian), "beautiful" and sought after or, as here, fashionable – from a slightly different perspective (such as the bourgeois viewpoint represented by Aunt Julia) all these qualities are suspect, and the apparent praise can be read as criticism: an aristocrat is likely to chafe against a middle-class lifestyle, singling out physical beauty implies a possible absence of moral qualities, mentioning her male admirers raises a doubt about whether she will remain faithful to her husband, fashionable activities waste money. Even Hedda's continued absence is an implied slight – as mistress of the house she should be present to receive such a valued guest. At the same time the way Tesman emphasizes her insistence on taking such an extended trip raises quite a different set of questions: was Hedda's demand a way of asserting dominance in the marriage? Evidence that she (like Tesman) is completely self-centered? A sign of an obsessive need to escape, either from her past, or from the provincial society embodied in Christiana (and in Tesman's family)? A device to postpone the demands of married life?

24 See note 21 for commentary on Tesman's sexual naivety and self-absorption.

25 As Gosse comments in a footnote to his translation, in the original the description is far more precise in its social designation: " 'Statsrådinde Falks villa' – showing that it had belonged to the widow of a cabinet minister."

MISS TESMAN. Oh, I can't even guess until all the accounts come in.[26]

TESMAN. Well, fortunately, Judge Brack has secured the most favourable terms for me, – so he said in a letter to Hedda.

MISS TESMAN. Yes, don't be uneasy, my dear boy. – Besides, I have given security for the furniture and all the carpets.

TESMAN. Security? You? My dear Aunt Julia – what sort of security could you give?

MISS TESMAN. I have given a mortgage on our annuity.

TESMAN. [*Jumps up.*] What! On your – and Aunt Rina's annuity!

MISS TESMAN. Yes, I knew of no other plan, you see.

TESMAN. [*Placing himself before her.*] Have you gone out of your senses, Auntie! Your annuity – it's all that you and Aunt Rina have to live upon.

MISS TESMAN. Well, well – don't get so excited about it. It's only a matter of form you know – Judge Brack assured me of that. It was he that was kind enough to arrange the whole affair for me. A mere matter of form, he said.[27]

TESMAN. Yes, that may be all very well. But never-the-less –

MISS TESMAN. You will have your own salary to depend upon now. And, good heavens, even if we did have to pay up a little – ! To eke things out a bit at the start – ! Why, it would be nothing but a pleasure to us.

TESMAN. Oh Auntie – will you never be tired of making sacrifices for me.

MISS TESMAN. [*Rises and lays her hand on his shoulders.*] Have I any other happiness in this world except to smooth your way for you, my dear boy? You, who have had neither father nor mother to depend on. And now we have reached the goal, George! Things have looked black enough for us, sometimes; but, thank heaven, now you have nothing to fear.[28]

TESMAN. Yes, it is really marvellous how everything has turned out for the best.

26 This short dialogue about finances offers a prime example of the way every detail in the play is interrelated, creating a dense pattern beneath the apparently everyday surface. Ibsen continues to build up a picture of Aunt Julia's future control over the household, and Tesman's unworldliness. At the same time it underlines potential costs of Hedda's extravagance. The fact that Aunt Julia has paid for the furnishings also retrospectively throws a different light on her surprise that the "chintzes" have been removed. The fact that the lifestyle he has adopted to suit Hedda could reduce his aunt to penury unless his salary increases puts Tesman under extreme pressure which will later help to motivate his abdication of moral responsibility concerning Løvborg's manuscript, which could lose him the competition for the professorship.

27 While on the surface a perfectly normal comment, the exchange raises questions about Judge Brack's probity and the nature of his "kindness," suggesting he may have a habit of reversing form and substance, which will later become obvious in his treatment of Hedda.

28 Hubris again. Aunt Julia is revealed as no less blind to possible disaster than Tesman was earlier; while her mention of Løvborg and comparison of his book to Tesman's, immediately preceding Hedda's entrance, subtly inserts an ominous linkage that will play out in the subsequent action, demonstrating how carefully this Naturalistic text is in fact structured.

MISS TESMAN. And the people who opposed you – who wanted to bar the way for you – now you have them at your feet. They have fallen, George! Your most dangerous rival – his fall was the worst. – And now he has to lie on the bed he has made for himself – poor misguided creature.

TESMAN. Have you heard anything of Eilert? Since I went away, I mean.

MISS TESMAN. Only that he is said to have published a new book.

TESMAN. What! Eilert Løvborg! Recently – eh?

MISS TESMAN. Yes, so they say. Heaven knows whether it can be worth anything! Ah, when your new book appears – that will be another story, George! What is it to be about?

TESMAN. It will deal with the domestic industries of Brabant during the Middle Ages.[29]

MISS TESMAN. Fancy – to be able to write on such a subject as that!

TESMAN. However, it may be some time before the book is ready. I have all these collections to arrange first, you see.

MISS TESMAN. Yes, collecting and arranging – no one can beat you at that. There you are my poor brother's own son.

TESMAN. I am looking forward eagerly to setting to work at it; especially now that I have my own delightful home to work in.

MISS TESMAN. And, most of all, now that you have got the wife of your heart, my dear George.

TESMAN. [*Embracing her.*] Oh yes, yes, Aunt Julia. Hedda – she is the best part of it all! [*Looks towards the doorway.*] I believe I hear her coming – eh?

[HEDDA *enters from the left through the inner room. She is a woman of nine-and-twenty. Her face and figure show refinement and distinction. Her complexion is pale and opaque. Her steel-grey eyes express a cold, unruffled repose. Her hair is of an agreeable medium brown, but not particularly abundant. She is dressed in a tasteful somewhat loose-fitting morning gown.*[30]

29 Tesman's choice of subject for his research is of course doubly ironic. On the one hand, his earlier incomprehension that Hedda might be pregnant and obvious inability to deal with his own household finances has demonstrated that he can have no real understanding of the domesticity he is researching. On the other, this can be seen as a parody of the work of nationalistic historians and etymologists, paralleling their search for a uniquely Norwegian heritage and language in the distant past using archaic formulas (see Seip, **p. 6**), though Tesman's work is plainly irrelevant to nation-building since it focuses on Flanders, not Norway. In dealing with materialistic physical details and a period over 500 years in the past, Tesman's book is also the complete opposite of Løvborg's (as we are to learn below, **p. 127**), as is his purely factual method – compiling and collating already existing materials – which represents the most pedantically academic form of scholarship.

30 All the adjectives chosen to describe Hedda are cool, and lacking in vitality – exactly expressing the concept defined in Ibsen's working notes (see **p. 33**). They are summed up in one of Ibsen's recurring tropes of thin, neutral colored hair. Etiolated and aesthetic, she appears to correspond to the ideal image of a wife, defined by this male-dominated nineteenth-century society as a "decorative household plant" (see Hovde, **p. 10**). At the same time the stress on control suggests repression and a desire for the "joy of life" – Ibsen's standard phrase for self-fulfillment – that she is constitutionally unable to experience, while the "loose-fitting" gown suggests concealment or possibly a denial of her own sexuality, one aspect of which is almost immediately picked up on in the dialogue.

MISS TESMAN. [*Going to meet* HEDDA.] Good morning, my dear Hedda! Good morning, and a hearty welcome!

HEDDA. [*Holds out her hand.*] Good morning, dear Miss Tesman! So early a call! That is kind of you.

MISS TESMAN. [*With some embarrassment.*] Well – has the bride slept well in her new home?

HEDDA. Oh yes, thanks. Passably.

TESMAN. [*Laughing.*] Passably! Come, that's good, Hedda! You were sleeping like a stone when I got up.

HEDDA. Fortunately. Of course one has always to accustom one's self to new surroundings, Miss Tesman – little by little. [*Looking towards the left.*] Oh – there the servant has gone and opened the veranda door, and let in a whole flood of sunshine.

MISS TESMAN. [*Going towards the door.*] Well, then we will shut it.

HEDDA. No, no, not that! Tesman, please draw the curtains.[31] That will give a softer light.

TESMAN. [*At the door.*] Alright – alright. – There now, Hedda, now you have both shade and fresh air.

HEDDA. Yes, fresh air we certainly must have, with all these stacks of flowers – . But – won't you sit down, Miss Tesman?

MISS TESMAN. No, thank you. Now that I have seen that everything is all right here – thank heaven! – I must be getting home again. My sister is lying longing for me, poor thing.

TESMAN. Give her my very best love, Auntie; and say I shall look in and see her later in the day.

MISS TESMAN. Yes, yes, I'll be sure to tell her. But bye-the-bye, George – [*Feeling in her dress pocket.*] – I had almost forgotten – I have something for you here.

TESMAN. What is it, Auntie? Eh?

MISS TESMAN. [*Produces a flat parcel wrapped in newspaper and hands it to him.*] Look here, my dear boy.

TESMAN. [*Opening the parcel.*] Well, I declare! – Have you really saved them for me, Aunt Julia! Hedda! isn't this touching – eh?

HEDDA. [*Beside the what-not*[32] *on the right.*] Well, what is it?

TESMAN. My old morning-shoes! My slippers.[33]

HEDDA. Indeed. I remember you often spoke of them while we were abroad.

31 It is significant that Hedda's first action should be to blot out the morning light – associated with happiness and hopeful new beginnings – and even if, here, this seems to be nothing more than a fashionable reflex, softer light showing the complexion to advantage, its implications of concealment and withdrawal are picked up in the subsequent action.

32 Display stand (see note on **p. 114**).

33 The importance Tesman gives to his broken-down slippers is not only comic but a tangible demonstration of his narrowness of vision. These slippers also go along with his research into "domestic industries" and signal the primacy of his allegiance to the family group, rather than to his wife (see Ibsen's letter to Stern, **p. 32**).

TESMAN. Yes, I missed them terribly. [*Goes up to her.*] Now you shall see them, Hedda!

HEDDA. [*Going towards the stove.*] Thanks, I really don't care about it.[34]

TESMAN. [*Following her.*] Only think – ill as she was, Aunt Rina embroidered these for me. Oh you can't think how many associations cling to them.

HEDDA. [*At the table.*] Scarcely for me.

MISS TESMAN. Of course not for Hedda, George.

TESMAN. Well, but now that she belongs to the family, I thought –

HEDDA. [*Interrupting.*] We shall never get on with this servant, Tesman.[35]

MISS TESMAN. Not get on with Berta?

TESMAN. Why, dear, what puts that in your head? Eh?

HEDDA. [*Pointing.*] Look there! She has left her old bonnet[36] lying about on a chair.

TESMAN. [*In consternation, drops the slippers on the floor.*] Why, Hedda –

HEDDA. Just fancy, if anyone should come in and see it!

TESMAN. But Hedda – that's Aunt Julia's bonnet.

HEDDA. Is it!

MISS TESMAN. [*Taking up the bonnet.*] Yes, indeed it's mine. And, what's more, it's not old, Madam Hedda.

HEDDA. I really did not look closely at it, Miss Tesman.

MISS TESMAN. [*Trying on the bonnet.*] Let me tell you it's the first time I have worn it – the very first time.

TESMAN. And a very nice bonnet it is too – quite a beauty!

MISS TESMAN. Oh, it's no such great thing, George. [*Looks around her.*] My parasol – ? Ah, here. [*Takes it.*] For this is mine too – [*mutters*] – not Berta's.

TESMAN. A new bonnet and a new parasol! Only think, Hedda!

HEDDA. Very handsome indeed.

34 See Elizabeth Robins's comment that although Hedda is initially presented as enviable, "she wasn't on the scene sixty seconds" before showing her deep dissatisfaction with her circumstances (**p. 58**).

35 The fact that Hedda addresses her husband by his surname while the rest of the family address each other – and her – by Christian names is intended to be startling, as the brief dialogue exchange sketched out in Ibsen's scenario indicates (see **p. 34**). It is a form of distancing and signals that she is, or would like to be, an outsider to this close-knit family group.

36 Although it is left unclear as to whether Hedda's "mistake" is honest, the evident newness and "gorgeous" decoration of this bonnet stressed by Tesman's reaction right at the beginning of the play clearly indicate that her comment is malicious. In attacking Aunt Julia's (bourgeois) taste as unsophisticated and asserting her own superiority – all in a single, seemingly inconsequential phrase – Hedda rejects and attempts to break up the "unity" that she feels as "inimical" (see Ibsen's letter to Stern, **p. 32**); and indeed does succeed, momentarily, in imposing her dominance as Tesman's dropping of his slippers demonstrates. He almost immediately turns the tables by raising the possibility of her pregnancy – though in the next scene he is still innocently referring to Hedda's weight-gain as the healthy result of travel – which of course re-engages Aunt Julia's family ties and promises to encircle Hedda even more closely. This is also one of the incidents that have been used to point out the comic elements in the play (see Suzman, **p. 101**).

TESMAN. Yes, isn't it? Eh? But Auntie, take a good look at Hedda before you go! See how handsome she is!

MISS TESMAN. Oh, my dear boy, there's nothing new in that. Hedda was always lovely.

[*She nods and goes towards the right.*

TESMAN. [*Following.*] Yes, but have you noticed what splendid condition she is in? How she has filled out on the journey?

HEDDA. [*Crossing the room.*] Oh, do be quiet – !

MISS TESMAN. [*Who has stopped and turned.*] Filled out?

TESMAN. Of course you don't notice it so much now that she has that dress on. But I, who can see –

HEDDA. [*At the glass door, impatiently.*] Oh, you can't see anything.[37]

TESMAN. It must be the mountain air in the Tyrol –

HEDDA. [*Curtly, interrupting.*] I am exactly as I was when I started.

TESMAN. So you insist; but I'm quite certain you are not. Don't you agree with me, Auntie?

MISS TESMAN. [*Who has been gazing at her with folded hands.*] Hedda is lovely – lovely – lovely. [*Goes up to her, takes her head between both hands, draws it downwards, and kisses her hair.*] God bless and preserve Hedda Tesman – for George's sake.[38]

HEDDA. [*Gently freeing herself.*] Oh – ! Let me go.

MISS TESMAN. [*In quiet emotion.*] I shall not let a day pass without coming to see you.

TESMAN. No you won't, will you, Auntie? Eh?

MISS TESMAN. Good-bye – good-bye!

[*She goes out by the hall door.* TESMAN *accompanies her. The door remains half open.* TESMAN *can be heard repeating his message to Aunt Rina and his thanks for the slippers.*

[*In the meantime,* HEDDA *walks about the room, raising her arms and clenching*

37 In a literal sense Hedda may be correct: quite apart from the concealing looseness of her gown, she is clearly at most only four or five months pregnant and not "showing" yet. However the signs are there for Aunt Julia's experienced eye; and Hedda's insistence that she is unchanged physically shades into a defence of her psychological coherence as an individual, effectively denying the change in social status that marriage represents. Notably it is not critics, but the actresses who have played Hedda, who bring out the psychological effect of her physiological condition (see Nazimova and Suzman, **pp. 68–9, 99**). In his production Ingmar Bergman made Hedda's pregnancy the keynote of her character (see **p. 90**).

38 Aunt Julia's mode of address – "Hedda Tesman" – contrasts strikingly with the play's title, and the way Hedda has been called simply by her personal name up to now, indicating the loss of individual identity and subordination to Tesman (and his family) that motherhood will bring.

her hands as if in desperation.[39] *Then she flings back the curtains from the glass door, and stands there looking out.*

[*Presently* TESMAN *returns and closes the door behind him.*

TESMAN. [*Picks up the slippers from the floor.*] What are you looking at, Hedda?

HEDDA. [*Once more calm and mistress of herself.*] I am only looking at the leaves. They are so yellow – so withered.

From Act 1: Hedda Versus Thea

Thea's entry is, like Hedda's if not nearly to the same extent, built up to by discussion of Thea (her marriage, a former relationship between her and Tesman, her – to Hedda – "irritating hair"), and in the introductory stage direction Ibsen stresses that Thea is Hedda's physical opposite: with prominent blue eyes and strikingly blonde, "unusually abundant and wavy" hair. In her opening comments when Tesman is present, Thea describes Løvborg's recently published book ("dealing with the march of civilization – in broad outline": a sharp contrast to the intimate and pedantic detail of Tesman's research).

This scene may seem little more than exposition, yet James McFarlane for one identifies it as "the focal point of the play" (see **p. 102**). Although her behavior is presented as apparently normal and entirely socially acceptable, thus providing a context for the increasing blatant and disastrous manipulations that Hedda carries out, this dialogue is the first clear indication of Hedda's manipulativeness, and the way she disguises self-serving aims (here to discover the true relationship between Thea and Løvborg) beneath apparent altruism. At the same time Ibsen exploits the irony that the essentially subservient and conventional Thea has been capable of freeing herself from a constricting marriage – and of pursuing her true soulmate – while the dominant and apparently individualistic Hedda is, as her reaction suggests, too governed by convention and fearful of her reputation to take the same escape.

It is also in this scene that Ibsen establishes the fire imagery, which surrounds Hedda, although this is done by seemingly "natural" and minor (in referring back to childhood activities) comments. Similarly, indicating the degree to which every detail of the play is given thematic significance, the "red-haired singing woman" whom Thea describes as dominating Løvborg's past (when it is already

39 Hedda's silent "desperation" physically demonstrates Ibsen's contention that, even though Norway might have achieved national liberty, this has not brought freedom or independence for individuals; and although Hedda is as much trapped by biology as by marriage, what she fears is clearly much the same as the meaningless life to which an early feminist writer like Camilla Collet perceived she was "destined" (see **pp. 24–5** and **25**). All Hedda can focus on are the "withered" and discolored autumn leaves, representing how she sees her future life (see Suzman and Lester, **pp. 94** and **99**).

clear that it was Hedda herself) becomes fleshed out in later scenes as the prostitute whom Løvborg will accuse of stealing his manuscript. This Madame Diana is also presented as an analogue to Hedda – linked not only by her pistols, but by her red hair (an intensification of Hedda's neutral brown, which relates to the fire imagery surrounding Hedda) – and can be seen as a possible alternative existence that Hedda is incapable of realizing (as le Gallienne noted, see Lester, **p. 94**). In the preceding conversation, with Tesman present, Thea attempts to disguise the fact that she has left her husband to follow Løvborg, arousing Hedda's suspicions.

MRS. ELVSTED.[1] [*Apprehensively.*] But there is nothing more Mrs. Tesman! Absolutely nothing!

HEDDA. Oh yes, but there is. There is a great deal more – I can see that. Sit here – and we'll have a cosy, confidential chat.

[*She forces* MRS. ELVSTED *to sit in the easy-chair beside the stove, and seats herself on one of the footstools.*

MRS. ELVSTED. [*Anxiously, looking at her watch.*] But, my dear Mrs. Tesman – I was really on the point of going.

HEDDA. Oh, you can't be in such a hurry. – Well? Now tell me something about your life at home.

MRS. ELVSTED. Oh, that is just what I care least to speak about.

HEDDA. But to me, dear – ? Why, weren't we schoolfellows?

MRS. ELVSTED. Yes, but you were in the class above me. Oh, how dreadfully afraid of you I was then!

HEDDA. Afraid of me?

MRS. ELVSTED. Yes, dreadfully. For when we met on the stairs you used always to pull my hair.

HEDDA. Did I, really?

MRS. ELVSTED. Yes, and once you said you would burn it off my head.[2]

HEDDA. Oh that was all nonsense, of course.

MRS. ELVSTED. Yes, but I was so silly in those days. – And since then,

1 It is significant that Thea is always listed by her married name, ironically underlining the status that (as Hedda is shortly to elicit from her) she has rejected. It also emphasizes the difference with the way Ibsen always identifies Hedda herself as a person in her own right, rather than as MRS. TESMAN. The contrast between the two characters is also underlined by the physical description of Thea in the stage direction when she enters, which stresses her large and slightly protruding blue eyes as well as her luxuriant blonde hair.

2 This relates to the physical characteristics Ibsen envisaged for these women, and suggests Hedda's envy of "normal" people, who have the sexual vitality (signaled by hair) that she lacks. As Archer points out, not only Hedda's threat to burn Thea's hair but even the emphasis on its luxuriance are very late additions to the text, only inserted in the final draft (see **p. 36**). As such they assume added significance, as well as showing the way Ibsen shaped the play.

too – we have drifted so far – far apart from each other. Our circles have been so entirely different.

HEDDA. Well then, we must try to drift together again. Now listen! At school we said *du*[3] to each other; and we called each other by our Christian names –

MRS. ELVSTED. No, I am sure you must be mistaken.

HEDDA., No, not at all! I can remember quite distinctly. So now we are going to renew our old friendship – [*Draws the footstool closer to* MRS. ELVSTED.] There now! [*Kisses her cheek.*] You must say *du* to me and call me Hedda.

MRS. ELVSTED. [*Presses and pats her hands.*] Oh, how good and kind you are! I am not used to such kindness.

HEDDA. There, there, there! And I shall say *du* to you, as in the old days, and call you my dear Thora.

MRS. ELVSTED. My name is Thea.[4]

HEDDA. Why, of course! I meant Thea. [*Looks at her compassionately.*] So you are not accustomed to goodness and kindness, Thea? Not in your own home?

MRS. ELVSTED. Oh, if I only had a home! But I haven't any; I have never had a home.

HEDDA. [*Looks at her for a moment.*] I almost suspected as much.

MRS. ELVSTED. [*Gazing helplessly before her.*] Yes – yes – yes.

HEDDA. I don't quite remember – was it not as house-keeper that you first went to Mr. Elvsted's?

MRS. ELVSTED. I really went as governess.[5] But his wife – his late wife – was an invalid, – and rarely left her room. So I had to look after the housekeeping as well.

HEDDA. And then – at last – you became mistress of the house.

MRS. ELVSTED. [*Sadly.*] Yes, I did.

HEDDA. Let me see – about how long ago was that?

MRS. ELVSTED. My marriage?

HEDDA. Yes.

MRS. ELVSTED. Five years ago.

HEDDA. To be sure; it must be that.

3 As Gosse points out in a footnote, "'Du' = 'thou'; the familiar instead of formal address," which here underlines the falsity of Hedda's behavior to Thea, particularly since she cannot even remember her name.

4 Gosse notes the pronunciation of these names as *Tora* and *Taya*. Hedda's "mistake" reveals the falsity of her claim to friendship and underlines the irony of her insistence on the intimate address of "*du*." However, Tora is a homonym for Nora – not only the heroine of *A Doll's House* who, just as Thea has done, walks out on her marriage; but also the name given to the female emblem for Norway, and as a blue-eyed blonde Thea corresponds to the national ideal – and the "mistake" therefore shows the connection between the two plays in Ibsen's mind (in *A Doll's House* Nora also briefly contemplates suicide), as well as reflecting his concern with the illusoriness of the freedom offered by national liberation (see Ibsen's letter to Bjørnson, **p. 24**).

5 See Hovde on the "dreary" options available to a single woman in nineteenth-century Scandinavia, the only escape being marriage, which explains why Thea's willingness to become the wife of an older man she finds (as she later comments) "repellent" is presented as a logical progression (**p. 10**).

MRS. ELVSTED. Oh those five years – ! Or at all events the last two or three of them! Oh, if you could only imagine –

HEDDA. [*Giving her a little slap on the hand.*] *De*?[6] Fie, Thea!

MRS. ELVSTED. Yes, yes, I will try – Well, if – you only imagine and understand –

HEDDA. [*Lightly.*] Eilert Løvborg has been in your neighbourhood about three years, hasn't he?

MRS. ELVSTED. [*Looks at her doubtfully.*] Eilert Løvborg? Yes – he has.

HEDDA. Had you known him before, in town here?

MRS. ELVSTED. Scarcely at all. I mean – I knew him by name of course.

HEDDA. But you saw a good deal of him in the country?

MRS. ELVSTED. Yes, he came to us every day. You see, he gave the children lessons; for in the long run I couldn't manage it all myself.

HEDDA. No, that's clear. – And your husband – ? I suppose he is often away from home?

MRS. ELVSTED. Yes. Being sheriff, you know, he has to travel about a good deal in his district.

HEDDA. [*Leaning against the arm of the chair.*] Thea – my poor, sweet Thea – now you must tell me everything – exactly as it stands.

MRS. ELVSTED. Well then, you must question me.

HEDDA. What sort of a man is your husband, Thea? I mean – you know – in everyday life. Is he kind to you?

MRS. ELVSTED. [*Evasively.*] I am sure he means well in everything.[7]

HEDDA. I should think he must be altogether too old for you. There is at least twenty years' difference between you, is there not?

MRS. ELVSTED. [*Irritably.*] Yes, that is true, too. Everything about him is repellent to me! We have not a thought in common. We have no single point of sympathy – he and I.

HEDDA. But is he not fond of you all the same? In his own way?

MRS. ELVSTED. Oh I really don't know. I think he regards me simply as a useful property.[8] And then it doesn't cost much to keep me. I am not expensive.

HEDDA. That is stupid of you.

MRS. ELVSTED. [*Shakes her head.*] It cannot be otherwise – not with him. I don't think he really cares for anyone but himself – and perhaps a little for the children.

HEDDA. And for Eilert Løvberg, Thea.

---

6 As Gosse's translation makes clear, though he has to resort to Norwegian since there is no equivalent usage in English, Mrs. Elvsted has used the formal pronoun for "you" ("*de*"), whereupon Hedda rebukes her. In her next speech Mrs. Elvsted says "*du*" ("thou").

7 The parallels between Thea's marriage and Hedda's become clear when Hedda uses almost the same terms to describe her "boredom" with Tesman to Brack in Act 2.

8 Even Thea, with far less sensitivity than Hedda, is fully aware of her legal status (in the 1860s at least: wife as chattel) – and the position of an unmarried woman, or even worse, one who had abandoned her marriage was still more menial (see Hovde, **p. 10**), which helps to explain the way towards the end she later latches on to Tesman when robbed of Løvborg. Note, too, Hedda's response: the only way she can conceive of being valued in marriage is materially.

MRS. ELVSTED. [*Looking at her.*] For Eilert Løvborg? What puts that into your head?

HEDDA. Well, my dear – I should say, when he sends you after him all the way to town – [*Smiling almost imperceptibly.*] And besides, you said so yourself, to Tesman.

MRS. ELVSTED. [*With a little nervous twitch.*] Did I? Yes, I suppose I did. [*Vehemently, but not loudly.*] No – I may just as well make a clean breast of it at once! For it must all come out in any case.

HEDDA. Why, my dear Thea – ?

MRS. ELVSTED. Well, to make a long story short: My husband did not know that I was coming.

HEDDA. What! Your husband didn't know it!

MRS. ELVSTED. No, of course not. For that matter, he was away from home himself – he was travelling. Oh, I could bear it no longer, Hedda! I couldn't indeed – so utterly alone as I should have been in future.

HEDDA. Well? And then?

MRS. ELVSTED. So I put together some of my things – what I needed most – as quietly as possible. And then I left the house.

HEDDA. Without a word?

MRS. ELVSTED. Yes – and took the train straight to town.

HEDDA. Why, my dear, good Thea – to think of you daring to do it![9]

MRS. ELVSTED. [*Rises and moves about the room.*] What else could I possibly do?

HEDDA. But what do you think your husband will say when you go home again?

MRS. ELVSTED. [*At the table, looks at her.*] Back to him?

HEDDA. Of course.

MRS. ELVSTED. I shall never go back to him again.

HEDDA. [*Rising and going towards her.*] Then you have left your home – for good and all?

MRS. ELVSTED. Yes. There was nothing else to be done.

HEDDA. But then – to take flight so openly.

MRS. ELVSTED. Oh, it's impossible to keep things of that sort secret.

HEDDA. But what do you think people will say[10] of you, Thea?

MRS. ELVSTED. They may say what they like, for aught *I* care. [*Seats herself wearily and sadly on the sofa.*] I have done nothing but what I had to do.

9 Ironically, Hedda's repeated labeling of Thea's action as "daring" reverses the image of the two characters: "daring" being an adjective that critics have reserved for Hedda (see Gosse's interpretation of her character as "devoid of any moral sense," though Shaw among others stresses her moral "cowardice", **pp. 55, 56–7**).

10 It is these kind of responses that led Glenda Jackson to emphasize that, despite her unconventional behavior, Hedda is "committed to a very old-fashioned set of values" and brings Jackson to an interesting comparison between Hedda and Thea on feminist grounds (see **p. 96**). Hedda's response here also prepares us for later inability to openly reject Brack's sexual blackmail.

HEDDA. [*After a short silence.*] And what are your plans now? What do you think of doing?

MRS. ELVSTED. I don't know yet. I only know this, that I must live here, where Eilert Løvborg is – if I am to live at all.

HEDDA. [*Takes a chair from the table, seats herself beside her, and strokes her hands.*] My dear Thea – how did this – this friendship – between you and Eilert Løvborg come about?

MRS. ELVSTED. Oh it grew up gradually. I gained a sort of influence over him.[11]

HEDDA. Indeed?

MRS. ELVSTED. He gave up his old habits. Not because I asked him to, for I never dared do that. But of course he saw how repulsive they were to me; and so he dropped them.

HEDDA. [*Concealing an involuntary smile of scorn.*] Then you have reclaimed him – as the saying goes – my little Thea.

MRS. ELVSTED. So he says himself, at any rate. And he, on his side, has made a real human being of me – taught me to think, and to understand so many things.

HEDDA. Did he give you lessons too, then?

MRS. ELVSTED. No, not exactly lessons. But he talked to me – talked about such an infinity of things. And then came the lovely, happy time when I began to share in his work[12] – when he allowed me to help him!

HEDDA. Oh he did, did he?

MRS. ELVSTED. Yes! He never wrote anything without my assistance.

HEDDA. You were two good comrades, in fact?

MRS. ELVSTED. [*Eagerly.*] Comrades![13] Yes, fancy, Hedda – that is the very word he used! – Oh, I ought to feel perfectly happy; and yet I cannot; for I don't know how long it will last.

HEDDA. Are you no surer of him than that?

MRS. ELVSTED. [*Gloomily.*] A woman's shadow stands between Eilert Løvberg and me.

HEDDA. [*Looks at her anxiously.*] Who can that be?

MRS. ELVSTED. I don't know. Some one he knew in his – in his past. Some one he has never been able wholly to forget.

HEDDA. What has he told you – about this?

---

11 See Elizabeth Robins's analysis of Hedda's motivation, and the effect this discovery has on her later actions (**p. 60**).

12 In the light of an earlier statement (to Tesman) implying that as a woman she has practically no understanding of either his, or Løvborg's work, this claim retrospectively demonstrates that Thea is as capable of manipulating people as Hedda, although in contrast to Hedda she does so through playing on male clichés of femininity.

13 In the Christopher Hampton translation "Comrades" is rendered as "Soulmates." Clearly this term corresponds more to a modern concept of the relationship Thea has described, and might be the sort of word Løvborg would use, yet Hedda is hardly likely to admit the existence of such intimacy (and in 1890 "comrade" had not yet taken on any of the political overtones that it now carries).

MRS. ELVSTED. He has only once – quite vaguely – alluded to it.

HEDDA. Well! And what did he say?

MRS. ELVSTED. He said that when they parted, she threatened to shoot him with a pistol.

HEDDA. [*With cold composure.*] Oh nonsense! No one does that sort of thing here.

MRS. ELVSTED. No. And that is why I think it must have been that red-haired singing-woman[14] whom he once –

HEDDA. Yes, very likely.

MRS. ELVSTED. For I remember they used to say of her that she carried loaded firearms.

From Act 2: Hedda Versus Brack

As with the physical contrast between Hedda and Thea, the stage description of Brack earlier in Act 1 is extremely precise and contrasts with Tesman, Brack's physique signaling upper-class status ("aristocratic profile," monocle), self-indulgence (plump face, thick moustache), vitality (lively sparkling eyes), and perhaps a certain duplicity or at least self-deception (a suit "a little too youthful for his age"). Although there is a clear time gap, in terms of the action Act 2 follows directly, since Hedda's last comment, in reaction to the news that the prospective loss of the professorship will mean restricting the lifestyle Tesman had promised her, was that there is now only one thing "to kill time with [. . .] General Gabler's pistols."

Symbolism is an integral part of Ibsen's Naturalism (as he told Archer, "life is one tissue of symbols;" and Hedda with pistol in hand is the visual symbol that dominates the play: see the images of Act 2 and Act 4 (**p. 97** and frontispiece). In addition, Steiner singles out the pistol as the primary organizing object in this play (**p. 85**), though a variant reading of this symbol is offered by Elenore Lester's labeling of Hedda's guns as "the penis-pistols" (**p. 93**). The weapon is, of course, a duelling pistol (not a service revolver) which is why there is a matched pair. The image is precise: Hedda is indeed engaged in a duel for her life against the society around her, of which Brack will emerge as the most threatening representative. As Chekhov once remarked (with respect to his play *Uncle Vanya*, 1899), dramatic economy requires that if as "symbolically loaded" an

14 An earlier draft of the play explicitly identifies the woman in Løvborg's early life to be Hedda and this is still clearly implied by her reaction to Thea's account, as well as later being confirmed by Løvborg himself (see **p. 146** below). However, since it would not be credible for a woman like Thea to confide in Hedda, let alone approach her or even Tesman for help in finding him, if she already knew that it was to her that Løvborg had been romantically committed, another figure is introduced. Hedda's curt response is an excellent example of the way an apparently simple sentence is made to carry ambiguous meanings. Note too that Thea's description of Madame Diana "threatening to shoot" Løvborg exactly parallels Hedda's firing of a pistol at Brack in Act 2, while her response of "No one does that sort of thing" is almost exactly echoed by Brack in the last line of the play.

object as a pistol is introduced on the stage, then it must eventually be fired. Here, since the gun is fired immediately, attention is being directed to apparently minor aspects – Brack's ability to identify the weapon, and the fact that there is a second gun in the pistol-case – both of which will emerge as crucial elements in the trap that closes around Hedda.

As background to this conversation, it is worth noting that the year the play was written – 1890 – was also the year the Norwegian Parliament first debated a proposal to allow women the vote; and arguments against doing so had emphasized that taking any role whatsoever in public life (even expressing a political opinion through casting a ballot) would be "the utmost disgrace" to femininity. (See Ida Blom, **p. 11**.)

Act Second[1]

The room at the TESMANS' *as in the first Act, except that the piano has been removed, and an elegant little writing-table with book-shelves put in its place. A smaller table stands near the sofa on the left. Most of the bouquets have been taken away.* MRS. ELVSTED'S *bouquet is upon the large table in front. It is afternoon.* HEDDA, *dressed to receive callers, is alone in the room. She stands by the open glass door, loading a revolver.*[2] *The fellow to it lies in an open pistol-case on the writing-table.*

HEDDA. [*Looks down the garden, and calls:*] here again, Judge!

BRACK. [*Is heard calling from a distance.*] As you see, Mrs. Tesman!

HEDDA. [*Raises the pistol and points.*] Now I'll shoot you, Judge Brack!

BRACK. [*Calling unseen.*] No, no, no! Don't stand aiming at me!

HEDDA. This is what comes of sneaking in by the back way.[3]

[*She fires.*

BRACK. [*Nearer.*] Are you out of your senses – !

HEDDA. Dear me – did I happen to hit you?

BRACK. [*Still outside.*] I wish you would let these pranks alone!

1 Muriel Bradbrook gives a succinct outline of the different movements and shifts in focus signaled by each Act division (see **pp. 78–9**).

2 Hedda's casual resort to gun-play is also one of the most overt reasons (in addition to her attitude to pregnancy) that led the initial British reviewers to label her with disgust as an "unwomanly woman" – and justifies Eric Bentley's more recent validation of precisely the same quality as linked to the heroic world of Ibsen's early Viking dramas, where Hedda would have had scope for her "energies and dreams" (see **pp. 63** and **82**).

3 In his translation Gosse notes that the term used by Ibsen ("*bagveje*") means both "back ways" and "underhand courses" – a pun that encapsulates Brack's duplicitous dealings: his attempt to "cash in" on the loans he has arranged for Tesman by attempting to seduce Hedda (as he does in this scene), or his later threat of exposure to blackmail her for sexual favors – and it is remarkable as the sole instance of this kind of literary pointing in the play.

HEDDA. Come in then, Judge.

[JUDGE BRACK, *dressed as though for a men's party, enters by the glass door. He carries a light overcoat over his arm.*

BRACK. What the deuce – haven't you tired of that sport, yet? What are you shooting at?

HEDDA. Oh, I am only firing in the air.

BRACK. [*Gently takes the pistol out of her hand.*] Allow me, madam! [*Looks at it.*] Ah – I know this pistol well![4] [*Looks around.*] Where is the case? Ah, here it is. [*Lays the pistol in it, and shuts it.*] Now we won't play at that game any more today.

HEDDA. Then what in heaven's name would you have me do with myself?[5]

BRACK. Have you had no visitors?

HEDDA. [*Closing the glass door.*] Not one. I suppose all our set are still out of town.

BRACK. And is Tesman not at home either?

HEDDA. [*At the writing-table, putting the pistol-case in a drawer which she shuts.*] No. He rushed off to his aunt's directly after lunch; he didn't expect you so early.

BRACK. H'm – how stupid of me not to have thought of that!

HEDDA. [*Turning her head to look at him.*] Why stupid?

BRACK. Because if I had thought of it I should have come a little – earlier.

HEDDA. [*Crossing the room.*] Then you would have found no one to receive you; for I have been in my room changing my dress ever since lunch.

BRACK. And is there no sort of little chink[6] that we could hold a parley through?

HEDDA. You have forgotten to arrange one.

BRACK. That was another piece of stupidity.

HEDDA. Well, we must just settle down here – and wait. Tesman is not likely to be back for some time yet.

4 The recognition of the gun here is the basis for Brack's later identification of it, that traps Hedda, the symbol of her dominance becoming the very instrument that subjects her to his power. However, certain critics have found this kind of carefully constructed dramaturgy too artificial (see Nigel Dennis, **p. 83**).

5 There is literally no role for Hedda in this society, except as sexual object: wife (to a husband incapable of understanding or satisfying her needs) or mother (which would trap her in a marriage she despises) or secret mistress (as Brack proposes in the following conversation). All her destructive behavior – graphically signaled here by the way she shoots at Brack – is a reaction to this situation; and, as James McFarlane observes, is at least in part motivated by an attempt to win some sort of significance for her life (see **p. 103**).

6 Brack is displaying his culture: playing off Shakespeare (*A Midsummer Night's Dream*) and casting himself as the romantic lover Pyramus who secretly courted Thisbe through a "crannied hole or chink." But, while there is no indication that he is thinking of such implications, the story ends with Thisbe's suicide – stabbing herself through the breast with a sword – which also forecasts Hedda's fate.

BRACK. Never mind; I shall not be impatient.

[HEDDA *seats herself in the corner of the sofa.* BRACK *lays his overcoat over the back of the nearest chair, and sits down, but keeps his hat in his hand. A short silence. They look at each other.*

HEDDA. Well?

BRACK. [*In the same tone.*] Well?

HEDDA. I spoke first.

BRACK. [*Bending a little forward.*] Come, let us have a cosy little chat, Mrs. Hedda.[7]

HEDDA. [*Leaning further back in the sofa.*] Does it not seem like a whole eternity since our last talk? Of course I don't count those few words yesterday evening and this morning.

BRACK. You mean since our last confidential talk? Our last *tête-à-tête*?

HEDDA. Well yes – since you put it so.

BRACK. Not a day has passed but I have wished that you were home again.

HEDDA. And I have done nothing but wish the same thing.

BRACK. You? Really, Mrs. Hedda? And I thought you had been enjoying your tour so much!

HEDDA. Oh yes, you may be sure of that!

BRACK. But Tesman's letters spoke of nothing but happiness.

HEDDA. Oh, Tesman! You see, he thinks nothing so delightful as grubbing in libraries and making copies of old parchments, or whatever you call them.

BRACK. [*With a spice of malice.*] Well, that is his vocation in life – or part of it at any rate.

HEDDA. Yes, of course; and no doubt when it's your vocation – . But *I*! Oh, my dear Mr. Brack, how mortally bored I have been.

BRACK. [*Sympathetically.*] Do you really say so? In downright earnest?

HEDDA. Yes, you can surely understand it – ! To go for six whole months without meeting a soul that knew anything of our circle[8] or could talk about the things we are interested in.

7 The modes of address Ibsen's characters use are extremely precise, particularly in this play, so much so that although usages such as this sound oddly archaic today, they caused even more problems for the early translators, when the play was contemporary and in no way a period piece. This is reflected in Gosse's note to the first English version: "As this form of address is contrary to English usage, and as the note of familiarity would be lacking in 'Mrs. Tesman,' Brack may, in stage representation, say 'Miss Hedda,' thus ignoring her marriage and reverting to the form of address no doubt customary between them of old."

8 Note Hedda's dependency on the society that constricts her, though she is attempting to set up an opposition between her previous "circle" and the one she has married into. In those days, of course, a young woman of any social standing was not expected to go out on the streets alone; and with no established contacts in a foreign country, she is indeed limited to her husband for escort, even to go sightseeing. This conversation clarifies the irony that Tesman's research into domesticity has prevented any possible bonding with his new wife, and, referring back to the opening exchange between Tesman and his Aunt in Act 1, demonstrates the close interweaving of the various strands in this play that contributes to the impression of claustrophobic enclosure.

BRACK. Yes, yes – I too should feel that a deprivation.

HEDDA. And then, what I found most intolerable of all –

BRACK. Well?

HEDDA. – was being everlastingly in the company of – one and the same person –

BRACK. [*With a nod of assent.*] Morning, noon, and night, yes – at all possible times and seasons.

HEDDA. I said "everlastingly."[9]

BRACK. Just so. But I should have thought, with our excellent Tesman, one could –

HEDDA. Tesman is – a specialist, my dear Judge.

BRACK. Undeniably.

HEDDA. And specialists are not at all amusing to travel with. Not in the long run at any rate.

BRACK. Not even – the specialist one happens to love?

HEDDA. Faugh – don't use that sickening word!

BRACK. [*Taken aback.*] What do you say, Mrs. Hedda?

HEDDA. [*Half laughing, half irritated.*] You should just try it! To hear of nothing but the history of civilisation, morning, noon, and night –

BRACK. Everlastingly.

HEDDA. Yes, yes, yes! And then all this about the domestic industry of the middle ages – ! That's the most disgusting[10] part of it!

BRACK. [*Looks searchingly at her.*] But tell me – in that case, how am I to understand your – ? H'm –

HEDDA. My accepting George Tesman, you mean?

BRACK. Well, let us put it so.

HEDDA. Good heavens, do you see anything so wonderful in that?

BRACK. Yes and no – Mrs. Hedda.

HEDDA. I had positively danced myself tired, my dear Judge. My day was done[11] – [*With a slight shudder.*] Oh no – I won't say that; nor think it either!

9 This stress on precision clearly covers a response to Brack's mention of nights together with her husband, indicating the extreme nature of Hedda's rejection of sexuality that leads her to react even to such a standard expression as "morning, noon, and night" and becomes explicit with her following repudiation of love as "sickening." This is one of the main factors that has led critics to see Hedda as a psychological case: "hyperaesthesia" at the turn of the century; a "patient on the couch" of Freudian psychology in the 1950s; or the depiction of "alienation and spiritual nausea" in Ingmar Bergman's 1964/1979 stagings (see Archer, Lester, and Marker and Marker, **pp. 66, 93** and **90**). At the same time, however, Hedda's visceral distaste for sexuality can be seen as merely an exaggerated form of the nineteenth-century emphasis on ideals of feminine "purity."

10 While this devaluing of Tesman's professional work relates back to the incongruity of preferring historical research to his wife during their honeymoon, which has already been established early in the previous act, the choice of adjective Hedda is given here also illuminates her disgust at sex (interpreting "domestic industry" as code for procreation).

11 Ibsen's preliminary scenario for the play is explicit about Hedda's reasons for marrying – repudiated by the fashionable world after her father's retirement, facing poverty after his death, fearing that (at the age of 25 or 26) she may already be (in the modern expression) "on the shelf" (see **p. 34**) – and although, given her personality, in Naturalistic terms she would never admit her real situation, perhaps even to herself, the truth does emerge between the lines of her subsequent comments.

BRACK. You have assuredly no reason to.

HEDDA. Oh, reasons – [*Watching him closely.*] And George Tesman – after all, you must admit that he is correctness itself.

BRACK. His correctness and respectability are beyond all question.

HEDDA. And I don't see anything absolutely ridiculous[12] about him. – Do you?

BRACK. Ridiculous? N – no – I shouldn't exactly say so –

HEDDA. Well – and his powers of research, at all events, are untiring. – I see no reason why he should not one day come to the front, after all.

BRACK. [*Looks at her hesitatingly.*] I thought that you, like every one else, expected him to attain the highest distinction.

HEDDA. [*With an expression of fatigue.*] Yes, so I did. – And then, since he was bent, at all hazards, on being allowed to provide for me – I really don't know why I should not have accepted his offer?

BRACK. No – if you look at it in that light –

HEDDA. It was more than my other adorers were prepared to do for me, my dear Judge.

BRACK. [*Laughing.*] Well, I can't answer for all the rest; but as for myself, you know quite well that I have always entertained a – a certain respect for the marriage tie – for marriage as an institution, Mrs. Hedda.

HEDDA. [*Jestingly.*] Oh, I assure you I have never cherished any hopes with respect to you.

BRACK. All I require is a pleasant and intimate interior, where I can make myself useful in every way, and am free to come and go as – as a trusted friend –

HEDDA. Of the master of the house, do you mean?

BRACK. [*Bowing.*] Frankly – of the mistress first of all; but of course of the master too, in the second place. Such a triangular friendship[13] – if I may call it so – is really a great convenience for all parties, let me tell you.

HEDDA. Yes, I have many a time longed for some one to make a third on our travels. Oh – those railway-carriage *tête-à-têtes* – !

BRACK. Fortunately your wedding journey is over now.

HEDDA. [*Shaking her head.*] Not by a long-long way. I have only arrived at a station on the line.

12 The fear of ridicule – the obverse of her clinging to the rigid attitudes and sexual prudery of a stratified society – is one of the defining elements of Hedda's personality, picked up on in the final act by Brack who blackmails her specifically with the threat of scandal: here expressed obliquely (her dignity is dependent on her husband's reputation, which paradoxically she has been doing her best to undermine).

13 What is being suggested here, though at this point only as a playful form of seduction, is a *ménage à trois*, with the adulterer as Brack's favored role; and the egoism plus exploitiveness of this is captured in one interpretation of Ibsen's capsule note on his character as representing "the personal bourgeois point of view" (see Ibsen's scenario, **p. 34**). Brack is clearly the "*homme moyen sensuel*" frequently featured in other nineteenth-century novels and plays; and several critics have explored this aspect of his character, most interestingly James McFarlane (see **p. 104**).

BRACK. Well, then the passengers jump out and move about a little, Mrs. Hedda.

HEDDA. I never jump out.

BRACK. Really?

HEDDA. No – because there is always some one standing by to –

BRACK. [*Laughing.*] To look at your ankles, do you mean?

HEDDA. Precisely.

BRACK. Well but, dear me –

HEDDA. [*With a gesture of repulsion.*[14]] I won't have it. I would rather keep my seat where I happen to be – and continue the *tête-à-tête*.

BRACK. But suppose a third person were to jump in and join the couple.

HEDDA. Ah – that is quite another matter!

BRACK. A trusted, sympathetic friend –

HEDDA. – with a fund of conversation on all sorts of lively topics –

BRACK. – and not the least bit of a specialist!

HEDDA. [*With an audible sigh.*] Yes, that would be a relief indeed.

BRACK. [*Hears the front door open, and glances in that direction.*] The triangle is completed.

HEDDA. [*Half aloud.*] And on goes the train.

GEORGE TESMAN, *in a grey walking-suit, with a soft felt hat, enters from the hall. He has a number of unbound books under his arm and in his pockets.*

From Act 2: Hedda Versus Løvborg

Entering as he does, over half-way through Act 2, yet having been a recurrent subject of conversation since the middle of Act 1, Løvborg is given a longer "build-up" even than Hedda, or indeed any other character in Ibsen's plays. This signals his centrality in the action, becoming Hedda's obsessive focus and the catalyst for her destruction, as well as a foil to her husband. The latter is emphasized in Ibsen's stage direction describing his person, where he is stated as being exactly the same age as Tesman, but lean (instead of plump), pale-faced with dark-hair and beard (rather than round-faced and fair), having patches of high color on his cheekbones signaling intensity (the opposite of Tesman's laid-back attitude), and being formally, even elegantly, dressed all in black (in contrast to Tesman's comfortable indoor clothes or gray suits) as well as carrying a silk top-hat (versus Tesman's soft homburg).

14 Nineteenth-century women's fashions dictated dresses down to the ground, so that even the ankle became an erotic object (in the words of a popular song: "A glimpse of stocking/Was something shocking") and Victorians even covered the legs of their tables with "skirts." But again Hedda's reaction betrays both her conventionality and her repulsion at anything remotely sexual, which implicitly extends to shame for her body and physical nature.

He brings with him the manuscript on which the plot of the whole play turns, describing this as dealing with the future; "the book I have put my true self into." In his 1970 version (the most recent adaptation of the play), Christopher Hampton has Løvborg add that the future developments he describes flow from "the underground revolution in women's thoughts." This certainly corresponds with our sensibilities today, and may possibly be a correct assumption since the whole play revolves around a woman in rebellion against the social restrictions of a gender role she is unable to break, while the only other young woman depicted has been forced to sacrifice position and reputation to escape. It is of course ironic, and from Tesman's limited viewpoint inconceivable, that a historian (by definition concerned with the past) should forecast the future. But this associates Løvborg's work with Ibsen's own aims as an author. In his view the present could only be accurately understood through an extensive knowledge of history; and what he aimed at – promoting a "revolution of the spirit of man" (see Ibsen's letters to Paulsen and Brandes, **pp. 8** and **24**). Indeed this link between the study of reality and changing the future, as a "fresh start" for both art and society, was something Zola pointed to as a fundamental basis for Naturalism (see **p. 27**). However, although his working notes explicitly describe Løvborg's subject as "Upward, forwards towards the bearer of light. Life on the present foundation of society is not worth living" (**p. 34**), as elsewhere in the play, Ibsen is careful to retain ambiguity, and leaves the question of Løvborg's ideas completely open. While most interpretations of the play unquestioningly assume that this manuscript is an intellectual and ethical masterpiece, with the potential to revolutionize society, Ibsen is careful not to give even a hint of its contents or quality in the dialogue. And that open question, upon which so much of our evaluation of Løvborg's character depends, was picked up by Ingmar Bergman, who reduced the manuscript he waves around to "a pitifully few sheets of paper" in his strikingly postmodernist production, justifying this on grounds of realistic credibility (see Frederick and Lise Lone Marker, **p. 91**).

This section of the play is remarkable for the way it portrays the oppressive restrictions of society through the almost Foucaultian (male) gaze of Tesman and Brack from the inner room. It also demonstrates the destructiveness of Hedda's will to self-assertion, which she defines time and again in terms of psychological or mental control over the actions of others – and which she is later to exercise with devastating effect, making her a female Zwingali (the hypnotist villain of *Trilby*, George Du Maurier's highly popular 1895 novel) – and indeed a critic like McFarlane sees this as encapsulating the wider meaning of the play (**pp. 102–3**), pointing out that Ibsen's attack on this sort of manipulation, particularly when undertaken in the name of altruism or morality (both of which are appealed to here by Hedda), is a recurrent theme in Ibsen's other plays. The section also offers the clearest picture of Hedda's sexuality. Elizabeth Robins was the first to point out that Hedda's motivation for breaking up with Løvborg reveals her disgust at "vulgar sensuality" (see **p. 60**) and suggests that she married the "decent" Tesman on the rebound. While she "thirsts" for "life" at second hand, when faced with performing the same acts physically she immediately rejects the experience. Yet the fear of "scandal" (being found out) seems altogether too insufficient for the violence of her reaction, leaving us to speculate that the real reason may be a repulsion against her own physical nature, and that her choice of husband may have been due to Tesman, with his immaturity, being the least sexually threatening husband possible. And she could hardly have turned from Løvborg to him, since – even if their break-up was the immediate cause of Løvborg's flight to the country – he has been with Thea for at least three years before the play opens. Shaw's insight into what this brief *tête-à-tête* implies about Hedda's view of Løvborg, which motivates the whole of her subsequent treatment of him, is particularly perceptive: that "when Løvborg tried to seduce her he was a hero, and that in allowing Thea to reform him he has played the miscreant" (**p. 57**).

Even this late in the play – over half-way through Act 2 – almost all of the dialogue between Hedda and Løvborg is exposition, though the way the details of past events is used to focus attention on their developing relationship makes it an active element, exemplifying Edmund Gosse's insight into Ibsen's technical mastery in conveying information (**p. 54**). This interweaving of past and present is also what Arthur Miller singled out as one of the most "dynamic" elements in Ibsen's dramaturgy, as well as epitomizing an "evolutionary" view of life (**pp. 76–7**), which expresses the Darwinism that fueled the whole Naturalistic movement. The extract here opens immediately after Løvborg has refused an invitation to dinner with Brack and Tesman.

HEDDA. [*Pointing towards the inner room.*] Will you not take a glass of cold punch, gentlemen?

BRACK. [*Looking at his watch.*] A stirrup-cup? Yes, it wouldn't come amiss.

TESMAN. A capital idea, Hedda! Just the thing! Now that the weight has been taken off my mind –

HEDDA. Will you not join them, Mr. Løvborg?

LØVBORG. [*With a gesture of refusal.*] No, thank you.

BRACK. Why bless me – cold punch is surely not poison.[1]

LØVBORG. Perhaps not for everyone.

HEDDA. I will keep Mr. Løvborg company in the meantime.

TESMAN. Yes, yes, Hedda dear, do.

[*He and* BRACK *go into the inner room, seat themselves, drink punch, smoke*

1 Given the force of this word, Hedda can have no doubt that by later manipulating Løvborg into drinking precisely this punch, she will be literally forcing poison on him – but it also reminds us that there are other, more metaphorical forms of mental and moral poisoning that from this point on gather impetus in the action.

cigarettes, and carry on a lively conversation during what follows. EILERT LØVBORG *remains standing beside the stove.* HEDDA *goes to the writing-table.*

HEDDA. [*Raising her voice a little*] Do you care to look at some photographs,[2] Mr. Løvborg? You know Tesman and I made a tour in the Tyrol on our way home?

[*She takes up an album, and places it on the table beside the sofa, in the further corner of which she seats herself.* ELIERT LØVBORG *approaches, stops, and looks at her. Then he takes a chair and seats himself to her left, with his back towards the inner room.*

HEDDA. [*Opening the album.*] Do you see this range of mountains, Mr. Løvborg? It's the Ortler group. Tesman has written the name underneath. Here it is: "The Ortler group near Meran."

LØVBORG. [*Who has never taken his eyes off her, says softly and slowly*:] Hedda – Gabler!

HEDDA. [*Glancing hastily at him.*] Ah! Hush.

LØVBORG. [*Repeats softly.*] Hedda Gabler!

HEDDA. [*Looking at the album.*] That was my name in the old days – when we two knew each other.

LØVBORG. And I must teach myself never to say Hedda Gabler again – never, as long as I live.

HEDDA. [*Still turning over the pages.*] Yes, you must. And I think you ought to practise in time. The sooner the better, I should say.

LØVBORG. [*In a tone of indignation.*] Hedda Gabler married? And married to – George Tesman!

HEDDA. Yes – so the world goes.

LØVBORG. Oh, Hedda, Hedda – how could you[3] throw yourself away!

HEDDA. [*Looks sharply at him.*] What? I can't allow this!

LØVBORG. What do you mean?

[TESMAN *comes into the room and goes towards the sofa.*

HEDDA. [*Hears him coming and says in an indifferent tone.*] And this is

2 However common holiday snapshots may be today, in the 1890s the camera was still a relatively new invention – and this is therefore yet another instance of Hedda displaying her sophistication.

3 As Gosse notes, in this first direct address to Hedda with no one else present, Løvborg uses the familiar "*du*," clearly indicating the closeness of their previous relationship – which Hedda had earlier taken pains to conceal from Thea. However, as in earlier passages where Ibsen plays on the difference between familiar and formal pronouns in the original Norwegian text (e.g. Hedda's insistence that Thea address her with "*du*" in the attempt to win confidences from her by insinuating an intimacy that never existed), this has far more than merely linguistic significance. As Løvborg himself does, one would normally understand Hedda's response to be a rejection of the *substance* of Løvborg's remark – his criticism of her marriage and contempt for her husband – but, as her comment following Tesman's interruption shows, it is the *surface* level of language and convention that concerns her.

a view from the Val d'Ampezzo, Mr. Løvborg. Just look at these peaks! [*Looks affectionately up at* TESMAN.] What's the name of these curious peaks, dear?

TESMAN. Let me see. Oh, those are the Dolomites.

HEDDA. Yes, that's it! – Those are the Dolomites, Mr. Løvborg.

TESMAN. Hedda dear, – I only wanted to ask whether I shouldn't bring you a little punch after all? For yourself at any rate – eh?

HEDDA. Yes, do, please; and perhaps a few biscuits.

TESMAN. No cigarettes?

HEDDA. No.

TESMAN. Very well.

[*He goes into the inner room and out to the right.* BRACK *sits in the inner room, and keeps an eye from time to time on* HEDDA and LØVBORG.[4]

LØVBORG. [*Softly, as before.*] Answer me, Hedda – how could you go and do this?

HEDDA. [*Apparently absorbed in the album.*] If you continue to say *du* to me I won't talk to you.

LØVBORG. May I not say *du* even when we are alone?

HEDDA. No. You may think it; but you mustn't say it.

LØVBORG. Ah, I understand. It is an offence against George Tesman, whom you[5] – love.

HEDDA. [*Glances at him and smiles.*] Love? What an idea!

LØVBORG. You don't love him then!

HEDDA. But I won't hear of any sort of unfaithfulness![6] Remember that.

LØVBORG. Hedda – answer me one thing –

HEDDA. Hush!

[TESMAN *enters with a small tray from the inner room.*

TESMAN. Here you are! Isn't this tempting?[7]

4 This grouping, with one or more characters in the inner room, capable of observing but not hearing a couple in the foreground who are forced to conceal the true nature of their conversation, is repeated in the final act (see **p. 163** below) – a parallelism that illustrates Ibsen's unusually careful structuring of the action in this play.

5 From this point in the dialogue up until his final comment to her, after Hedda has implied that she in fact might previously have welcomed his advances despite her apparent rejection of him at that time, Løvborg uses the formal "*de*," signaling his acceptance of her status as a married woman (compare note 3 above).

6 Given her admitted lack of any love for her husband, which reveals the affection she has just shown to be an empty display, Hedda's assertion of her morality here is perhaps the clearest instance of the way she habitually substitutes appearances for inner truth. It also suggests a repulsion against her own physical sexuality, and possibly that she is incapable of forming an emotional bond with anyone else.

7 Typically, as with the earlier passing reference to poison, Ibsen uses apparently innocuous statements (here by an uninvolved third party) to key attention to the underlying thematic significance of the action that is to come. And indeed this scene is shortly to become Hedda's "temptation" of Løvborg.

[*He puts the tray on the table.*

HEDDA. Why do you bring it yourself?

TESMAN. [*Filling the glasses.*] Because I think it's such fun to wait upon you, Hedda.

HEDDA. But you have poured out two glasses. Mr. Løvborg said he wouldn't have any –

TESMAN. No, but Mrs. Elvsted will soon be here, won't she?

HEDDA. Yes, by-the-bye – Mrs. Elvsted –

TESMAN. Had you forgotten her? Eh?

HEDDA. We were so absorbed in these photographs. [*Shows him a picture.*] Do you remember this little village?

TESMAN. Oh, it's that one just below the Brenner Pass. It was there we passed the night –

HEDDA. – and met that lively party of tourists.

TESMAN. Yes, that was the place. Fancy – if we could only have had you with us, Eilert! Eh?

[*He returns to the inner room and sits beside* BRACK.

LØVBORG. Answer me this one thing, Hedda –

HEDDA. Well?

LØVBORG. Was there no love in your friendship for me either? Not a spark – not a tinge of love in it?

HEDDA. I wonder if there was? To me it seems as though we were two good comrades – two thoroughly intimate friends. [*Smilingly.*] You especially were frankness itself.

LØVBORG. It was you that made me so.

HEDDA. As I look back upon it all, I think there was really something beautiful, something fascinating – something daring – in – in that secret intimacy – that comradeship which no living creature so much as dreamed of.

LØVBORG. Yes, yes, Hedda! Was there not? – When I used to come to your father's in the afternoon – and the General sat over at the window reading his papers – with his back towards us –

HEDDA. And we two on the corner sofa[8] –

LØVBORG. Always with the same illustrated paper before us –

HEDDA. For want of an album yes.

LØVBORG. Yes, Hedda, and when I made my confessions to you – told you about myself, things that at that time no one else knew! There I

8 Past and present merge in this confidential dialogue. And while Ingmar Bergman's staging was unrealistic – particularly for the historical period – in making Løvborg's gestures sexually explicit, while Hedda's reaction was presented as initially acquiescent then a rejection in strongly physical terms (see Frederick and Lise Lone Marker, p. 91), such a reading exposes the erotic subtext that indeed underlies the scene, and also brings out the voyeuristic nature of Brack's watching gaze.

would sit and tell you of my escapades[9] – my days and nights of devilment. Oh, Hedda – what was the power in you that forced me to confess these things?

HEDDA. Do you think it was any power in me?

LØVBORG. How else can I explain it? And all those – those roundabout questions you used to put to me –

HEDDA. Which you understood so particularly well –

LØVBORG. How could you sit and question me like that? Question me quite frankly –

HEDDA. In roundabout terms, please observe.

LØVBORG. Yes, but frankly nevertheless. Cross-question me about – all that sort of thing?[10]

HEDDA. And how could you answer, Mr. Løvborg?

LØVBORG. Yes, that is just what I can't understand – in looking back upon it. But tell me now, Hedda – was there not love at the bottom of our friendship? On your side, did you not feel as though you might purge my stains away – if I made you my confessor? Was it not so?

HEDDA. No, not quite.

LØVBORG. What was your motive, then?

HEDDA. Do you think it quite incomprehensible that a young girl – when it can be done – without any one knowing –

LØVBORG. Well?

HEDDA. – should be glad to have a peep, now and then, into a world[11] which –

LØVBORG. Which – ?

HEDDA. – which she is forbidden to know anything about?

LØVBORG. So that was it?

HEDDA. Partly. Partly – I almost think.

9 Although Løvborg's speech sounds superficially like a down-market and domesticized version of Othello's tales to Desdemona "of dangers he had passed," the implications here for Hedda are more far-reaching. They relate not only to her desire for "power," but also to her obvious dissatisfaction with her life, suggesting that the "boredom" to which she so frequently refers long pre-dates her marriage.

10 Clearly the "nights of devilment" that Løvborg has referred to are his visits to Madame Diana's establishment, and his sexual exploits with prostitutes, which makes Hedda's curiosity prurient – and led to nineteenth-century reviewers condemning her (along with Thea) as "harlots at heart" (see William Archer, p. 63).

11 As a nineteenth-century lady subject to moral expectation and social requirements that controlled every aspect of her behavior, Hedda would not have been even allowed outside her father's house except with a respectable female chaperone, except perhaps for riding (hence the importance placed on her horse: both Aunt Julia's memory of her in a riding-dress, and her insistence in the marital agreement on having her own horse – now ruled out by their financial circumstances); and the same is true for her now. As Hedda has reported, she had to stay alone in their lodgings while Tesman was working in libraries; and it is no coincidence that she never leaves her new home during the play. To do so without her husband or his aunt, who are precisely the people she wants to escape, would sacrifice her reputation – putting her in a similar position to Thea – since only servants or women past the age of childbearing (like Aunt Julia) were allowed to come and go freely by themselves. So living a surrogate existence through others is Hedda's only opportunity to experience all the aspects of life "forbidden" to women of her class and time.

LØVBORG. Comradeship in the thirst for life. But why should not that, at any rate, have continued?

HEDDA. The fault was yours.

LØVBORG. It was you that broke with me.

HEDDA. Yes, when our friendship threatened to develop into something more serious. Shame upon you, Eilert Løvborg! How could you think of wronging your – your frank comrade?

LØVBORG. [*Clenching his hands.*] Oh, why did you not carry out your threat? Why did you not shoot[12] me down?

HEDDA. Because I have such a dread of scandal.

LØVBORG. Yes, Hedda, you are a coward at heart.

HEDDA. A terrible coward. [*Changing her tone.*] But it was a lucky thing for you. And now you have found ample consolation at the Elvsteds'.

LØVBORG. I know what Thea has confided to you.

HEDDA. And perhaps you have confided to her something about us?

LØVBORG. Not a word. She is too stupid to understand anything of that sort.

HEDDA. Stupid?

LØVBORG. She is stupid about matters of that sort.

HEDDA. And I am cowardly. [*Bends over towards him, without looking him in the face, and says more softly:*] But now I will confide something to you.

LØVBORG. [*Eagerly.*] Well?

HEDDA. The fact that I dared not shoot you down –

LØVBORG. Yes!

HEDDA. – that was not my most arrant cowardice[13] – that evening.

LØVBORG. [*Looks at her a moment, understands, and whispers passionately.*] Oh, Hedda! Hedda Gabler! Now I begin to see a hidden reason beneath our comradeship! You[14] and I – ! After all, then, it was your craving for life[15] –

12 Compare Thea's earlier retelling of Løvborg's story about a woman who drove him away by threatening him with a pistol, whom Thea has mistakenly identified with the prostitute Diana (see **p. 133** above).

13 Shaw's analysis of Hedda's moral standards – her reaction against her earlier conformism to conventional behavior that leads to a reversal of standards of right and wrong – is extremely perceptive (see **pp. 56–7**).

14 As Gosse notes, in this speech Løvborg once more says "*du*," with this reversion to the intimate pronoun in the original Norwegian betraying the reawakening of his passion for her, or perhaps his renewed hopes of seducing her. Hedda by contrast demonstrates her continued clinging to conventionality by addressing him throughout as "*de*" (the impersonal, plural pronoun).

15 The "craving for life" or for "the joy of life" is a key theme for Ibsen. As Muriel Bradbrook suggests, Hedda's destructive impulse is the inverse of this "craving for life," which lies behind all Hedda's actions (see **p. 78**). However, given the kind of sentiments expressed by Hedda throughout the play, one has to take seriously the insight of Janet Suzman. One of the few English actresses to play Hedda who was able to read the text in the original Norwegian, she points out that much of Hedda's vocabulary is "provincial and mundane" as a tangible demonstration that she has failed to attain the ideal existence she identifies with Løvborg's escapades (see Suzman, **p. 99**).

HEDDA. [*Softly, with a sharp glance.*] Take care! Believe nothing of the sort!

[*Twilight has begun to fall. The hall door is opened from without by* BERTA.

HEDDA. [*Closes the album with a bang and calls smilingly:*] Ah, at last! My darling Thea, – come along!

[MRS. ELVSTED *enters from the hall. She is in evening dress. The door is closed behind her.*

HEDDA. [*On the sofa, stretches out her arms towards her.*] My sweet Thea – you can't think how I have been longing for you!

[MRS. ELVSTED, *in passing, exchanges slight salutations with the gentlemen in the inner room, then goes up to the table and gives* HEDDA *her hand.* EILERT LØVBORG *has risen. He and* MRS. ELVSTED *greet each other with a silent nod.*

MRS. ELVSTED. Ought I to go in and talk to your husband for a moment?

HEDDA. Oh, not at all. Leave those two alone. They will soon be going.

MRS. ELVSTED. Are they going out?

HEDDA. Yes, to a supper-party.

MRS. ELVSTED. [*Quickly, to* LØVBORG.] Not you?

LØVBORG. No.

HEDDA. Mr. Løvborg remains with us.

MRS. ELVSTED. [*Takes a chair and is about to seat herself at his side.*] Oh, how nice it is here!

HEDDA. No, thank you, my little Thea! Not there! You'll be good enough to come over here to me. I will sit between you.[16]

MRS. ELVSTED. Yes, just as you please.

[*She goes round the table and seats herself on the sofa on* HEDDA'S *right.* LØVBORG *re-seats himself on his chair.*

LØVBORG. [*After a short pause, to* HEDDA.] Is not she lovely to look at?

HEDDA. [*Lightly stroking her hair.*] Only to look at?

LØVBORG. Yes. For we two – she and I – we are two real comrades. We have absolute faith in each other; so we can sit and talk with perfect frankness –

HEDDA. Not round about, Mr. Løvborg?

LØVBORG. Well –

16 As elsewhere in the play, Ibsen uses the physical placement of the characters to express their relationships, providing a visual image of the motives and psychological state.

MRS. ELVSTED. [*Softly clinging close to* HEDDA.] Oh, how happy I am, Hedda! For, only think, he says I have inspired[17] him too.

HEDDA. [*Looks at her with a smile.*] Ah! Does he say that, dear?

LØVBORG. And then she is so brave, Mrs. Tesman!

MRS. ELVSTED. Good heavens – am I brave?

LØVBORG. Exceedingly – where your comrade is concerned.

HEDDA. Ah yes – courage! If one only had that![18]

LØVBORG. What then? What do you mean?

HEDDA. Then life would perhaps be liveable – after all. [*With a sudden change of tone.*] But now, my dearest Thea, you really must have a glass of cold punch.

MRS. ELVSTED. No, thanks – I never take anything of that kind.

HEDDA. Well then, you, Mr. Løvborg.

LØVBORG. Nor I, thank you.

MRS. ELVSTED. No, he doesn't either.

HEDDA. [*Looks fixedly at him.*] But if I say you shall?

LØVBORG. It would be no use.

HEDDA. [*Laughing.*] Then I, poor creature, have no sort of power over you?[19]

LØVBORG. Not in that respect.

HEDDA. But seriously, I think you ought to – for your own sake.

MRS. ELVSTED. Why, Hedda – !

LØVBORG. How so?

HEDDA. Or rather on account of other people.[20]

LØVBORG. Indeed?

HEDDA. Otherwise people might be apt to suspect that – in your heart of hearts – you did not feel quite secure – quite confident in yourself.

MRS. ELVSTED. [*Softly.*] Oh please, Hedda – !

LØVBORG. People may suspect what they like – for the present.

MRS. ELVSTED. [*Joyfully.*] Yes, let them!

HEDDA. I saw it plainly in Judge Brack's face a moment ago.

---

17 The implication that the ideas in Løvborg's new manuscript come from Thea is not lost on Hedda, leading her to identify it with their "child" and motivating her to burn it.

18 As in their earlier dialogue, the capacity to go against society's moral standards versus the appearance of independence is explored through the contrast between Hedda and Thea, reversing audience expectations, with the seemingly conventional Thea's ability to act outside the frame being used by Ibsen as a standard for evaluating Hedda (see editor's headnote to Act 1 above, **p. 127**).

19 The origin of this "test" may well have a real-life source in an episode, recounted by William Archer, which occurred around the time Ibsen was writing the play (see **p. 37**). But this episode has always been seen as the key to Hedda's personality and one of the defining moments in the way an audience responds to her – as Ibsen underlined in one of his notes while composing the play, "The demonic thing about Hedda is that she wants to exert an influence over another person" (see **p. 102**).

20 Characteristically, after appealing unsuccessfully to the love that Løvborg has implicitly shown for her, Hedda's next "temptation" is based on her own primary motivation: the moral "cowardice" that makes it impossible for her to contemplate going against social convention – not something Løvborg would be affected by, going on his previous bohemianism; but in remaining steadfast in the face of purported social contempt he in fact suggests that he has not changed. Despite his newly respectable clothing and sobriety, he is just as open to temptation as in his earlier phase.

LØVBORG. What did you see?

HEDDA. His contemptuous smile, when you dared not go with them into the inner room.

LØVBORG. Dared not? Of course I preferred to stop here and talk to you.

MRS. ELVSTED. What could be more natural, Hedda?

HEDDA. But the Judge could not guess that. And I saw, too, the way he smiled and glanced at Tesman when you dared not accept his invitation to this wretched little supper-party of his.

LØVBORG. Dared not! Do you say I dared not?

HEDDA. *I* don't say so. But that was how Judge Brack understood it.

LØVBORG. Well, let him.

HEDDA. Then you are not going with them?

LØVBORG. I will stay here with you and Thea.

MRS. ELVSTED. Yes, Hedda – how can you doubt that?

HEDDA. [*Smiles and nods approvingly to* LØVBORG.] Firm as a rock! Faithful to your principles,[21] now and for ever! Ah, that is how a man should be! [*Turns to* MRS. ELVSTED *and caresses her*.] Well now, what did I tell you, when you came to us this morning in such a state of distraction –

LØVBORG. [*Surprised.*] Distraction!

MRS. ELVSTED. [*Terrified.*] Hedda – oh Hedda – !

HEDDA. You can see for yourself! You haven't the slightest reason to be in such mortal terror – [*Interrupting herself.*] There! Now we can all three enjoy ourselves!

LØVBORG. [*Who has given a start.*] Ah – what is all this, Mrs. Tesman?

MRS. ELVSTED. Oh my God, Hedda! What are you saying? What are you doing?

HEDDA. Don't get excited! That horrid Judge Brack is sitting watching you.

LØVBORG. So she was in mortal terror! On my account!

MRS. ELVSTED. [*Softly and piteously.*] Oh, Hedda – now you have ruined everything!

LØVBORG. [*Looks fixedly at her for a moment. His face is distorted.*] So that was my comrade's frank confidence in me?[22]

21 Hedda's testing of Løvborg throughout has clearly been designed to undermine his vow of abstinence; and despite her approving nod – which is shown to be false by her blatantly hypocritical caress of Thea – this praise is of course highly ambiguous, reminding Løvborg in fact of his previous principles of self-realization and "thirst for life" that they had shared and have just been discussing, which are the opposite of the conventional and self-denying principles he has adopted under Thea's guidance.

22 Ibsen may well have biblical symbolism in mind, having Løvborg able to withstand two temptations, only to fall to the third. As some commentators have pointed out, this temptation of Løvborg operates on a double level: on the Naturalistic surface Hedda's is malicious and destructive; but in terms of the Apollo/Dionysus imagery, where Thea and Tesman stand for the Apollonian values of rational self-control epitomized by Victorian society, Hedda might be seen as right to be putting Løvborg in touch with the anarchic Dionysian creativity of his inner nature (see Elenore Lester, p. 94).

MRS. ELVSTED. [*Imploringly.*] Oh, my dearest friend – only let me tell you –

LØVBORG. [*Takes one of the glasses of punch, raises it to his lips, and says in a low, husky voice.*] Your health, Thea!

[*He empties the glass, puts it down, and takes the second.*

MRS. ELVSTED. [*Softly.*] Oh, Hedda, Hedda – how could you do this?

HEDDA. *I* do it? *I*? Are you crazy?

LØVBORG. Here's to your health too, Mrs. Tesman. Thanks for the truth. Hurrah for the truth!

[*He empties the glass and is about to re-fill it.*

HEDDA. [*Lays her hand on his arm.*] Come, come – no more for the present. Remember you are going out to supper.

From Act 3: Hedda Versus Tesman

One of the key phrases of the play is highlighted in this extract. George Steiner points out that Hedda's proposal to crown Løvborg with vine leaves is a "symbolic act which argues a specific vision of life," while Nigel Dennis identifies the image as specifically feminine (see **pp. 85** and **83**). It is derived from traditional Classical images of Dionysus and Bacchic revelry, with which Ibsen could confidently assume his audience were familiar, representing visionary experience and the liberation of the subconscious rather than ordinary alcoholic intoxication. However, here, where the person to be crowned with vine leaves has in fact a history of alcoholism, the image becomes highly ambiguous – and indeed the expression was rapidly adopted by the English public in the 1890s as an ironic way of referring to physical drunkenness. Elizabeth Robins, the first English actress to perform the role, insisted that Hedda is referring solely to inspired vision. Yet the way she forces Løvborg to break his pledge of sobriety in Act 2 also indicates an awareness of the Dionysian ritual where wine was the tool to unlock the spirit, which perhaps adds another layer of motivation that might cause us to retrospectively re-evaluate her malicious manipulation of Løvborg into drinking (see **p. 61**).

The overtly poetic, even emblematic, nature of the phrase contrasts very obviously with the extreme flatness and broken syntax of the prose spoken throughout the rest of the play, and therefore draws attention as much to its form as to its meaning. This has led a critic like Eric Bentley (see **p. 88**), who sees the strength of Ibsen's style as being in the construction of a subliminal and non-verbal poetry from the most ordinary phrases, to propose that Ibsen has inserted such a rhetorical image precisely to undermine this sort of idealism. The anti-poetic language surrounding Hedda's vine leaves thus exposes her vision as illusory, indeed self-deceptive and dangerously idealistic, simply because the phrase is revealed as linguistically incongruous and artificial – which would correspond exactly with Shaw's point (see **p. 56**) about the problematic nature of idealism as Ibsen depicts it.

In terms of *fin-de-siècle* imagery, it is no accident that "vine leaves" are associated with Hedda: an association leading to her being identified with the biblical Salome – Eva le Gallienne remarks that "she must have loved [. . .] Beardsley's illustrations for [Oscar Wilde's play] *Salome*" – whose figure had already become an icon of dangerous female sexuality in the late Romantic and Symbolist art of the last decades of the nineteenth century, and identifies Hedda with the "decadent" poetry of Baudelaire, whose *Fleurs du Mal* had become a byword for perversion (see **p. 74**). Another aspect of decadence, the neurotic fastidiousness, which Archer singled out as the cause of Hedda's tragedy (**p. 66**) and led to Gosse labeling her the epitome of "*fin de siècle* woman," is also indicated in this extract by Hedda's refusal to visit Tesman's dying aunt.

TESMAN. [*Sitting on a footstool near the stove.*] Oh Hedda, you can't conceive what a book that is going to be! I believe it is one of the most remarkable things that have ever been written.[1] Fancy that!

HEDDA. Yes yes; I don't care about that –

TESMAN. I must make a confession to you, Hedda. When he had finished reading – a horrid feeling came over me.

HEDDA. A horrid feeling?

TESMAN. I felt jealous of Eilert for having had it in him to write such a book. Only think, Hedda!

HEDDA. Yes, yes, I am thinking![2]

TESMAN. And then how pitiful to think that he – with all his gifts – should be irreclaimable, after all.

HEDDA. I suppose you mean that he has more courage than the rest?

TESMAN. No, not at all – I mean that he is incapable of taking his pleasures in moderation.

HEDDA. And what came of it all – in the end?

1 What is clear here is that Tesman himself would have been incapable of even conceiving, let alone writing such a work. However, we have only Tesman's word that it is so "remarkable"; and Tesman's intellect has hardly been shown as outstanding. This is typical of Ibsen's objectivity, which precluded him from inserting his own opinions (see **p. 29**). Whether this extraordinarily superlative praise is a true evaluation of Løvborg's book, or not – and in at least one interpretation of the play it is discredited (see **p. 91**) – such potential places additional weight on its destruction at the end of this Act, since Hedda has no reason to disbelieve her husband's estimate.

2 A repeated refrain of Hedda's in response to Tesman's automatism (see, for instance, **p. 165** below). While the verbal formula of "Only think, Hedda! /[. . .] I am thinking!" is a normal way of expressing contempt, such verbal parallelism is an example of the subtle patterning beneath the play's Naturalistic surface. It also serves as a measure of the developing situation, later signaling her increasing desperation as she is forced to think in ever more serious terms about the ultimate human concern: self-preservation.

TESMAN. Well, to tell the truth, I think it might best be described as an orgy, Hedda.

HEDDA. Had he vine-leaves in his hair?[3]

TESMAN. Vine-leaves? No, I saw nothing of the sort.[4] But he made a long, rambling speech in honour of the woman who had inspired him in his work – that was the phrase he used.

HEDDA. Did he name her?

TESMAN. No, he didn't; but I can't help thinking he meant Mrs. Elvsted. You may be sure he did.

HEDDA. Well – where did you part from him?

TESMAN. On the way to town. We broke up – the last of us at any rate – all together; and Brack came with us to get a breath of fresh air. And then, you see, we agreed to take Eilert home; for he had had far more than was good for him.

HEDDA. I daresay.

TESMAN. But now comes the strange part of it, Hedda; or, I should rather say, the melancholy part of it. I declare I am almost ashamed – on Eilert's account – to tell you –

HEDDA. Oh, go on – !

TESMAN. Well, as we were getting near town, you see, I happened to drop a little behind the others. Only for a minute or two – fancy that![5]

HEDDA. Yes yes yes, but – ?

TESMAN. And then, as I hurried after them – what do you think I found by the wayside? Eh?

HEDDA. Oh, how should I know!

TESMAN. You mustn't speak of it to a soul, Hedda! Do you hear! Promise me, for Eilert's sake. [*Draws a parcel, wrapped in paper, from his coat pocket.*] Fancy, dear – I found this.

HEDDA. Is not that the parcel he had with him yesterday?

TESMAN. Yes, it is the whole of his precious, irreplaceable manuscript! And he had gone and lost it,[6] and knew nothing about it. Only fancy, Hedda! So deplorably –

3 This phrase, which Hedda uses repeatedly when speaking of Løvborg, becomes one of the major thematic motifs associated with her character. As William Archer notes (see **p. 36**), it is a late addition to the text, which does not occur in any of the versions before the final script – and therefore has particular significance as an explanatory gloss on her motives and the vision that animates her.

4 Even the simplest statement in Ibsen's dialogue is multi-layered, making this – as various critics have remarked – one of his most densely textured plays (see, for instance, Archer's comment that "Ibsen's brain never worked at higher pressure," **p. 66**, or John Northam's evaluation that "the tension was highest [. . .] in *Hedda Gabler*," **p. 87**). Thus such a literal-minded response not only demonstrates Tesman's complete lack of imagination, as well as insensitivity to his wife's concerns. It is also factual and accurate, underlining that, rather than being an ideal Løvborg just fails to live up to (as she is about to discover), Hedda's vision is intrinsically illusory.

5 See the earlier comment on Tesman's verbal "tics" in footnote 2 on **p. 151** above.

6 Although almost everything else in Ibsen's orginal conception changed as his ideas developed, the lost manuscript was retained, though shifted from Act 2 to here in Act 3. As such it has to be seen as the key element in the play: the incident that, corresponding to Archer's report on Ibsen's method of composition, crystallized the "*idea*" upon which the whole work is based (see **p. 36**).

HEDDA. But why did you not give him back the parcel at once?

TESMAN. I didn't dare to – in the state he was then in –

HEDDA. Did you not tell any of the others that you had found it?

TESMAN. Oh, far from it! You can surely understand that, for Eilert's sake, I wouldn't do that.

HEDDA. So no one knows that Eilert Løvborg's manuscript is in your possession?

TESMAN. No. And no one must know it.

HEDDA. Then what did you say to him afterwards?

TESMAN. I didn't talk to him again at all; for when we got in among the streets, he and two or three of the others gave us the slip and disappeared.[7] Fancy that!

HEDDA. Indeed! They must have taken him home then.

TESMAN. Yes, so it would appear. And Brack, too, left us.

HEDDA. And what have you been doing with yourself since?

TESMAN. Well, I and some of the others went home with one of the party, a jolly fellow, and took our morning coffee with him; or perhaps I should rather call it our night coffee – eh? But now, when I have rested a little, and given Eilert, poor fellow, time to have his sleep out, I must take this back to him.

HEDDA. [*Holds out her hand for the packet.*] No – don't give it to him! Not in such a hurry, I mean. Let me read it first.

TESMAN. No, my dearest Hedda, I mustn't, I really mustn't.

HEDDA. You must not?

TESMAN. No – for you can imagine what a state of despair he will be in when he wakens and misses the manuscript.[8] He has no copy of it, you must know! He told me so.

HEDDA. [*Looking searchingly at him.*] Can such a thing not be reproduced? Written over again?

TESMAN. No, I don't think that would be possible. For the inspiration, you see –

7 Passing references indicate that Løvborg's destination (the brothel run by Madame Diana) has been deliberately organized by Brack. Recounting the evening's events, Tesman has remarked that he and Løvborg were left alone at the beginning since "Brack had all sorts of arrangements to make"; and – although Tesman himself (typically) makes nothing of it – Brack later admits to having "had special reasons for keeping track of my guests – or rather of some of my guests – last night." If he is responsible for setting Løvborg up, then the fact that it is he who subsequently insists on the public banning of Løvborg has to be seen as more sinister than moral outrage.

8 In contrast to Ibsen's original intentions – when it was to be Tesman who decided to keep the manuscript: first because of a "passing remark" of Hedda's intended to "test" his morality, then because she makes him jealous of Løvborg (see **p. 36**) – in the final text his only concern is to return it without anyone being aware that it has been lost, in order not to expose Løvborg's drunkenness. This reversal offers a good illustration of Ibsen's dramaturgy and the way he developed the play. By preserving Tesman's naïve (and bumbling) self-righteousness, the change both heightens the dramatic tension through intensifying Tesman's eventual horror when he discovers Hedda's destruction of the manuscript and emphasizes Hedda's sole responsibility for everything that stems from its retention and concealment.

HEDDA. Yes, yes – I suppose it depends on that – [*Lightly.*] But, by-the-bye – here is a letter for you.[9]

TESMAN. Fancy –!

HEDDA. [*Handing it to him.*] It came early this morning.

TESMAN. It's from Aunt Julia! What can it be? [*He lays the packet on the other footstool, opens the letter, runs his eye through it, and jumps up.*] Oh, Hedda – she says that poor Aunt Rina is dying!

HEDDA. Well, we were prepared for that.

TESMAN. And that if I want to see her again, I must make haste. I'll run in to them at once.

HEDDA. [*Suppressing a smile.*] Will you run?

TESMAN. Oh, my dearest Hedda – if you could only make up your mind to come with me! Just think!

HEDDA. [*Rises and says wearily, repelling the idea.*] No, no, don't ask me. I will not look upon sickness and death. I loathe all sorts of ugliness.[10]

TESMAN. Well, well, then – ! [*Bustling around.*] My hat – ? My overcoat – ? Oh, in the hall – . I do hope I mayn't come too late, Hedda! Eh?

HEDDA. Oh, if you run –

[BERTA *appears at the hall door.*

BERTA. Judge Brack is at the door, and wishes to know if he may come in.

TESMAN. At this time! No, I can't possibly see him.

HEDDA. But I can. [*To* BERTA.] Ask Judge Brack to come in.

[BERTA *goes out.*

HEDDA. [*Quickly, whispering.*] The parcel, Tesman!

[*She snatches it up from the stool.*

TESMAN. Yes, give it to me!

HEDDA. No, no, I will keep it till you come back.

[*She goes to the writing-table and places it in the bookcase.* TESMAN *stands in a flurry of haste, and cannot get his gloves on.*

9 The letter is the sort of stock device – another letter having been used already in *A Doll's House* for even more pivotal effect – that led H. L. Mencken to label Ibsen a "journeyman dramatist," and which others, such as Nigel Dennis, have criticized as artificial (see **pp. 75** and **83**).

10 As one of the clearest instances of Hedda's egoism and rejection of emotional involvement, this refusal to face human suffering goes along with her denial of her own pregnancy, and her one-time rejection of Løvborg's sexual advances. The sense that she is repulsed by all physical aspects of life (also expressed in her idealistic vision of Løvborg with "vine leaves in his hair") causes the extreme nature of the actions she takes after learning of his actual drunkenness and demeaning sexual indulgence, and later when she discovers the "mess" he has made of his own death.

From Act 3: Burning the Book

This episode represents the moral climax of the play, with its graphic but purely symbolic violence. It is this book-burning that most clearly identifies Hedda as evil. Being explicitly presented as infanticide, it points forward to a crucial aspect of her suicide at the end: that she also kills her unborn child (something that remains unmentioned by the characters). At the same time, commentators from Bernard Shaw to George Steiner have identified idealism to be the ultimate sin in Ibsen's plays – a "cancer" of self-deception that makes any idealist a "villain" (see **pp. 85** and **56**) – and while Hedda now recognizes that her image of vine leaves is illusory, she switches it for the far more damaging ideal of a "beautiful" death.

The way she urges Løvborg to kill himself is of course an anticipation of her own suicide; and while his motive is never explicitly stated, the reasons are clearly given in Ibsen's notes. After his complete debasement – drunkenness, whoring, physical rioting, police arrest; all of which have been made only too public by his appearance in court – Løvborg is indeed a "lost soul." He has not only sacrificed any reputation of being a "man of culture" that he needs if his book is to be taken seriously, but also invalidated the "ethics of the future" that his book proposes (see **pp. 33** and **35**). This is the sense in which he announces that he has "utterly destroyed" his manuscript. And it is Hedda's perception of the truth of this that partly motivates her reinforcement of Løvborg's desire to "make an end," and perhaps also her burning of the manuscript, which is now valueless because of his actions. Hedda is associated with fire throughout, so much so that one critic has labeled her "the bomb in the living room" (see **p. 94**). And the hellish suggestion of the flames is perhaps given an additional weight for more modern spectators, than it had even for the audiences of Ibsen's day, prefiguring as it does the burning of books by the Nazis almost half a century after the play was written as well as the more recent destruction of irreplaceable art by the Taliban. Even so it is still possible to argue that Hedda is justified in burning the book, as Wilson Knight does in pointing out that the "greatness" she desires for Løvborg was very different from an academic work (maybe not even his own), which would detract from the act she has sent him out to perform (see **p. 80**). At the same time, however extreme or melodramatic it may seem, as Archer reported, there was a real-life equivalent to Hedda's action in the burning of a symphonic score by the jealous wife of a Norwegian composer (see **p. 36**).

LØVBORG. I have torn my own life to pieces. So why should I not tear my life-work too – ?

MRS. ELVSTED. And you did this last night?

LØVBORG. Yes, I tell you! Tore it into a thousand pieces – and scattered them on the fiord – far out. There, there is cool sea-water at any rate – let them drift upon it – drift with the current and the wind. And then presently they will sink – deeper and deeper – as I shall, Thea.

MRS. ELVSTED. Do you know, Løvborg, that what you have done with the book – I shall think of it to my dying day as though you had killed a little child.

LØVBORG. Yes, you are right. It is a sort of child-murder.[1]

MRS. ELVSTED. How could you, then – ! Did not the child belong to me too?

HEDDA. [*Almost inaudibly.*] Ah, the child –

MRS. ELVSTED. [*Breathing heavily.*] It is all over then. Well, well, now I will go, Hedda.

HEDDA. But you are not going away from town?

MRS. ELVSTED. Oh, I don't know what I shall do. I see nothing but darkness before me.

[*She goes out by the hall door.*

HEDDA. [*Stands waiting for a moment.*] So you are not going to see her home, Mr. Løvborg?

LØVBORG. I? Through the streets? Would you have people see her walking with me?[2]

HEDDA. Of course I don't know what else may have happened last night. But is it so utterly irretrievable?

LØVBORG. It will not end with last night – I know that perfectly well. And the thing is that now I have no taste for that sort of life either. I won't begin it anew. She has broken my courage and my power of braving life out.

HEDDA. [*Looking straight before her.*] So that pretty little fool has had her fingers in a man's destiny.[3] [*Looks at him.*] But all the same, how could you treat her so heartlessly.

1 This association between the book and a child, immediately picked up by Hedda and repeated several times during her conversation with Løvborg after Thea's exit, carries through to Hedda's burning of the manuscript at the very end of the Act.

2 Given Løvborg's history of flouting moral norms, his sudden acceptance of social censure may seem surprising. It could either be argued that this demonstrates the rigidity and inescapability of conventions in this society (helping to justify Hedda's "cowardice," as well as reinforcing the weight of Brack's blackmail, and underlining the independence, or desperation of Thea in abandoning her husband and step-children for a lover), or alternatively that it is evidence of hypocritical double standards (the crime being publicly *seen* together, just as Brack and Løvborg himself perceive nothing wrong in his visiting a brothel: it is only being found out through arrest that results in ostracization).

3 Ibsen's note that "The demonic thing about Hedda is that she wants to exert an influence over another person" – for Ibsen a very rare moral judgment on a character – has been discussed with reference to Act 2 (see **pp. 140** and **148** above). However, the concept is made even stronger here by the word "destiny" with its ominous connotations of final fate.

At the same time, as her following comments indicate, this manipulativeness is a reflection on Hedda's actual powerlessness, and her inability to achieve independent self-fulfillment. Jealous already of her rival for Løvborg, this demonstration that Thea has succeeded at precisely what Hedda desired for herself is perhaps the crucial factor motivating her to push Løvborg into suicide: death being the ultimate form of control over another person.

LØVBORG. Oh, don't say that it was heartless!

HEDDA. To go and destroy what has filled her whole soul for months and years! You do not call that heartless!

LØVBORG. To you I *can* tell the truth, Hedda.

HEDDA. The truth?

LØVBORG. First promise me – give me your word – that what I now confide to you Thea shall never know.

HEDDA. I give you my word.

LØVBORG. Good. Then let me tell you that what I said just now was untrue.

HEDDA. About the manuscript?

LØVBORG. Yes. I have not torn it to pieces – nor thrown it into the fiord.

HEDDA. No, no – . But – where is it then?

LØVBORG. I have destroyed it none the less – utterly destroyed it, Hedda!

HEDDA. I don't understand.

LØVBORG. Thea said that what I had done seemed to her like a child-murder.

HEDDA. Yes, so she said.

LØVBORG. But to kill his child – that is not the worst thing a father can do to it.

HEDDA. Not the worst?

LØVBORG. No. I wanted to spare Thea from hearing the worst.

HEDDA. Then what is the worst?

LØVBORG. Suppose now, Hedda, that a man – in the small hours of the morning – came home to his child's mother after a night of riot and debauchery,[4] and said: "Listen – I have been here and there – in this place and in that. And I have taken our child with me – to this place and to that. And I have lost the child – utterly lost it. The devil knows into what hands it may have fallen – who may have had their clutches on it."

HEDDA. Well – but when all is said and done, you know – this was only a book –

LØVBORG. Thea's pure soul was in that book.[5]

HEDDA. Yes, so I understand.

4 According to William Archer, a real-life model existed for the episode recounted here: a young Danish writer who told Ibsen about losing the manuscript of a book he had just finished during the course of a night of debauchery – and who, once the play appeared, even adopted the pseudonym of "Eilert Løvborg" (see **pp. 36–7**)!

5 In Blanche Yurka's production this moment was used to both humanize Hedda and underline her motivation for what follows. Yurka's actions suggested that Hedda had been about to return the book, until Løvborg identified it with Thea (see **p. 71**). However, by doing so, Yurka ignored the point that restitution would be useless now that Løvborg's actions have discredited the ideas in the book, thus reducing Hedda's motive simply to jealousy – in other words, Yurka's attempt to suggest generosity led to a more purely negative reading of Hedda than Ibsen had intended.

LØVBORG. And you can understand, too, that for her and me together no future is possible.

HEDDA. What path do you mean to take then?

LØVBORG. None. I will only try to make an end of it all – the sooner the better.

HEDDA. [*A step nearer him.*] Eilert Løvborg – listen to me. – Will you not try to – to do it beautifully?

LØVBORG. Beautifully? [*Smiling.*] With vine-leaves in my hair, as you used to dream in the old days – ?

HEDDA. No, no. I have lost my faith in the, the vine-leaves. But beautifully nevertheless! For once in a way! – Good-bye! You must go now – and do not come here any more.

LØVBORG. Good-bye, Mrs. Tesman. And give George Tesman my love.

[*He is on the point of going.*

HEDDA. No, wait! I must give you a memento[6] to take with you.

[*She goes to the writing-table and opens the drawer and the pistol-case; then returns to* LØVBORG *with one of the pistols.*

LØVBORG. [*Looks at her.*] This? Is this the memento?

HEDDA. [*Nodding slowly.*] Do you recognise it? It was aimed at you once.

LØVBORG. You should have used it then.

HEDDA. Take it – and do you use it now.

LØVBORG. [*Puts the pistol in his breast pocket.*] Thanks!

HEDDA. And beautifully, Eilert Løvborg. Promise me that!

LØVBORG. Good-bye, Hedda Gabler.

[*He goes out by the hall door.*

[HEDDA *listens for a moment at the door. Then she goes up to the writing-table, takes out the packet of manuscript, peeps under the cover, draws a few of the sheets half out, and looks at them.*[7] *Next she goes over and seats herself in the*

6 Having lost faith in "vine leaves," Hedda's idealism is given tangible shape in the pistol, which, as Muriel Bradbrook has observed, is "consciously theatrical," not only for an audience but also to Hedda herself (see **p. 77**).

7 As William Archer notes, Ibsen's original stage direction in one of the final drafts for the play states that she "opens the packet, sorts out the white leaves from the blue, puts the white back in the cover again, and keeps the blue in her lap," then just burns the blue. Archer puts this division into different colored pages down to "some earlier phase" in the play's development that has been omitted (see **p. 36**). However, when Løvborg first mentions his manuscript he stresses that it "falls into two parts" – and it would be logical to assume that the white leaves contain his comments on the "civilising forces of the future" (in other words the analysis of present-day society) while the blue contain his forecast of "the probable line of development" (his vision of the future itself).

The earlier version stresses Hedda's self-control leading up to this climactic moment of violence, and possibly her rejection of a future that her actions (though she may not yet fully grasp this) have made impossible for her. The change brings out the completeness of her destructive impulse.

arm-chair beside the stove, with the packet in her lap. Presently she opens the stove door, and then the packet.

HEDDA. [*Throws one of the quires into the fire and whispers to herself.*] Now I am burning your child, Thea! – Burning it, curly-locks! [*Throwing one or two more quires into the stove.*] Your child and Eilert Løvborg's. [*Throws the rest in.*] I am burning – I am burning your child.[8]

From Act 4: Entrapment and Liberation

There is no concept of "tragic fate" underlying this play: while it is certainly the case that the restrictions and attitudes of society wall her in claustrophobically and threaten her very personality, it is Hedda herself who creates the circumstances that lead to her destruction. At the same time the tone of this final sequence is hardly "tragic" in a conventional sense, as one of the pivotal actions in this excerpt shows: the alliance between Thea and Tesman to reconstitute Løvborg's book.

This whole situation – Thea's immediate "discovery" of the notes, the avidity with which Tesman seizes on them, and the extreme rapidity of their getting together so immediately after the news of Løvborg's death (which undermines the intense concern she has shown for him, since one would have expected at least some signs of mourning!) – exemplifies the unsettlingly rapid switch between tragic moments and farce in the play (see **p. 98**). Looking at the scene on a purely realistic level, William Archer and other early commentators criticized it as improbable, even unnatural; however, more recently it has come to be seen as "acidly comic" (see Muriel Bradbrook, **p. 79**). The quickness with which she abandons her grief for Løvborg as well as her, in these circumstances, unseemly eagerness are what led some of the early reviewers to classify her together with Hedda as "harlots at heart" (see **p. 63**). The same contradictory merging of deeply serious issues and broad farcical elements becomes increasingly marked from this point right up to the ending, where the incongruity and sheer disproportion of the response to Hedda's violent death makes the closing lines brutally comic – and together with the language, it is this highly

8 This act is designed to crystallize our view of Hedda. It is a prime example of the quality James singled out, where the psychology and the action are inextricably interfused (see **p. 64**). But as Janet Suzman showed, the exact way this action is performed creates a quite specific interpretation of Hedda's state of mind, which can vary significantly, depending on the presentation (see **p. 100**).

Glenda Jackson noted that it can hardly be construed as an actual crime, particularly since Hedda has to be aware that what she burns is indeed only papers, having earlier pointed out to Løvborg the "absurdity" of equating a book with a baby. As Blanche Yurka says, structurally the scene is only a "springboard" to the final tragedy. Yet it inevitably associates Hedda with the demonic; and Yurka, who staged this action in such a way as to produce the most visceral reaction possible, set the tone for most subsequent productions, ranging from Joan Greenwood to Glenda Jackson. (See **pp. 98** and **71**.)

untraditional mixture that qualifies *Hedda Gabler* as the most modernistic of all Ibsen's plays.

This excerpt also contains the longest speech in the play – and only though just 100 words, it is almost 20 percent longer than the single other extensive speech: Løvborg's comparison of having mislaid his manuscript to the loss of a child (see **p. 157** above). That speech expresses his psychological state. By contrast this is an external description of physical circumstances. Hedda is given no words to explain her feelings in any depth. We can only deduce her motives or emotional state from the outside, which represents Ibsen's principle that "the style must conform to the degree of ideality which pervades the representation" of life in a play (see **p. 30**). This lack of self-explanation is unmatched by any other playwright up to Harold Pinter and David Mamet. The externalization also corresponds with Ibsen's principle of objectivity (see **p. 29**). We are expected to learn about Hedda in exactly the same way that we get to know ordinary people in our daily lives, by building up a picture of her/their personality through observing their behavior.

Finally one should note that in Act 4, Aunt Rina having died, the Tesman family is in mourning. So Hedda is dressed in black, corresponding to the iconic image of her.

MRS. ELVSTED. Oh, at least tell me what has happened to him? What is it?

TESMAN. You don't mean to say[1] that he has himself – Eh?

HEDDA. Yes, I am sure he has.

TESMAN. Hedda, how can you?

BRACK. [*Keeping his eyes fixed upon her.*] Unfortunately you have guessed quite correctly, Mrs. Tesman.

MRS. ELVSTED. Oh, how horrible!

TESMAN. Himself, then! Fancy that!

BRACK. Rightly guessed again, Mrs. Tesman.

MRS. ELVSTED. [*With an effort at self-control.*] When did it happen, Mr. Brack?

BRACK. This afternoon – between three and four.

TESMAN. But, good Lord, where did he do it? Eh?

BRACK. [*With some hesitation.*] Where? Well – I suppose at his lodgings.

MRS. ELVSTED. No, that cannot be; for I was there between six and seven.

BRACK. Well then, somewhere else. I don't know exactly. I only know that he was found – . He had shot himself – in the breast.

1 The evasiveness and lack of honesty in this society is encapsulated in this whole discussion about Løvborg's death, where it takes fourteen speeches before anyone actually says that he committed suicide.

MRS. ELVSTED. Oh, how terrible! That he should die like that!

HEDDA. [*To* BRACK.] Was it in the breast?

BRACK. Yes – as I told you.

HEDDA. Not in the temple?[2]

BRACK. In the breast, Mrs. Tesman.

HEDDA. Well, well – the breast is a good place, too.

BRACK. How do you mean, Mrs. Tesman?

HEDDA. [*Evasively.*] Oh, nothing – nothing.

TESMAN. And the wound is dangerous, you say – eh?

BRACK. Absolutely mortal. The end has probably come by this time.

MRS. ELVSTED. Yes, yes, I feel it. The end! The end! Oh, Hedda – !

TESMAN. But tell me, how have you learnt all this?

BRACK. [*Curtly.*] Through one of the police. A man I had some business with.

HEDDA. [*In a clear voice.*] At last a deed worth doing![3]

TESMAN. [*Terrified.*] Good heavens, Hedda! what are you saying?

HEDDA. I say there is beauty in this.

BRACK. H'm, Mrs. Tesman –

TESMAN. Beauty! Fancy that!

MRS. ELVSTED. Oh, Hedda, how can you talk of beauty in such an act!

HEDDA. Eilert Løvborg has himself made up his account with life. He has had the courage[4] to do – the one right thing.

MRS. ELVSTED. No, you must never think that was how it happened! It must have been in delirium that he did it.

TESMAN. In despair!

HEDDA. That he did not. I am certain of that.

MRS. ELVSTED. Yes, yes! In delirium! Just as when he tore up our manuscript.

BRACK. [*Starting.*] The manuscript? Has he torn that up?

MRS. ELVSTED. Yes, last night.

TESMAN. [*Whispers softly.*] Oh, Hedda, we shall never get over this.

BRACK. H'm, very extraordinary.

TESMAN. [*Moving about the room.*] To think of Eilert going out of the

2 When sending Løvborg out to die at the end of Act 3, Hedda had demanded that he kill himself "beautifully" (see **p. 158** above) – this defines what she meant by that romantically vague designation: a "cerebral" death, ignoring the physical realities of the body (as distinct from the head). And it is precisely this romantic ideal that she will carry out at the end, as the parallel wording of Tesman's last speech in the play makes clear.

3 Hedda's reaction is not just startlingly inappropriate, as Thea's response shows, but dangerously self-revealing, as even Tesman is capable of perceiving. However, it is also possible to interpret this positively, as Wilson Knight does in asserting that her honesty and reckless independence here are what raise Hedda to heroic and tragic status (see **p. 81**).

4 Note Hedda's stress on "courage," which contrasts with her sense of her own "cowardice" as well as contradicting the conventional view of suicide as "the coward's way out." Her aestheticization of death through associating it with "beauty" is used to justify an act that by conventional standards (as the reaction of Thea and Tesman shows) is so taboo that it can only be seen as the result of insanity. All of this will subsequently become the rationale for her own suicide (though when she takes that step, it remains unexpressed).

world in this way! And not leaving behind him the book[5] that would have immortalised his name –

MRS. ELVSTED. Oh, if only it could be put together again!

TESMAN. Yes, if it only could! I don't know what I would not give –

MRS. ELVSTED. Perhaps it can, Mr. Tesman.

TESMAN. What do you mean?

MRS. ELVSTED. [*Searches in the pocket of her dress.*[6]] Look here. I have kept all the loose notes he used to dictate from.

HEDDA. [*A step forward.*] Ah – !

TESMAN. You have kept them, Mrs. Elvsted! Eh?

MRS. ELVSTED. Yes, I have them here. I put them in my pocket when I left home. Here they still are –

TESMAN. Oh, do let me see them!

MRS. ELVSTED. [*Hands him a bundle of papers.*] But they are in such disorder – all mixed up.

TESMAN. Fancy, if we could make something out of them, after all! Perhaps if we two put our heads together –

MRS. ELVSTED. Oh yes, at least let us try –

TESMAN. We will manage it! We must! I will dedicate my life to this task.

HEDDA. You, George? Your life?

TESMAN. Yes, or rather all the time I can spare. My own collections must wait in the meantime. Hedda – you understand, eh? I owe this to Eilert's memory.

HEDDA. Perhaps.

TESMAN. And so, my dear Mrs. Elvsted, we will give our whole minds to it. There is no use in brooding over what can't be undone – eh? We must try to control our grief as much as possible, and –

MRS. ELVSTED. Yes, yes, Mr. Tesman, I will do the best I can.

TESMAN. Well then, come here. I can't rest until we have looked through the notes. Where shall we sit? Here? No, in there in the back room. Excuse me, my dear Judge. Come with me, Mrs. Elvsted.

MRS. ELVSTED. Oh, if only it were possible![7]

[TESMAN *and* MRS. ELVSTED *go into the back room. She takes off her hat and*

5 It is, of course Tesman's willingness to lie in order to cover for Hedda – and for himself, since he alone profits by her burning of the manuscript, and he has been persuaded that she did it for him – that makes him accept Thea's offer of the "notes." So Hedda herself is ultimately responsible for the pairing that will shut her out and finally leaves her no other option but her own death.

6 The incongruity of a woman carrying such a "bundle of papers" in a pocket – and not mentioning them earlier, when Løvborg was still around and might have used them himself to reconstitute the book he has lost – is one of the aspects of the action that has been specifically attacked as evidence of the artificiality and contrivance beneath Ibsen's apparently realistic dramaturgy (see Nigel Dennis, p. 83).

7 It was not uncommon in the nineteenth century for women writers to publish under a male name, and in the case of such an unconventional and intellectual work as this analysis of the future, clearly Thea's only way to get her ideas taken seriously (if they are indeed hers) is to get them adopted as the work of someone with the right academic qualifications.

cloak. They both sit at the table under the hanging lamp, and are soon deep in an eager examination of the papers.[8] HEDDA *crosses to the stove and sits in the arm-chair. Presently* BRACK *goes up to her.*

HEDDA. [*In a low voice.*] Oh, what a sense of freedom it gives one, this act of Eilert Løvborg's.

BRACK. Freedom, Mrs. Hedda? Well, of course, it is a release for him –

HEDDA. I mean for me. It gives me a sense of freedom[9] to know that a deed of deliberate courage is still possible in this world, – a deed of spontaneous beauty.

BRACK. [*Smiling.*] H'm – my dear Mrs. Hedda –

HEDDA. Oh, I know what you are going to say. For you are a kind of specialist too, like – you know!

BRACK. [*Looking hard at her.*] Eilert Løvborg was more to you than perhaps you are willing to admit to yourself.[10] Am I wrong?

HEDDA. I don't answer such questions. I only know that Eilert Løvborg has had the courage to live his life after his own fashion. And then – the last great act, with its beauty! Ah! that he should have the will and the strength to turn away from the banquet of life – so early.

BRACK. I am sorry, Mrs. Hedda, – but I fear I must dispel an amiable illusion.

HEDDA. Illusion?[11]

BRACK. Which could not have lasted long in any case.

HEDDA. What do you mean?

BRACK. Eilert Løvborg did not shoot himself – voluntarily.

HEDDA. Not voluntarily?

BRACK. No. The thing did not happen exactly as I told it.

HEDDA. [*In suspense.*] Have you concealed something? What is it?

BRACK. For poor Mrs. Elvsted's sake I idealised the facts a little.

HEDDA. What are the facts?

BRACK. First, that he is already dead.

HEDDA. At the hospital?

BRACK. Yes – without regaining consciousness.

HEDDA. What more have you concealed?

8 Since it has already been clearly suggested that Thea is not just an amanuensis, but the inspiration and perhaps even the actual author of Løvborg's book this should be seen as an exact replay of her relationship with Løvborg, as Hedda later explicitly points out.

9 Ironically this declaration of liberation is precisely what reduces Hedda, once the actual situation has been made clear and her faith in Løvborg revealed as illusory, to slavery. This continues the pattern of hubristic reversal established early in Act 1 of the play (see note 20 on **p. 119** above).

10 Ibsen's careful, even mathematical construction of the play can be seen in the placing of the characters in this scene, with Hedda in a secretive conversation (about Løvborg) which both participants must hide from a couple who can oversee them from the inner room, which exactly duplicates her *tête-à-tête* with Løvborg in Act 2, where it was Brack who watched from behind, sitting with Tesman.

11 The extent to which performance can give a new interpretation, which clarifies an underlying meaning in the text, can be seen in the way Elizabeth Robins used these lines to show the degree to which Hedda clings to her ideals, and is capable of ignoring reality (see William Archer, **p. 66**).

BRACK. This – the event did not happen at his lodgings.

HEDDA. Oh, that can make no difference.

BRACK. Perhaps it may. For I must tell you – Eilert Løvborg was found shot in – in Mademoiselle Diana's boudoir.[12]

HEDDA. [*Makes a motion as if to rise, but sinks back again.*] That is impossible, Judge Brack! He cannot have been there again today.

BRACK. He was there this afternoon. He went there, he said, to demand the return of something which they had taken from him. Talked wildly about a lost child –

HEDDA. Ah – so that was why –

BRACK. I thought probably he meant his manuscript; but now I hear he destroyed that himself. So I suppose it must have been his pocket-book.[13]

HEDDA. Yes, no doubt. And there – there he was found?

BRACK. Yes, there. With a pistol in his breast-pocket, discharged. The ball had lodged in a vital part.

HEDDA. In the breast – yes!

BRACK. No – in the bowels.[14]

HEDDA. [*Looks up at him with an expression of loathing.*] That too! Oh, what curse is it that makes everything I touch turn ludicrous and mean?

BRACK. There is one point more, Mrs. Hedda – another disagreeable feature in the affair.

HEDDA. And what is that?

BRACK. The pistol he carried –

HEDDA. [*Breathless.*] Well? What of it?

BRACK. He must have stolen it.

HEDDA. [*Leaps up.*] Stolen it! That is not true! He did not steal it![15]

BRACK. No other explanation is possible. He must have stolen it – Hush!

[TESMAN *and* MRS. ELVSTED *have risen from the table in the back room, and come into the drawing-room.*

12 Beyond her disgust at prostitution, Hedda's horrified reaction to Madame Diana's name reminds us that Ibsen has established significant parallels between the two through the imagery of pistols and hair (the red hair reported of Diana echoing the association of Hedda with fire). The connections between Løvborg, Diana, and death are already present in the real-life story of the young Danish writer and the Last Will in which he named Ibsen as his executor, recounted by Archer as one of the sources for the play (see **p. 37**).

13 Wallet, or billfold.

14 It is an open question whether Brack is also sanitizing his account for Hedda as he has done earlier for Thea. Some commentators have suggested that "bowels" might be a synonym for genitals. But in either case it is the most fundamental bodily functions that are conjured up – and Hedda's reaction of "loathing" is excessive for simply the breakdown of illusions about a "beautiful" death. It links with her denial of her own pregnancy and rejection of Løvborg's one-time physical advances, to complete the picture of a woman who fears and is repulsed by her own physicality. 

15 Hedda's repeated refusal to lie about the pistol, even later after all the consequences of not doing so have been made clear by Brack, can be viewed (like her earlier self-betraying honesty about the "beauty" she mistakenly perceives in his suicide) as noble (see Eva le Gallienne, **p. 74**).

TESMAN. [*With the paper in both his hands.*] Hedda dear, it is almost impossible to see under that lamp. Think of that!

HEDDA. Yes, I am thinking.[16]

TESMAN. Would you mind our sitting at your writing-table – eh?

HEDDA. If you like. [*Quickly.*] No, wait! Let me clear it first!

TESMAN. Oh, you needn't trouble, Hedda. There is plenty of room.

HEDDA. No, no, let me clear it, I say! I will take these things in and put them on the piano. There!

[*She has drawn out an object, covered with sheet music, from under the bookcase, places several other pieces of music upon it, and carries the whole into the inner room, to the left.* TESMAN *lays the scraps of paper on the writing-table, and moves the lamp there from the corner table. He and* MRS. ELVSTED *sit down and proceed with their work.* HEDDA *returns.*

HEDDA. [*Behind* MRS. ELVSTED'S *chair, gently ruffling her hair.*] Well, my sweet Thea, – how goes it with Eilert Løvborg's monument?

MRS. ELVSTED. [*Looks dispiritedly up at her.*] Oh, it will be terribly hard to put in order.

TESMAN. We must manage it. I am determined. And arranging other people's papers is just the work for me.[17]

[HEDDA *goes over to the stove, and seats herself on one of the footstools.* BRACK *stands over her, leaning on the arm-chair.*

HEDDA. [*Whispers.*] What did you say about the pistol?

BRACK. [*Softly.*] That he must have stolen it.

HEDDA. Why stolen it?

BRACK. Because every other explanation ought to be impossible, Mrs. Hedda.[18]

HEDDA. Indeed?

BRACK. [*Glances at her.*] Of course Eilert Løvborg was here this morning. Was he not?

16 This has been Hedda's response before (see pp. 151–2 above). The triviality of Tesman's concerns, and his inability (represented by his stock phrase) to "think" about anything significant, is underlined by the contrast with the issue that Hedda is being forced into "thinking" about: the evidence of the pistol, and its implications for her very survival. That she is already aware of the potential for blackmail in Brack's insinuation, and has considered how she might have to respond is clear from the way she immediately takes the chance to remove the other pistol (the "*object, covered with sheet music*") to the inner room.

17 This confirmation of Tesman's pedantic nature and lack of intellectual initiative demonstrates that, even if it might not have been quite the case with Løvborg, what he produces with Thea will be her work. More immediately, his self-evaluation makes it obvious that Hedda will not be able to count on him – even though as her husband he is officially responsible for protection – to save her from Brack.

18 Since Hedda has already betrayed the truth, this interrogation should be seen as Brack's attempt to corrupt her: note the way his position, leaning over Hedda, might be interpreted as the biblical Serpent tempting Eve from the tree.

HEDDA. Yes.

BRACK. Were you alone with him?

HEDDA. Part of the time.

BRACK. Did you not leave the room whilst he was here?

HEDDA. No.

BRACK. Try to recollect. Were you not out of the room a moment?

HEDDA. Yes, perhaps just a moment – out in the hall.

BRACK. And where was your pistol-case during that time?

HEDDA. I had it locked up in –

BRACK. Well, Mrs. Hedda?

HEDDA. The case stood there on the writing-table.

BRACK. Have you looked since, to see whether both the pistols are there?

HEDDA. No. –

BRACK. Well, you need not. I saw the pistol found in Løvborg's pocket, and I knew it at once as the one I had seen yesterday – and before, too.

HEDDA. Have you it with you?

BRACK. No; the police have it.

HEDDA. What will the police do with it?

BRACK. Search till they find the owner.

HEDDA. Do you think they will succeed?

BRACK. [*Bends over her and whispers.*] No, Hedda Gabler – not so long as I say nothing.

HEDDA. [*Looks frightened at him.*] And if you do not say nothing, – what then?

BRACK. [*Shrugs his shoulders.*] There is always the possibility that the pistol was stolen.

HEDDA. [*Firmly.*] Death rather than that.

BRACK. [*Smiling.*] People say such things – but they don't do them.[19]

HEDDA. [*Without replying.*] And supposing the pistol was not stolen, and the owner is discovered? What then?

BRACK. Well, Hedda – then comes the scandal.

HEDDA. The scandal!

BRACK. Yes, the scandal[20] – of which you are so mortally afraid. You

19 Brack's conviction in rational behavior (as defined by the norms of the society he represents) is what leads him to ignore the warning in Hedda's preference for dying over self-betrayal. His words also point forward to his final speech.

20 It is a striking mark of Ibsen's technique that this is the longest speech in the whole play. But it is significant not just for its length, and what that reveals about Ibsen's technique, but also thematically. Referring back to Thea's first conversation with her in Act 1, it sets Hedda in an explicit (and demeaning) parallel with the brothel madam, equating their "moral" status, as well as giving a concrete context for Hedda's inability to free herself from the conventions of acceptable behavior. Prison is an accurate metaphor for the social conventions that restrict Hedda's actions and prevent her from attaining self-fulfillment; and the now open intimidation is Brack's way of caging her in so that, blackmailed to buy his silence, she will be deprived of her sexual independence as well. (On a strictly realistic level it is worth noting that at this time suicide was considered almost as serious a crime as murder – and having provided the weapon, Hedda is certainly liable to punishment as an accessory before the fact.)

will, of course, be brought before the court – both you and Mademoiselle Diana. She will have to explain how the thing happened – whether it was an accidental shot or murder. Did the pistol go off as he was trying to take it out of his pocket, to threaten her with? Or did she tear the pistol out of his hand, shoot him, and push it back into his pocket? That would be quite like her; for she is an able-bodied young person, this same Mademoiselle Diana.

HEDDA. But *I* have nothing to do with all this repulsive business.

BRACK. No. But you will have to answer the question: Why did you give Eilert Løvborg the pistol? And what conclusions will people draw from the fact that you did give it to him?

HEDDA. [*Lets her head sink.*] That is true. I did not think of that.

BRACK. Well, fortunately, there is no danger, so long as I say nothing.

HEDDA. [*Looks up at him.*] So I am in your power, Judge Brack. You have me at your beck and call, from this time forward.

BRACK. [*Whispers softly.*] Dearest Hedda – believe me – I shall not abuse my advantage.

HEDDA. I am in your power none the less. Subject to your will and your demands. A slave, a slave then! [*Rises impetuously.*] No, I cannot endure the thought of that! Never!

BRACK. [*Looks half-mockingly at her.*] People generally get used to the inevitable.

HEDDA. [*Returns his look.*] Yes, perhaps. [*She crosses to the writing-table. Suppressing an involuntary smile, she imitates* TESMAN'S *intonations.*[21]] Well? Are you getting on, George? Eh?

TESMAN. Heaven knows, dear. In any case it will be the work of months.

HEDDA. [*As before.*] Fancy that! [*Passes her hands softly through* MRS. ELVSTED'S *hair.*] Doesn't it seem strange to you, Thea? Here are you sitting with Tesman – just as you used to sit with Eilert Løvborg?

MRS. ELVSTED. Ah, if I could only inspire your husband in the same way!

HEDDA. Oh, that will come too – in time.

TESMAN. Yes, do you know, Hedda – I really think I begin to feel something of the sort. But won't you go and sit with Brack again?

HEDDA. Is there nothing I can do to help you two?

TESMAN. No, nothing in the world.[22] [*Turning his head.*] I trust to you to keep Hedda company, my dear Brack.

21 Contrasting with her earlier contemptuous imitation of Tesman's clichéd expressions, this corresponds to Ibsen's note that her attitude to her husband changes, so that by the end she finds him pitiful rather than ridiculous (see **p. 34**). Compare too her previous threat to burn Thea's hair off, with the way she "*passes her hands softly through*" Thea's hair here, and the shift in emotional state this implies.

22 It is a sign of Hedda's desperation that she should turn to the husband she despises – and to the rival she considers so far beneath her – to find some way of escape. However, it is her own actions, in first concealing, then burning, Løvborg's manuscript and using its destruction to manipulate Tesman through guilt that have driven him to join forces with Thea in an activity that necessarily

BRACK. [*With a glance at* HEDDA.] With the very greatest of pleasure.

HEDDA. Thanks. But I am tired this evening. I will go in and lie down a little on the sofa.

TESMAN. Yes, do dear – eh?

[HEDDA *goes into the back room and draws the curtains.*[23] *A short pause. Suddenly she is heard playing a wild dance on the piano.*

MRS. ELVSTED. [*Starts from her chair.*] Oh – what is that?

TESMAN. [*Runs to the doorway.*] Why, my dearest Hedda – don't play dance-music to-night![24] Just think of Aunt Rina! And of Eilert too!

HEDDA. [*Puts her head out between the curtains.*] And of Aunt Julia. And of all the rest of them. – After this, I will be quiet. [*Closes the curtains again.*]

TESMAN. [*At the writing-table.*] It's not good for her to see us at this distressing work. I'll tell you what, Mrs. Elvsted, – you shall take the empty room at Aunt Julia's, and then I will come over in the evenings, and we can sit and work there – eh?

HEDDA. [*In the inner room.*[25]] I hear what you are saying, Tesman. But how am *I* to get through the evenings out here?[26]

excludes her. And his response, which delivers her precisely to the fate from which she is appealing for his protection (though the conventions that control her mean she cannot mention Brack's sexual designs explicitly), is a damning demonstration of his insensitivity, naivety, and egoism.

His phrasing – "nothing in the world" – is of course a cliché, throwaway expression. But here its literal meaning has ominous significance: without even his support indeed there is nothing left for Hedda – apart, that is, from the baby she denies even having.

23 As Eva le Gallienne (one of the American actresses who made Hedda her trademark role) noted, these curtains are very much the equivalent of stage curtains (see **p. 100**). And the wild dance music she plays is the exact equivalent of Nora frenziedly dancing the Tarantella in *A Doll's House* at the point where she too believes suicide is her only way out, although in Ingmar Bergman's production the music was reduced to a few dissonant chords to bring out Hedda's neurotic state and frustration (see Frederick and Lise Lone Marker's description on **p. 92**).

24 The reference to Aunt Rina's death is intended to remind us that, as Glenda Jackson observes (**p. 96**), the whole action only takes just thirty-six hours from Hedda's return after her honeymoon to her suicide. While the text is longer than his other Naturalistic plays, *Hedda Gabler* is by far the most compressed of all Ibsen's drama. It is one of the very few plays in the whole theatrical repertoire to follow the "tragic unities" of Aristotle so closely, which not only gives the action an unusual intensity, but also reinforces the claustrophobic nature of the society Ibsen is depicting.

25 As Ingmar Bergman's strikingly modernistic production of the play emphasized, this inner room is not just a personal retreat, but Hedda's psychic space (see **p. 89**). While remaining a realistic physical space in terms of the play's setting, its function as the heroine's interior psychological state is marked by the objects it contains. These are specifically: her father's pistols, with their connotations of the heritage lost to her and masculine symbolism of penis-transference, and her piano – representing not only her cultural aspirations, or aesthetic sensibility, but (as expressed in the wild music in this, the first and only time she plays) her desperation and need for the vitality she has been deprived of.

26 This is the nearest thing to a soliloquy for Hedda. It is this absence of any self-evaluation or explanation of why she acts as she does that leads some critics, like Muriel Bradbrook, to conclude that Hedda "is hardly self-conscious enough to suffer," and allows others, like H. L. Mencken, to present Ibsen as interested solely in technique and "not with the propagation of ethical ideas" or problems (see **pp. 78** and **75**). But it is also possible to defend this avoidance of inner insight as both realistic and the expression of a modern individualistic sense of moral relativism (see Geoffrey Brereton, **p. 86**).

TESMAN. [*Turning over the papers.*] Oh, I daresay Judge Brack will be so kind as to look in[27] now and then, even though I am out.

BRACK. [*In the arm-chair, calls out gaily.*] Every blessed evening, with all the pleasure in life, Mrs. Tesman! We shall get on capitally together, we two!

HEDDA. [*Speaking loud and clear.*] Yes, don't you flatter yourself we will, Judge Brack? Now that you are the one cock in the basket[28] –

[*A shot is heard within.* TESMAN, MRS. ELVSTED, *and* BRACK *leap to their feet.*

TESMAN. Oh, now she is playing with those pistols again.

[*He throws back the curtains and runs in, followed by* MRS. ELVSTED. HEDDA *lies stretched on the sofa, lifeless. Confusion and cries.* BERTA *enters in alarm from the right.*

TESMAN. [*Shrieks to* BRACK.] Shot herself! Shot herself in the temple![29] Fancy that!

BRACK. [*Half-fainting in the arm-chair.*] Good *God*! – people don't do such things.[30]

27 From a female viewpoint, as Elizabeth Robins so perceptively remarks, Tesman is delivering Hedda into a form of sexual slavery that a woman like her would find particularly humiliating – a form of "enslavement" that men (both the male characters here and the critics of the time who found Hedda an "unnatural" character) were incapable of recognizing because of their patriarchal assumptions – from which suicide is the only escape (see **p. 61**, and the reviews cited by Archer on **pp. 62–3**).

28 A proverbial Norwegian expression, for which there is no precise equivalent in English; other translations have rendered it as a "bull in the pen" (Christopher Hampton) or "cock on the roost" (John Osborne). It points to her major reason for committing suicide, though many of Hedda's previous comments had toyed with the idea (as with her superficially playful assertion in Act 2 that the only talent she has is "boring myself to death"), as the only way left to escape his advances. It also places the guilt for her act on him.

29 It is specifically the supposedly noble manner of her death – shooting herself in the forehead, the mind being seen as "the spirit's right antagonist and target" (note Tesman's use of the word "temple") – that leads a critic such as Wilson Knight to assert that Hedda's act is "positive" and heroic (see **p. 81**).

30 This single sentence is one of the most discussed elements of the play.

It is ambiguous since the "things" people don't do could relate to either one of Tesman's preceding statements: the suicide itself, or the manner of it – that she has succeeded in killing herself "beautifully" where Løvborg so signally messed up his own death. The latter would suggest that Løvborg's failure to serve as a surrogate (as always in the past, when she "lived" through his exploits) causes her to kill herself – and to do so in the precise way she had urged him to follow. In other words that it is her romantic ideals that destroy her. Beyond that, since "people" in this case refers to pregnant mothers, it also emphasizes the "unnatural" quality of Hedda's act: in committing suicide, she has also perpetrated infanticide.

For Janet Suzman, Brack's words are a natural expression of shock, even if they also show that "he was too self-engrossed to read the signals she gave him" (see **p. 101**). But what has disturbed many commentators, and continues to shock audiences today almost as much as when *Hedda Gabler* was first performed over a century ago, is the sheer insufficiency of the response to something as significant in dramatic – and human – terms as the self-destruction of a protagonist on whom our attention has been so closely focused.

A rather different way of reading the last line is suggested by Bernard Shaw, who declared Brack "on the whole right" since, if enough people followed Hedda's example, then the society that deformed her ideals and destroyed her would be forced to change (see **p. 57**) – in other words that if Hedda's situation is representative of women in general, as William Archer, Edmund Gosse, and Elizabeth Robins all reported people at the time indeed assumed (see **pp. 63, 55,** and **61**), then they should rise up against the norms Brack epitomizes in order to prevent such tragedies in the real world.

It is a striking contrast to the conventions of tragedy, which traditionally concludes with a moral (as in the final injunction to "Count no man happy until he has lived his life free from pain" of *Oedipus Rex*) or a eulogy (such as the "flights of angels" that sing Hamlet "to his rest"). At the very least, as in *King Lear*, the assumption is that the tragic action forces survivors to a cathartic recognition: "The weight of this sad time we must obey/Speak what we feel, not what we ought to say." Looking at this play in terms of the principles of tragedy, as Geoffrey Brereton suggests, the avoidance of tragic recognition denies the existence of any "moral law based on absolutes" (see **p. 86**).

Yet at the same time Ibsen's approach here is exactly the same as in his earlier play *Ghosts* which, he asserted, "preaches nothing at all" (see **p. 29**); and it is representative of Naturalistic drama, much the same truncated closure being copied by Chekhov in *The Seagull*. However, the comparison shows how far Ibsen was ahead of his contemporaries, since Chekhov gives his characters a comprehensible and even generous motive for their muted response to the death of the central figure (attempting to minimize the grief of Konstantine's mother by pretending nothing has happened in order to break the news to her gently). By contrast Ibsen's two-line ending is ruthlessly revealing, but unsettlingly noncommittal. This absence of general commentary is largely what led Henry James to decide that the play was purely a psychological study where the only explanations to be found are in the character of Hedda herself; while it is also Brack's last words that led Muriel Bradbrook to assert that "There is no answer to Hedda" (see **p. 64** and **p. 77**).

Even so, on a subtextual level clear moral verdicts are indeed being communicated. The extreme brevity of the speeches following Hedda's death is so disproportionate to the sight of her body, or even the definitive noise of the gun-shot, and the sentiments expressed so incongruous that the ending serves as a devastating indictment of this society: these people being so morally corrupted, self-serving, and insensitive that they are incapable of responding appropriately. This was made explicit by a striking directorial intervention by Ingmar Bergman's staging, where Brack pulled up Hedda's head by her hair to stare contemptuously into her dead face before stating that "people don't do such things" (see **p. 92**). Ibsen's unequivocal assertion of the importance of motherhood (see **p. 26**) implies a condemnation of Hedda's suicide, which also kills the only real baby in the play. However, it is also possible that

Ibsen may have intended the infanticide to indicate that – as he had earlier remarked in a letter to Georg Brandes (see **p. 8**) – "the whole race is on the wrong track." Either way this suggests that such a society has quite literally no future.

4

Further Reading

Further Reading

This selection makes no attempt to be comprehensive, and works that have already been reproduced in this book are not listed here, assuming readers will realize that these are all recommended. Although there is a great mass of writing on Ibsen, in the critical Interpretations section only those books or articles that specifically feature *Hedda Gabler* are included, except in a few cases where it would distort the critical history to omit them.

Editions and Text

There are over a dozen translations of *Hedda Gabler*. Until 1950, all editions, including William Archer's edition of *The Collected Works of Henrik Ibsen* (translated by Charles Archer, New York: Charles Scribner's, 1906–12, 12 vols), reprinted Edmund Gosse's 1890 text. Then in 1950, as she announced in her Introduction, Una Ellis-Fermor made the "attempt to translate [Ibsen's plays] into the English of today" (Harmondsworth: Penguin Books). Her version is somewhat less than colloquial, since it is specifically designed as a version for reading and – although popular at the time and reissued in 1961 – today sounds linguistically dated. Almost all the subsequent translations were undertaken with the same aim of updating the language, while making it more actable, though Rolfe Fjelde (*The Complete Major Prose Plays*, New York: Farrar, Straus & Giroux, 1978) made the additional claim of complete linguistic accuracy. James McFarlane produced *The Oxford Ibsen* (London: Oxford University Press) between 1960 and 1970 (with Vol. VII, which contains *Hedda Gabler*, appearing in 1966), followed by Michael Meyer, whose *Hedda Gabler* was published in *Plays: Two* of the Methuen Ibsen series (London: Eyre Methuen) in 1967, and later by various translations of the play as a single text that have used "an American voice" (Nicholas Rudall, Chicago: I. R. Dee, 1992) or even Canadian English (Henry Beissel, Toronto: Playwrights Canada, 1983). In addition there have been two adaptations by well-known modern British playwrights: Christopher Hampton, whose version was performed in 1970 and published in 1989 (both by Faber & Faber Ltd.); and John Osborne, whose version was first performed in 1972 and published in 1989. These are interpretations of the play rather than straight translations, adding or distorting details in order to cater to contemporary sensibilities (Hampton) or to a personal agenda (Osborne).

Indeed, although some productions have set the play in contemporary dress and scenery, this has not proved effective; and none of the published translations to date has shifted the action to a different time or place. As a result, Edmund Gosse's initial 1890 translation has been preferred for this Sourcebook.

Background Reading

The best source of background context for *Hedda Gabler* is in biographies of Ibsen, and of these two are particularly rewarding. Altered and enhanced by new bibliographical data and Halvdan Koht's own fundamental shift in perspective, his second edition of *Life of Ibsen* (New York: Benjamin Blom, Inc., 1971) offers insights that make this still a standard text. Initially conceptualized (1928–9) within a purely historical framework – where Ibsen's contributions to, and positioning within, the history of drama were outlined – the second edition addresses the moral and psychological undercurrents of Ibsen's work. Combining the authority of biographical fact with critical interpretations of the plays, Koht presents a multi-faceted perspective: not merely Ibsen the man, or Ibsen the dramatist, but a fusion of the two.

While not possessing intimate familiarity with Ibsen himself (they are said to have met only once), Koht gained invaluable experience preparing notes for Ibsen's last volume of collected works and as editor of the playwright's letters. But other writers have criticized the work for its nationalistic or political bias, particularly Michael Meyer, whose *Ibsen: A Biography* (Garden City, N.Y.: Doubleday, 1971) was written specifically to correct inconsistency and factual omission in the first edition of Koht's *Life of Ibsen*. Meyer focuses on Ibsen's time as director of the Norwegian Theater, his experiences in Rome, the "truth" about his various relationships with women, the reactions he elicited from his contemporaries. Citing Koht's nationalistic bias and his preference to depict Ibsen as more the writer (of literature) than the dramatist (who revolutionized theater), Meyer further argues that the study of Ibsen and Ibsenism demands new critical treatment and insight from each successive generation. With this in mind, he shows how Ibsen influenced, and was influenced by, history: a history confined not merely to the prevailing currents or movements of the theater but one which pervaded all of nineteenth-century Europe with its startlingly innovative ideologies – social, political, philosophical, and existential.

Critical Interpretations

The works cited here have been chosen because they represent different approaches to *Hedda Gabler*. Since studies of Ibsen show a clear development, with critics frequently commenting on, or writing in opposition to, their predecessors, the books are listed chronologically, rather than in order of critical significance.

Havelock Ellis's chapter on Ibsen in *The New Spirit* (New York: Boni and Liveright, [1890] 1921) is the earliest critical perspective on his plays – predating Shaw's *Quintessence of Ibsenism.* Giving a brief historical account (political as well as artistic) up to the nineteenth century, Ibsen is situated amongst such artists as Whitman, Tolstoy, and Heine, who are presented as having had a singular influence in the development of modern writing. An outline of the cultural qualities and influences which nurture Ibsen's work is followed by a synoptical treatment of the artist's plays and poems, and the chapter concludes, slightly histrionically, with what Ellis (the controversial author of *Psychology and Sex*) presents as Ibsen's chief contribution to modernity: the dramatic development of the individualistic subject conceptualized within a humanistic context.

In *Ibsen: The Man, His Art and His Significance* (New York: Morgan Shepart, 1907), Haldane MacFall pays humble recognition to the fact that any genuine appreciation of Ibsen lies not with his (or anyone else's) critical and/or historic evaluation, but in personal observation and experience of the plays themselves. Curious as to what motivated the artist to write the plays he did, the author centers much of his biography on the plays themselves: the events leading up to their conception, their reception and subsequent influence, and, in turn, how these factors affected Ibsen and his later artistic contributions.

Brian W. Downs's *Ibsen: The Intellectual Background* (Cambridge: Cambridge University Press, 1946) is valuable for its objective survey of historical occurrences and intellectual movements, which illuminates the prevailing sociopolitical and philosophical climate during Ibsen's life. Beginning with the currents of revolution (and revolutionary thought) transversing Europe in the mid-nineteenth century, the time of Ibsen's early literary and intellectual maturation, then moving to the playwright's philosophical perspectives and political affiliations, Downs argues that Ibsen, far from being an anomaly, was a product of his time.

By contrast, the expressed purpose of Maurice Valency's trend-setting book, *The Flower and the Castle: An Introduction to Modern Drama* (New York: Macmillan, 1963), is to define the emergence of modern drama, which he does through a biographical and critical study of the life and works of both Ibsen and Strindberg. Choosing the playwrights for their respective innovations, Valency argues that both men precipitated an aesthetic revolution that benefitted (and was benefitted by) other artistic genres. Beginning with Ibsen's university career and his relationship, both professional and personal, with Björnson, Valency outlines Ibsen's influence upon Naturalism, which is traced to a unique brand of self-reflective characterization and social commentary that constitutes a paradigm shift in the history of drama.

A culmination of over three decades (1953–87) of Ibsen scholarship, James McFarlane's *Ibsen and Meaning: Studies, Essays and Prefaces* (Norwich: Norvik Press, 1989) provides a valuable chronological overview of Ibsen's drama. Detailed topics such as Ibsen's positioning within the history of drama, his dramatic strategies of composition, and the problematic nature of translation are complemented by the documentation and commentary on individual plays offered by the Introductions from *The Oxford Ibsen*, which are included.

Acknowledging that any useful feminist discussion of Ibsen's work must remain historically specific, Joan Templeton's *Ibsen's Women* (Cambridge: Cambridge University Press, 1997) underscores the strong and positive characterization of women in the plays. Using Ibsen's own insistence that his work (and more specifically his chief characters) are crafted from personal experience and self-reflection, a parallel is established between the construction of his female protagonists and the relationships he shared with the women around him: lovers, actresses, friends, relations. A close reading of the texts (*A Doll's House*, *Ghosts*, and *Hedda Gabler* in particular) is used to argue the presence of an Ibsenite ideology – one which questions societal expectations that confine or limit the potentiality of the human subject – as an embryonic form of modern feminist philosophy.

Index

Note: Bold numbers indicate extracts